Eviction

Jessica Field has a humanities PhD and is a research affiliate at the University of Manchester. Following her parents' eviction threat in 2017 and the community formation of #SaveOurHomesLS26, she ran the saveourhomesLS26.org campaign website and wrote for the *Guardian* and *Red Pepper*. In 2022, she won the Dawn Foster Memorial Essay Prize. This is her first book.

Eviction

A Social History of Rent

Jessica Field

VERSO
London • New York

This edition first published by Verso 2026
First published by Verso 2025

The manufacturer's authorized representative in the EU for product safety (GPSR) is LOGOS EUROPE, 9 rue Nicolas Poussin, 17000, La Rochelle, France
contact@logoseurope.eu

1 3 5 7 9 10 8 6 4 2

Verso
UK: 6 Meard Street, London W1F 0EG
US: 207 East 32nd Street, New York, NY 10016
versobooks.com

Verso is the imprint of New Left Books

ISBN-13: 978-1-83674-357-6
ISBN-13: 978-1-80429-889-3 (UK EBK)
ISBN-13: 978-1-80429-890-9 (US EBK)

British Library Cataloguing in Publication Data
A catalogue record for this book is available from the British Library

The Library of Congress Has Cataloged the Hardcover Edition as Follows:

Names: Field, Jessica author
Title: Eviction : a social history of rent / Jessica Field.
Description: London ; New York : Verso, 2025. | Includes bibliographical references and index.
Identifiers: LCCN 2025015479 (print) | LCCN 2025015480 (ebook) | ISBN 9781804298886 hardback | ISBN 9781804298909 ebook
Subjects: LCSH: Public housing—Great Britain—History | Rental housing—Great Britain—History | Housing policy—Great Britain—History | Tenants' associations—Great Britain—History
Classification: LCC HD7288.78.G7 F54 2025 (print) | LCC HD7288.78.G7 (ebook) | DDC 363.5/850941—dc23/eng/20250529
LC record available at https://lccn.loc.gov/2025015479
LC ebook record available at https://lccn.loc.gov/2025015480

Typeset in Sabon by MJ & N Gavan, Truro, Cornwall
Printed and bound by CPI Group (UK) Ltd, Croydon CR0 4YY

For Dad

Contents

Introduction

My head's a shed

'I'm a different person now,' Mum often says. For a time, she meant that in a good way: stronger, confident, less fearful of ruffling feathers. That's because for five years between 2017 and 2022 my mum, Hazell, was a leading figure in her community's campaign to prevent their mass eviction. The scale of the eviction made news. Television interviews, newspaper features, social media coverage – you name it, she appeared in it, alongside Dad and her close neighbour-friends. Mum's wide, round eyes, tousled mane of hair, and slight smile made her a beseeching subject of campaign features. It was a mistake to confuse her reserved smile with shyness, though. As coverage snowballed, Mum grew increasingly confident about vocalising the injustices faced by her private renting community.

Now though, Mum says it regretfully. She feels different all right, but burnt and bitter. And plain dog tired. 'My head's a shed' is another favourite phrase of hers, one that seems to caveat her capacity to deal with anything these days. The adrenaline of the campaign gave way to overwhelm, which gave way to burn out and cynicism. Mum longs to turn the clock back to before she was forced into fight-or-flight mode. Not just because they lost the fight in the end; not just because the community were evicted. Mum's been evicted before, and managed.

This time, it was the compounding weight of it all: uncertainty and anxiety as the fight dragged on with bureaucracy and appeals. The strain of campaigning on relationships,

Hazell Field (Mum), flanked by John Readman (left) and Robert Walker (right) outside Leeds City Council (Save Our Homes LS26).

friendships, and health. And the seeming inevitability of everyone losing their homes anyway. After all, eviction is baked into the way Britain manages its tenanted homes. All Mum feels she gained from fighting this one is worse mental health, more grey hairs, and a deep-seated mistrust of private and public individuals with power.

In late autumn 2017, my parents and sixty-nine other tenant households picked up an unaddressed leaflet that had been casually pushed through their letterbox. The glossy front page stated that their landlord, corporate investment company Pemberstone, was seeking planning permission to demolish their entire tenanted estate in south Leeds and build up to seventy-two new executive-style houses for sale.

It wasn't an eviction notice, and it wasn't directly addressed to tenants; the leaflet was a generic notification of a public consultation event inviting 'locals' (whoever they were, if not the tenants) to share ideas 'on how the scheme can help meet the needs of the local community prior to submission of a formal planning application'. As if they were invisible, this leaflet announced to residents that the landlord had plans for their homes that didn't involve them, the occupiers.

Mum felt bewildered at first. Initial hope that the new properties might be rentals for existing residents gave way to shock and anger when it dawned that current tenants were expected just to shuffle silently off elsewhere. My parents and brother had lived on the estate for eleven years by that point, and some of their neighbours had been there for decades longer. Residents were settled: they'd decorated and renovated, chosen jobs nearby, raised families, and made deep friendships and memories with neighbours – even drawn lifelong friends onto the estate. It was home.

By early 2022, all assured shorthold-tenancy homes had received their formal Section 21 'no fault' eviction notices. Section 21s give tenants just two months to pack up their homes of decades and find somewhere else to live. Dozens of families have now been forced off the estate, including my parents in April 2022. Others fled before receiving the notice, knowing what was coming down the line. At the time of writing, the last shorthold-tenancy family has moved out; those remaining are a handful of families and older residents protected by a pre-1989 tenancy agreement that prevents eviction without the provision of a comparable alternative. The vacant houses surrounding these remaining residents have been boarded up, inviting vandalism, break-ins, and frequent fly-tipping. Demolition and redevelopment of the estate will commence eventually.

There are efforts to ensure that the evicted families who'd lived longest on the estate can return if the promised portion of housing association houses – fewer and much smaller than the previous rentals – get built on the site. Residents have been campaigning hard for a bespoke local-lettings policy to circumvent existing rules that would see them all sent to the bottom of the council house waiting list. Leeds City Council have shown willing on this front, but it might only apply to around a dozen long-settled tenant households. And, based on previous dealings with the landlord and council, tenants won't believe it until they have the keys in their hands anyway. Whatever happens from here, my parents' neighbourly community has already been destroyed.

In many ways this is an unremarkable story for today's housing landscape: landlord rents out properties to tenants; landlord evicts tenants for renovations or redevelopment; tenants have to move to new rentals elsewhere. Yet, like most everyday stories, when you zoom in closer you see that even ordinary turns of events show something significant. In this case, our small Yorkshire housing estate stands as a microcosm of the nationwide public and private rented-housing swindles that ordinary tenants have had to face for more than a century. It is a hope or a promise of a secure forever home, broken by managed decline, weak tenant rights, and cycles of eviction.

Landlord power and tenant displacement have been fixtures of British housing for more than a century, even during the apparent welfare-focused years of council house building. This post-war era was the time when my parents' estate was first built. In fact, the estate's first landlord was the government's National Coal Board (NCB), though it was not inevitable that these homes should share the same decline and privatisation fate as the coal mines.

Cardboard City

My parents' two-street neighbourhood is the last-surviving part of a sizeable former Coal Board estate in Oulton, on the outskirts of south Leeds. The NCB built it in record time out of prefabricated materials in the early 1950s to house miners and their families employed by nearby collieries. It soon became like a village community in its own right, situated on the periphery of established towns and villages, although it had no shops or other basic community amenities of its own.

Rents for the 210 prefab houses were pegged to local authority rates for council houses to keep them affordable for workers. They were a form of public housing, but distinct from the conventional council house, as all Coal Board houses were state owned following the nationalisation of the coal industry in 1947. The neighbourhood was nicknamed (derogatorily) Cardboard City by outsiders, because of its draughty pre-cast concrete buildings. The name stuck and is now used with affection by some ex-residents, though many still hate the label.

After the decline of the mining industry and closure of local pits by the early 1980s, houses on our Oulton estate weren't sold to sitting tenants via the Coal Board as thousands of others had been; nor did they fall under Margaret Thatcher's Right to Buy scheme. Instead, in a sleight of hand, the estate was sold by the NCB to a private investment company ... which then sold it to another, and another, transitioning it into an estate for private tenants where rents have followed the market rather than the social housing sector.

As the 1990s' boom in house prices and rental rates started to take off, Cardboard City's new investor landlords hedged their bets. They served eviction or relocation notices to around 140 households, demolished that part of the estate, and redeveloped the land – building fancy new middle-class houses that were sold off for home ownership. In 1997, the remaining seventy prefab homes were sold to investment company Pemberstone as private rentals.

Rent rates in the 1980s were initially costly, comparable with the high rates charged in the well-serviced LS26 postcodes of nearby Oulton, Rothwell, and Woodlesford. But they eventually slowed in growth, falling slightly behind market rates. Costs reflected conditions. Since its construction, all Cardboard City landlords had undertaken only the bare minimum of maintenance on these factory-made buildings, even after the model was declared to have defects in the 1980s. Window frames rotted; heat dissipated through single-glazed panes; fences collapsed. Winters were damp and cold, heating bills high. Still, the poor condition of the houses was the only reason the private landlords kept the rent low(ish). By the 2010s, the managed decline of otherwise serviceable prefab stock made Cardboard City one of the last remaining affordable (in the genuine sense of the word) rental estates in the LS26 postcode for low-income households needing a family-sized home.

From post-war public housing to private rent; from shiny new stock to defective and dilapidated; from home to eviction – though Cardboard City is small in size, the history of my parents' estate reflects the national ebbs and flows of rented-housing policy, quality, and cost – whether private, industry, or municipal.

First, Cardboard City can be seen as part of a wider post-Second World War scramble to build quality homes for returning soldiers and future workers in Britain's rapidly

Four Airey semis on Wordsworth Drive in 2018 (Save Our Homes LS26).

expanding industries. This period is often romanticised as the start of a short-lived golden era for public housing. Local authorities constructed hundreds of thousands of homes each year, and 160,000 more were requisitioned or built by the newly nationalised Coal Board.

Both requisitioned and newbuild NCB stock were to be rentals, but with the state or, more accurately, state-run industry as landlord. Like council houses, these NCB homes provided people with somewhere secure, comfortable, and affordable to live while they helped get Britain back on its feet. Construction materials were limited, and demand was high. Off-the-peg prefabricated houses seemed the ideal solution – particularly for the Coal Board, which was in urgent need of houses for its workers.

Designers intended that a prefabricated house be quick to assemble, without requiring skilled labour. Components were made in factories from widely available materials such as aluminium, steel, and timber, before being shipped to the chosen site and set up in record time. The first prefabs produced in any significant number were the 156,623 temporary bungalows erected under the 1944 Temporary Housing Programme. These classic prefab bungalows were produced in multiple designs, including the steel-framed Arcon design and the timber-framed Uni-Seco, each with around a ten-year lifespan (though many remained occupied for decades longer).[1]

Many more prefab designs were commissioned in the decade after the war, primarily so-called 'permanent' designs that came with longer projected lifespans or technical guarantees. The Oulton estate – Cardboard City – was designed by Leeds industrialist Sir Edwin Airey, who first prototyped the houses in the grounds of his Oakwood home in Roundhay and the Leeds suburb Seacroft. Some 26,000 precast concrete Airey houses were built across England and Wales from the 1940s to the 1960s, each with a sixty-year design life.[2] Hundreds of thousands of other 'permanent' prefab houses, based on around two dozen prototypes, were built by competing manufacturers that are now household building industry names, such as Wimpey, Laing, and Taylor Woodrow. Most of these were built for municipal housing.

The total number of prefab houses constructed in this era – upwards of half a million – remained relatively small in the grand scheme of Britain's housing development. As a result, prefabricated housing typically only appears as a footnote in Britain's public housing past.[3] Yet many features of its conception have characterised the power and culture of private development and landlordism that have defined the British housing sector ever since. As I'll show in the early chapters of the book, post-war prefabricated housing was a knee-jerk housing programme influenced by powerful men in politics and industry. Some were in it for the apparently revolutionary innovation in cheap construction technologies. Others were in it for the contracts.

The house units were designed with working-class men and their housewives in mind, but in a functional sense: focused more on providing spacious kitchens for housewives' labour rather than considerations of structural longevity or community sustainability. In fact, hundreds of thousands of post-war prefabs, including the Airey design, had a limited lifespan and therefore an inbuilt guarantee of eviction. This planned obsolescence underlines a visualisation of their inhabitants, the renting class, as moveable masses needing shelter rather than home and community – an attitude that's manifest throughout modern renting history.

Activist women

While the government, the National Coal Board, and later Pemberstone wrote eviction and dispersal into the fate of Oulton's mining homes, Cardboard City's most recent residents had other ideas. Over the past six years, as Pemberstone backed tenants into a familiar corner of eviction, dispersal, and redevelopment, residents – especially the women – came out fighting. In 2017, this bunch of neighbours and friends formed the Save Our Homes LS26 Residents Action Group, and kickstarted a fierce campaign to preserve their beloved homes and community.

Named after Cardboard City's postcode, Save Our Homes LS26 rallied tenants and supporters together to protest the landlord's plans. They printed placards and banners, petitioned Leeds City Council, organised marches, raised funds, attracted media attention, and mobilised institutional backing to prevent forced eviction from their homes of decades. Residents regularly featured in local news, appeared on the BBC's *Newsnight*, and were even the subject of an award-winning documentary short film, *Hanging On*, which showed my dad and other neighbours strung from cranes, literally clinging on to the edges of their homes.[4] Save Our Homes LS26 was supported by trade unions, housing campaign organisations, and the National Union of Mineworkers, as several ex-miners and their descendants still lived on Cardboard City's surviving streets. This solidarity evoked decades of struggles by groups and individuals for decent and secure housing as part of decent and secure working conditions, locally and nationally.

Several women, including my mum, Hazell, and her friends Cindy, Mavis, Linda, and Susan, became the faces of the campaign, utilising modern tools of activism such as social media and blogs, as well as engaging with the appetite for twenty-four-hour online news to ensure sustained attention on the estate. This spotlight resulted in small victories, as well as creating PR problems for landlord Pemberstone and Leeds City Council, which forced them into making concessions.

Like other housing activists before them, Cardboard City's women-led protests were more than an isolated and temporary backlash against a local renting issue. To borrow from writer and trade union activist Pam Currie (describing the women-led Glasgow rent strikes in 1915), Save Our Homes LS26 should be seen as part of a 'wider continuum of women's political activism and radical social change'.[5] In other words, Cardboard City's women, and their families and neighbours, weren't just calling for their individual right to stay in their own homes. Like generations of women tenant activists before them, they were mobilising diverse political forces to fight for an entire estate: its people, all the homes, and the estate's long history as a friendly and affordable neighbourhood for low-income tenants. Rented houses, Save Our Homes LS26 forcefully argued, are *homes* for so many, and not wealth-making assets for the few; tenanted communities need rights and protections.

Yet, Save Our Homes LS26 was not a successful campaign, as the redevelopment is still going ahead; the tenants' beloved historic Airey homes are to be flattened, and the majority of displaced tenants will never be able to return. Nor was it a showy *spectacle* campaign, bringing to light great orators who could galvanise the masses on behalf of the similarly oppressed – the type that tends to make the history books.

My mum, Hazell, and other prominent campaigners such as Cindy, chair of Save Our Homes LS26, worked out their activist tactics on the hoof, juggling full-time jobs, family needs, illnesses, bereavements, and the stress of looming eviction. They spoke powerfully at meetings and rallies, but motivation peaked and troughed as drudgery set in and obstacles multiplied. As with all activists who are subsumed by the challenges they are fighting against, campaign leadership and visibility came with huge physical and emotional costs.

Chroniclers of activists and change-makers tend to lionise successful or 'charismatic' (read: loud, self-assured) activists – often men – and can miss the less showy grafters who might not win the big fight, but who succeed and fail in smaller-scale, more mundane ways that still have social and political significance.

No golden era for public housing

The material past and present of Cardboard City make up the backdrop of this book: a story of built-in obsolescence for renting workers' homes, lucrative development contracts that have always benefited the developer and rarely the tenant, the financialisation of housing, and endless cycles of eviction. To tell this story, I step around the well-trodden history of council house development from the 1940s and focus instead on the rise and fall of National Coal Board housing to show how private builders and commercial interests have always had their fingers deep in the national housing pie, to the detriment of tenants. I highlight how, for more than 150 years, ordinary renters have been seen by political leaders, housebuilders, investors, and industries as moveable masses – encouraged to make homes, then evicted and displaced in multiple cycles within lifetimes and between generations.

A spotlight on the history of housebuilding for rent in the UK, with a closer focus on the lives well-lived on my parents' ex–Coal Board estate, reveals a housing history of constant insecurity – not the public housing golden eras and private sector nadirs that populate many established narratives. The reality, as always, was much muddier. During the nineteenth and early twentieth centuries the state enabled profit-making through rented housing, turned a blind eye to the dereliction of rented properties, and then used moralising arguments to evict tenants and redevelop properties when they became slums. 'Redevelopment' became the acceptable term for tenant displacement and community dislocation.

Even after the Second World War, when Labour developed the notion of a welfare state and set lofty public housebuilding targets, housing policy fell between the cracks of national plans for health, wealth, and productivity. There was to be no national housing corporation. Responsibility for housing policy fell to Aneurin 'Nye' Bevan in 1945. Enthusiastic though he was about building more and better-quality council houses, he was first and foremost the health minister, responsible for implementing the National Health Service – a heavy portfolio without adding housing the nation to his list. In the face of post-war building-material shortages and under intense pressure to deliver numbers, Bevan had little choice but to be pragmatic: incentivising market competition, steering municipal procurement to favour particular private developers, and commissioning house designs that were never built to last.

Then, to win the 1951 election, the Conservatives promised to build more houses than Labour. After winning, Housing Minister Harold Macmillan met that target by overseeing a further drop in quality. Subsequent ministers across succeeding governments were then ideologically flexible about tenant selection, tenant rights, and rent rates. Council houses were increasingly limited to the poorest, and industry houses to physically able working men. Ideas about who was suitable (who *deserved*) to live in public housing narrowed, and all the while rent rates and evictions climbed.

So, even in this apparent golden era of public housing in the decade or two after the Second World War, mass housebuilding for ordinary renters was hamstrung by resource issues and political pragmatism, which lined developers' pockets and resulted in constant compromises over housing quality and tenure security. At times, ordinary people and their families fitted into what policymakers imagined an area needed – for example, where new mines needed labourers. Yet what's clear from the history of Cardboard City is that these estates – and their communities – were treated as impermanent in more ways than the houses' expedient design.

Taking a multi-generational perspective is key. When we speak about a golden era or get nostalgic about secure and affordable municipal housing, its expansion lasted a matter of years and serviced a relatively small number of people. By the late 1950s, council house waiting lists were growing as construction slowed. More people lived in private rentals than local authority housing (32 per cent to 25 per cent).[6] Councils neglected maintenance as budgets tightened, and rent rates rose while wages in many industries were declining. The NCB followed suit. Complaints of maintenance neglect dogged the Coal Board from the point of nationalisation, as they inherited dilapidated housing stock that they deemed too costly to replace. As early as the 1970s, thousands of these neglected houses were being sold off to tenants, then entire estates to speculators in the 1980s. All for peanuts.

By this decade, the term 'council estate' had become synonymous with poverty and crime. Also in the 1980s, hundreds of thousands of prefabs, including the Airey design, were declared defective – requiring extensive inspection and refurbishment or demolition and forcing tenants out in the process. This post-war pattern of shoddy construction, neglect, and eviction was little different to the slum landlordism, clearances, and redevelopments of the Victorian era.

In the grand scheme of modern housing, relatively few families had access to publicly funded homes and then stayed secure in them as council or Coal Board tenants for a single adult lifetime – let alone across multiple generations. All the while, private builders and investors have raked in profits, whichever way the wind blew.

Of course, at the heart of the book are the people affected by these shifts in housing security; in Cardboard City's case, it is the men and women – but particularly the women – who made this Oulton estate home over many generations, and who fought fiercely for it when a landlord sought to boot them out. Beyond Cardboard City's links to national policy, this is an everyday story about Yorkshire housing and community.

Histories of English housing, especially public housing, often centre on southern examples, particularly those in and around London.[7] Where Yorkshire housing developments feature in national histories, it's usually due to their striking designs – such as the 1930s' modernist Quarry Hill council block in Leeds – or as a means to talk about a noteworthy architect or town planner.[8] I want to shed light on a more ordinary Yorkshire estate and community, sharing experiences of housing quality and insecurity that would have been familiar in the North and Midlands across the mid- to late twentieth century because of their vast coal pits and mining communities. Yorkshire was also, of course, home to the Airey company that designed Cardboard City. The wider Leeds area saw the highest concentration of Airey houses in the country – reportedly some 10 per cent of the nation's 26,000 total of Airey stock.[9] That's a lot of people affected by changes in NCB housing policies and prefab design flaws over the years.

Neighbourly interdependence

The ebbs and flows of housing policies and quality have always created tsunami-like waves for ordinary people forced out of their homes. Not least because being evicted can feel catastrophic – like losing your grip on whatever keeps you grounded, at the exact moment you must hold yourself together to find somewhere new. Somewhere that you can live, but also keep your job, your kids' school places, and financial solvency while firefighting unexpected costs. Eviction can destabilise relationships as well as forcing you out of precious personal space. In Cardboard City, the efforts of my parents and their neighbours to protect their homes and community reveal the deep neighbourly friendships, kinships, and social safety nets that are essential for living, yet are constantly broken as tenants are dispersed at the whim of a landlord.

We saw during the COVID-19 pandemic and lockdowns that community support – neighbours helping neighbours – was vital for individual, family, and societal well-being. In Cardboard City throughout the pandemic, residents shopped for each other and met for tea and company in each other's gardens as rules and distance meant family visits were few and far between. These pandemic lifelines were built on long friendships, family links, and interconnected histories.

My 'auntie' Linda, a single woman now in her seventies, has been my mum's close friend for more than twenty years, and until eviction they lived at either end of the same street, Wordsworth Drive. Linda moved to the estate to be closer to Mum, and because the rents were affordable on a single pensioner's income. Another long-time friend of theirs, Susan, moved to Sugar Hill Close, the adjoining street, for similar reasons.

For more than a decade, Mum and Linda went shopping together at least once a week, followed by a ritual of tea and cake at the supermarket café – or, in winter, a midweek roast dinner at our local Toby Carvery. They spoke on the phone almost every day, and Linda spent every Christmas and her Boxing Day birthday with my family, exchanging gifts and fighting over leftovers. Until early 2022, my parents didn't own a working car so they borrowed Linda's for necessities – theirs and hers. During the pandemic, Mum's garden cups of tea with Linda, Susan, Cindy, and others were lifelines. These kinds of interdependent relationships, particularly between women, have characterised Cardboard City since it began. And now they are dispersed – broken. Following their eviction, my parents had to take a small private let in the centre of Rothwell, Linda a council bungalow on the outskirts. Cindy lives in another town, Susan nearly 100 miles away in Newcastle.

Neighbourly care is not a new social phenomenon. Neighbours have long been essential companions and caregivers, particularly for older people. Their reliable presence and proximity mean that even the smallest discomforts don't go unnoticed and opportunities for social exchanges are rarely missed. Neighbours shop for each other, babysit, pet sit, care, and teach their skills to others – as they always have.

Among the stories shared by former residents, one of my favourite Cardboard City characters from the late 1950s was a young piano virtuoso, Mike Terry, who loved honky-tonk music, and won a piano owned by Trinidadian music legend Winifred Atwell when he was just fifteen years old (Atwell was the first Black artist to have a UK number one, in 1954). Larger-than-life Mike Terry went on to become a club musician and at one stage was mentored by Atwell herself; he toured the world performing music and comedy, finally returning to nearby Wakefield, where he passed away in 2017. While living on Oulton Drive in Cardboard City, he used to give piano lessons to kids on the estate (presumably on that same piano!) and was a constant source of entertainment – and noise – for the neighbours.

The estate was full of characters like Mike, each with their own friendly offering of an ear to listen, a shoulder to cry on, a skill to share, or a haircut in a neighbour's shed-turned-barbershop. Many still stay in touch, decades after moving away. Sisters Lynn and Diane, whose family moved into an Oulton Drive Coal Board house before the estate's construction was fully completed in the mid-1950s, continue to meet fellow ex-tenants Gill, Janet, and Angela for regular lunches and to reminisce about their much-loved homes.

Despite these long-standing community relationships, housing policy looks on households as separate social units – especially when it comes to eviction. When it eventually became clear in 2021 that the Save Our Homes LS26 campaign was lost and most Cardboard City residents would have no chance of remaining on the estate, the imperative to keep neighbours together stopped featuring in institutional efforts to support those soon to be displaced. People and houses became detached concerns; Leeds City Council suddenly seemed to lack the funding, tools, and vocabulary to keep the community together outside of Cardboard City. Where it did step in to help rehouse families, it was a matter of every household for itself. Some got cash support, others didn't. Some got council housing, others didn't. None are neighbours any more.

Their house, my home

This blind spot about tenant community connections is not just a by-product of council (and now private rental) housing shortages; it has been central to a two-part logic that has long characterised the British rental sector. First is the idea that people *merely occupy* tenanted houses, so their personal lives are irrelevant to the management of what is legally someone else's property. Tenants are interchangeable in that sense, defined only by their ability to pay rent. Similarly, housing quality and maintenance are budget management issues, rather than a lived reality. Second is the belief that interdependence between neighbouring tenanted homes is happenstance neighbourliness rather than based on essential care relationships – and therefore also irrelevant to housing planning and management.

These two strands have characterised general attitudes towards the rental sector, private and public, for more than 150 years – even during the small post-war window when British political consensus seemed to be behind the state construction of homes and mixed communities. Today, it's jarringly visible in the leaflet pushed through the letterboxes of Wordsworth Drive and Sugar Hill Close – containing information about Pemberstone's proposed demolition of seventy beloved homes but disregarding the existence of the tenants who lived in them, and of their relationships.

This book charts the history and implications of that two-part logic, building up to a very personal story of homemaking in a tenanted estate and of fiery activism by a group of women and their families, who fought – and ultimately failed – to save their homes and community.

To get there, in Part I, I travel through the nineteenth to the mid-twentieth century to chart the rise and fall of slum landlordism, which accelerated a cycle of high rent charges (that bore no relation to accommodation quality), property dereliction, and state-sponsored eviction and dispersal for redevelopment. In Chapter 1, you can see the seeds of a state attitude that came to dominate across the twentieth century: that tenants can, and should, be displaced for their own good. Chapter 2 looks at the period immediately after the Second World War, and the emergence of the state as a house provider in search of quick wins. A combination of post-war pressures – time, resources, and industry interests – led to the costly development of a nationwide prefabricated housing policy and the birth of Cardboard City.

In popular housing histories, the Second World War remains a pivotal moment – a period of change where affordable, state-provided rented homes hit the government mainstream. I don't fully subscribe to that analysis. While the scale of public housing development certainly changed after 1945, approaches to building weren't so revolutionary. Industry rushed through developments to locate workers where they were needed. Private companies saw a boon in contracts at the taxpayers' expense. And tenants were shuffled across the country, oscillating between public and private housing based on availability and evictions. Rents rose as public housing availability declined, and private landlordism grew, bit by bit.

Part II is focused on the story of Cardboard City. In Chapter 3, we arrive in Yorkshire and I take you inside Airey homes. You'll get to meet past and recent members of the Cardboard City community – some of whom will justifiably scold me for still using that nickname for our Oulton estate (it's meant with affection – I promise!). And you'll see how this neighbourhood became a community despite its isolation from nearby towns. Chapters 4 and 5 zoom out to look at how the Coal Board managed Cardboard City and all their housing stock into a state of decline across the 1960s and 1970s. This, coupled with emerging defects in prefabricated houses, left some tenants living in conditions akin to Victorian slums.

From decline to devastation, Chapter 6 charts the nails (plural) in the coffin for NCB and public housing in Britain. While you might be familiar with Thatcher's fire sale of council housing in the 1980s, you might not know that the National Coal Board prefigured the Right to Buy scheme with their own cut-price mass sell-off of tens of thousands of Coal Board properties from 1976 – years before her election victory. Unlike their municipal counterparts, that did not mean Cardboard City tenants had the chance to become asset-rich homeowners. Cardboard City went through a series of murky sales between different companies in the late 1980s and early 1990s. You'll see how families fled, homes emptied, and the community was destroyed. Chapter 7 contextualises these shadowy sales against the financialisation of the rental sector as a whole, and explores the consequences for tenants: absentee landlords, increased rents, and subcontracted accountability.

Of course, tenants have never taken these changes lying down. Part III looks at the rise of tenant resistance in Cardboard City – first at a household level, and then, in more recent years, through the formation of Save Our Homes LS26. In Chapter 8, you'll get to know my mum (and social media whizz) Hazell, as well as Residents Action Group Chair Cindy, stalwart campaigners Mavis, Barry, John, and Mark (my dad), and a whole host of other family members, neighbours, friends, and supporters who brought the campaign to life and forced concessions from Pemberstone and Leeds City Council.

It is impossible to ignore the gendered element of this story: the fact that the Save Our Homes LS26 campaign – and so many housing fights that have come before it – have been spearheaded by women. So in Chapter 9, I'll explore the reasons for this, and its implications for housing history, tenant activism, and housing policy looking forward. At the time of writing, rent reform is again on the cards – this time via the Renters Rights Bill put forward by a newly elected Labour Party. While some reform is better than none, I will explain how this is just the latest in a long line of attempts to fiddle around the edges of a broken system.

To end, I reflect on what went wrong, why we lost the campaign to save our homes and what Cardboard City's demolition says about the ongoing state of all rented housing in the UK. Though housing laws and policies across the book relate to England and Wales rather than Scotland or Northern Ireland, the experiences of eviction and activism that run through the book tell a wider story.

Tying the history and threads of the book together, I conclude by calling out the destructive impacts of 150 years of broken promises for decent and secure rented homes. We've never moved beyond the idea that a house is at the grace and favour of a landlord, whether that landlord is private, a housing association, or the state. Nor have we ever challenged the notion that displacement of the poorest in the name of progress – and sometimes even welfare – is unavoidable. We fail to see relationships across tenanted households as integral to community life. This needs to change. I'll map out how.

PART I

EVICTION AS PROGRESS

1

It's for your own good

When Pemberstone's redevelopment leaflet was stuffed through my parents' letterbox in 2017, we should all have expected a mass eviction. After all, this glossy A5 sheet with its computer-generated estate plan was the first the residents heard that they'd be booted out, yet a lot of time and money had evidently gone into planning already. Pemberstone's strategists were clearly confident that eviction and demolition would be straightforward: the houses and land were for them to use however they liked.

This cocksure and unsympathetic approach solicited a lot of criticism from residents and their supporters, and, for a short time, Pemberstone's disregard of the tenant community looked like it might derail the plan. In October 2019, their planning application was rejected by Leeds City Council – partly on the grounds that demolition would break up a close-knit community who had nowhere else to go. But of course, there's always more in a landlord's armoury – particularly with the law on your side. As Nick Bano writes in his recent book *Against Landlords*, a landlord's power to evict, raise rents, and redevelop is the very foundation of Britain's housing sector – as well as its housing crisis.

In response to Leeds City Council's rejection of their proposals, Pemberstone appealed, kicking the can up to the Planning Inspectorate for review by an independent inspector. To win that appeal review, Pemberstone changed tack and doubled down on the moral aspects of their case: the landlord honourably asserted that they were '*not prepared to allow the current tenants, with the vulnerabilities, protected characteristics and health issues they live with, to continue to rent properties which are becoming unsafe, and which fall far below modern standards'*. What better way to get rid of tenants than to say 'it's for your own good'? For your own safety, even. It was stated without a hint of irony that it was Pemberstone who had been responsible for maintaining the safety and standards of these properties for decades. The argument was, of course, a winner.

In January 2021, a government inspector found in favour of the landlord, greenlighting evictions and demolition. Again with no hint of irony, the inspector reported:

> If no scheme [of structural intervention] for the existing houses is put in place, I anticipate that the dwellings would become unsafe to occupy. In this situation, it is reasonable to expect the Appellant [Pemberstone] would give notice to the existing occupiers.

In short: Pemberstone's neglect of the houses gave Pemberstone the right to evict, so there's no point stalling the inevitable. It's for the tenants' own good.

Eviction packaged as progress or beneficence has no culprit. Yet it clearly has victims: tenants. Renters whose lives are upended as they are forced to leave their homes and communities – these days with just two months' notice, as per the Section 21 'no fault' minimum timescale. This framing of necessity – whether for redevelopment or safety – is very hard to challenge for ordinary tenants. And because there's never been a meaningful parallel moral obligation to ensure decent and secure homes for the renting class, tenants have been subjected to cycles of eviction, generation after generation.

Scourge of the poor

Moralising landlordism grew significantly in the Victorian era, when slum tenants needed booting out for their own good. And slums abounded. In this period, land and property across

Britain were almost entirely in a small number of private hands. Owner-occupier rates remained low, and over 90 per cent of working people were tenants of individual private landlords – landowners and businessmen on various scales who, in the words of one contemporary builder, 'try any mode of making a profit'.[1] As industrialisation and urbanisation accelerated and expanded in Britain across the century, more and more people moved from the countryside to cities and vied for limited accommodation near their workplaces. Housing conditions deteriorated and became increasingly overcrowded. Multiple families occupied a single house – sometimes a single room – and multiple households shared dismal cooking facilities, limited storage spaces, and (if they were lucky enough to have one at all), a toilet area or outhouse.

Private landlords cashed in on this rapidly expanding renting economy but kept a distance from the day-to-day management of the property. In their stead were middlemen who acted as housing managers: letting out rooms, setting and collecting rents, evicting tenants, and – theoretically at least – overseeing repairs. These middlemen were the forerunners of today's letting agents, but with much less oversight. The middleman made his living from getting a share of the rent from all the occupants: the more families he packed into one landlord's property, the more money he made.

Overcrowding did not lower rent rates; at the end of the nineteenth century, many workers in poorer parts of London were shelling out between a quarter and half of their earnings on private rent. A study in York in 1900 highlighted that the poorest workers were paying 29 per cent of their income for these dire conditions.[2] Even scant council housing offered little better. At the turn of the twentieth century, workers were shelling out 23 per cent of average earnings to rent their council homes.[3] These were significant proportions of a poor family's income, when food took between 50 to 70 per cent of household expenditure.

If such hefty costs sound familiar today, that's because little has changed. The Office for National Statistics (ONS) wrote that at the end of 2021, a household in England with an average income (around £2,825 per month) could expect to pay 26 per cent of that on a median-priced private rent. Renters in Wales and Northern Ireland could expect to fork out 23 per cent of their pay packet. It's worse in Yorkshire and the Humber, where renters pay the second-highest percentage of their incomes on rent in the country (31.1 per cent) after London (39.8 per cent) – making Yorkshire more expensive for private rentals than the South East (30.5 per cent), despite having very different income levels.[4] The ONS crisply classes this ratio as 'unaffordable' – even by their own ungenerous measuring stick. (For decades, the unchallenged consensus has been that rent is affordable if it does not exceed 30 per cent of gross income. Yet that equates to roughly 43 per cent of disposable income for the average low-income, basic-rate taxpayer. Food may have got cheaper since 1900, but rents have gone the other way).

Also like today, Victorian tenants had little room to complain as, waiting behind them, there was a queue of willing or desperate replacements. Such was the demand for accommodation in urban industrial areas that poor tenants sub-rented rooms to those poorer still. A 1907 study of Middlesborough steelworkers found that almost a third of tenants were subletting floor spaces in their rented room, unbeknownst to their landlords.[5]

On the surface, thresholds for overcrowding appear to have shifted significantly in the last century and a half, as we don't see many bulging slums today. At the end of the nineteenth century, a dwelling was technically defined as overcrowded if a single room contained more than two adults – one-year-old children didn't count, and each child under ten years old counted as half an adult. As multiple families shared single properties, a four-roomed house (which included the kitchen area as one of the rooms) would be at maximum acceptable capacity in the 1890s with six adults, four children under ten, and any number of babies. Of course, these houses also lacked their own toilet facilities. Over 11 per cent of the population of England and Wales lived in dwellings that exceeded this limit in 1891, with vast differences between urban and rural areas.[6] In industrialised towns for example, overcrowding could affect nearer 35 per cent of households.

If we translate this benchmark to houses today, a four-roomed property would typically be a two-up, two-down. In other words, a two-bedroomed terraced house with an inside bathroom as well as a kitchen and living room downstairs. Imagine: six adults, four children and multiple babies sharing a two-bedroomed terraced house, and that being considered acceptable. Today, acceptable maximum capacity by law (which has not been statutorily updated since 1935) is two people to a room, as long as they're the same sex or in a relationship. The kitchen and living room can still be considered bedroom options if they can accommodate a bed.[7]

So far, pretty similar. The difference now is the space standard, which came in with the 1985 Housing Act. This calculation provides a maximum number of people in a household based on the number of rooms, which also must meet a minimum floor area. If a dwelling has one room of 110 square feet, it should house no more than two people (that is, two adults; or one adult and two children under ten). For two rooms, there is a three-person limit. For three rooms, there's a five-person limit, four rooms have a seven-person limit, and so on. Any room smaller than 70 square feet cannot be classed as a bedroom for an adult. Rooms of less than 50 square feet cannot count as a bedroom at all.

So, in theory, a two-up, two-down terraced house in England and Wales today could house upwards of ten people: five adults, four children, and any number of babies under twelve months. Two couples in two rooms; two boys under ten with one adult male in one room; two children of either sex under ten in the fourth room; and the babies anywhere, as they don't count. Just one baby would take the total up to ten people without exceeding the seven-person limit. That will *technically* be classed as acceptable according to the law today, even if guidelines acknowledge this standard is too low. Turns out, we can't be throwing stones at the Victorians on this one. Some 9 per cent of social-rented households were classed as overcrowded in 2021, along with 7 per cent of privately rented households, and 1 per cent of owner-occupied.[8]

In the moralising times of late-Victorian Britain, dense overcrowding increasingly became a social and health concern for the governing classes. Slum conditions were viewed as petri dishes for disease, crime, and immoral behaviour that, in the view of the well-to-do Victorian, impacted productivity as well as society. In urban areas, many slums stood in the way of industrial expansion, too. Political figures began inching towards change.

Tory leader Lord Salisbury criticised the miserable state of privately owned working-class slum housing in 1883. In 1884, a Royal Commission was established to investigate working-class housing conditions, though its recommendations were paltry in relation to the scale of the challenge. Then, when Salisbury became prime minister in 1885, he enacted minor housing legislation that gave local governments limited powers to build worker lodgings.[9] Rents for this publicly owned housing had to reflect market-rate building costs and they were meant to be sold off within ten years, foreshadowing late-twentieth-century trends to set market-level rent rates and eventually divest the state of its housing stock.

Alternative styles of housing management to the middleman's sardine-can approach also emerged from the mid-nineteenth century. Social reformer Octavia Hill is one of the most commonly cited examples; she acted as a housing manager for over 3,000 people by 1874 (many of whom lived in blocks purchased by her friend, the radical thinker John Ruskin – who was wealthy enough to be philanthropic). Through a direct management strategy, where she and her trained disciples got to know tenants personally as part of the job, Hill sought to improve the living conditions of their largely impoverished tenants.

Hill believed that women were uniquely placed to manage worker housing conditions professionally and with empathy, trying to ensure, for example, that difficult tenants were supported and only evicted as a last resort. She also sought to offer out-of-work tenants temporary employment in basic housing repairs to prevent them falling into arrears.[10] This social work style of management was neither revolutionary in approach nor lasting, however.

Hill retained a middle-class, moralising view of poverty, believing that people should work their way out of it through self-help, while largely ignoring structural factors that prevented social mobility.[11] Hill was also a product of her time, believing that women were uniquely suited to undertake social work; moreover, her reach was relatively limited and her approach was not adopted by other housing management organisations such as the Institute of Housing.

The Institute, a forerunner to the Chartered Institute of Housing, framed housing management as a sphere of (typically male) professional expertise – a technical and economic issue rather than a social responsibility, and one that gradually decreased the contact between rent collector and tenant through bureaucratisation.[12] This masculinised sphere of technical expertise was obviously no less reductive than Hill's notion of feminised social work, but it became the status quo. In the end, Hill's model was the exception rather than the norm for tenancy management, and the tenant came to be viewed as a paying occupier rather than a person living in a home and contributing to a community.

As private ownership dominated in the late-Victorian period, and consecutive governments took a laissez-faire, small-state approach to intervention, there was little chance to change anything at the systemic level. Where local authorities needed to clear slums, they were only able to do so in a few cases: first, as a rare and last-resort punishment for landlords who refused to improve their properties; or second, through the Artisans' and Labourers' Dwellings Improvement Act of 1875 – known as the Cross Act, after Home Secretary Richard Cross – which specified that, where individual improvements were not possible, local authorities *could* step in to undertake clearance (not *must* step in, but *could*).

The Act included an obligation to rehouse displaced residents elsewhere – preferably through philanthropy or private efforts. But this proved so costly that London's Metropolitan Board of Works attempted to lobby a Cross Act inquiry to drop the rehousing obligation and focus only on demolition. On the relatively rare occasions when local authorities did step in to demolish and rehouse, landlords were compensated for losses at market rates, based on their rent receipts.[13] Thus, wherever the Cross Act was applied, tenants were out on their ear, and the landlords who squeezed out most rent through dense overcrowding profited the most from the government compensation scheme.

Options that might have enabled existing rent-paying tenants to stay put were never on the table. Renovation of properties, the provision of basic facilities such as toilets and wash basins, or restrictions around occupancy numbers were barely considered for these slum properties. Instead, evictions, demolition, and rebuilding was the order of the day – a theme we'll see time and again. Ahead of her time, Octavia Hill criticised this fixation on demolition and redevelopment, viewing it as the scourge of the poor as it displaced families from communities, and the cost of rebuilding made the new rents unaffordable for former tenants.[14]

Local councils' stringent vetting procedures for new tenants additionally contributed to a situation where redevelopment tended to put public housing in the hands of better-off workers with predictable, albeit still meagre, incomes. Meanwhile, neighbouring private properties became even more overcrowded, as the poorest of the displaced residents sought any means to stay near their work. Ultimately, though, public housing provision remained relatively small in scale, accommodating around just 1 per cent of the population by 1914.[15] Private tenancies continued to dominate across Britain, and soon enough were exposed as seriously wanting.

Dealing with undesirables

With the onset of the First World War, manufacturing industries expanded production capacity and demand for workers. These workers and their families needed housing and, in already densely populated cities where war industries were concentrated, supply could not meet demand. Overcrowding and slum conditions continued to proliferate. Yet landlords kept increasing rents, even as food and living costs continued to rise.

The problem was particularly acute in Glasgow, which suffered severe housing shortages even before the expansion of the munitions industry. By 1914, the city was at breaking point, recording the highest population density in Britain.[16] Rentier landlords – those whose income comes from property investments – had a virtual monopoly over housing in the city and charged huge amounts, while their slumlord management rendered the houses unsanitary and barely liveable.[17] Some areas saw rent hikes of up to 25 per cent. Even in these abysmal conditions, tenants couldn't keep a roof over their heads, as landlords exercised an unprecedented level of evictions for any number of reasons – particularly non-payment of rapidly escalating rents. Displacement created a destabilising merry-go-round for impoverished workers and, unsurprisingly, anger grew.

A mass rent movement mobilised around the Glasgow Women's Housing Association (supported locally by the Independent Labour Party Housing Committee and Glasgow Women's Labour Party), prompting a groundswell of agitations. These culminated in a massive rent strike in 1915, where some 20,000–25,000 people refused to pay rent and collectively resisted punitive measures.

Rent strikes and agitations were also growing across England and Europe in the years running up to the First World War. Closer to home, in Leeds in 1914, around 300 tenants went on strike against a sixpence increase in rents.[18] The rise was imposed on more than 10,000 houses by the Leeds Property Owners Association (which returns as a bogeyman later in the book). The Labour-affiliated Leeds Trades Council formed a Tenants Defence League and led public meetings to canvass support, though its campaign against rises was ultimately defeated in the courts.

Even closer to home than Leeds, in my home area of Oulton and Woodlesford (and typical of other industrialising areas), concerns also grew about the quality and affordability of housing in 1915. The opening of a large quarry in the 1890s, then the creation of Armitage brickworks in 1907, followed by the sinking of Water Haigh Colliery from 1908, brought significant numbers of workers and their families to the district. But housing supply did not meet demand. The accommodation that was available was neglected, cramped, rat-infested, and lacked any basic amenities. Shared outdoor toilets were often just holes in the ground, covered by a board. Local historian Howard Benson writes that these crumbling cottages were built as investments by quarry owners, who then sold them on to landlords with no connection to the area. The only concern of these landlord investors was collecting rent.[19]

For years there was talk in the local council that private enterprise would fill the housing gap, but projects and houses were not forthcoming, leaving Oulton and Woodlesford's workers with excessively long commutes or dismal living conditions. While some of the area's prominent figures, such as the Armitage family, put effort into building terraced housing with their own bricks and improving sanitation and utilities for their workers, the supply was insufficient to meet overall need. Council members seemed reluctant to back any housebuilding policy that would increase their voters' rates bills (essentially council tax). But the dearth of supply was causing a local housing crisis affecting the poorest the most.

Prominent local figures from across the political spectrum railed against the rising inequalities. In 1915, Thomas Killingbeck (a member of the co-operative movement, Independent Labour Party supporter, and soon-to-be local councillor) wrote to the local newspaper, arguing:

> Sir, I notice in your issue of July 31st that the miners have sent a complaint to the Executive of the Yorkshire Miners' Association at Barnsley about the exorbitant rents charged to them at Woodlesford and district. One would naturally have thought this would be a most inopportune time to take advantage of the scarcity of houses, when all sections of the community are expected to show their patriotism by making some sacrifice for the benefit of the country ... [Yet] greedy property owners have been able to raise the rents to the extent they have ...
>
> If a man can borrow money to build houses with, and make a profit on the transaction by letting the houses to the workers, surely the district council can borrow the money which is required, especially when we realise that local authorities can borrow at a far cheaper rate than any private individual can ...[20]

Killingbeck and likeminded individuals did not achieve any immediate changes to housing in Oulton and Woodlesford. Nonetheless, it was clear that national unrest was growing. The 1915 Glasgow strikes were of such a scale and ferocity that they were key in forcing the government's hand nationally.[21] Rent restrictions were brought in that year to ameliorate the rocketing costs and protests. Rent was frozen to pre-war levels, and the law made it harder for landlords to evict tenants – a victory for the protestors. There was also a sop to landlords, though, as mortgage rates were frozen.

This strike and parallel nationwide agitations then provided some of the impetus for the 1919 Housing and Town Planning Act, which committed government subsidies to finance the construction of 500,000 new council houses over the following three years. Packaged as a programme that would create 'homes fit for heroes' – the returning soldiers – it placed housing firmly within the government's responsibility, promising the development of new rented homes to meet the needs of soldiers and labourers, rather than simply the reactive pre-war slum clearances. It was a policy envisaged as both a reward for war service and an incentive to ignore the temptations of revolutionary Bolshevism, which had taken hold in Russia and Eastern Europe. In other words, the political establishment was increasingly worried about the contagion of revolution.

Mirroring developments up and down the country, Rothwell – the neighbouring town to Oulton and Woodlesford – got its own share of new council homes in this period, with the building of the John O'Gaunt's (now John O'Gaunts) estate just off Haigh Road. Developed by Rothwell Urban District Council (RUDC), the land was given for free by the colliery-owning landowners on the condition that the several hundred new houses went mainly to miners and their families. Howard Benson describes this deal as benefiting both parties: RUDC wanted to take advantage of new government subsidies and develop housing; while the colliery company was too 'tight-fisted' to fund worker housing itself.[22]

While the 'homes fit for heroes' programme was not the first example of government-funded housing in the country, it was certainly one of the most significant in scale up to that point. Alongside housing targets, this post-war government pioneered better standards for working-class homes. The 1918

Tudor Walters Report recommended space standards that few working-class renters had ever imagined, let alone experienced: semi-detached properties rather than terraced; three bedrooms; an indoor toilet; and a scullery to keep bathing separate from the living room (or even a separate bathroom for the higher class of worker). The Report recommended external façades adhere to the long-standing English preference for 'cottage'-style houses – in other words, groups of buildings blending neatly into the semi-rural local landscape. The Tudor Walters Report set the quality standard for council houses for nearly a century afterwards, particularly after the Second World War. But no break is a clean break, and the government then failed to realise (or care) that targets and standards are meaningless without secured state investment protected against economic shocks and weathervane politics.

Soon enough, as the economic situation in the 1920s deteriorated, the housing programme faltered, and the government met less than half of its housing goal – building just 213,000 houses in total. While the Tudor Walters Committee sought to mitigate labour shortages and rising building costs in their initial planning, they had not factored in a post-war depression that sent housebuilding costs soaring.[23] Labour's Charles Latham griped in the House of Lords some two decades later that a lack of government power over price controls in 1921 meant that 'housing was shut down, and local authorities actually paid out to contractors sums of money, not for building houses, but for refraining from building them. Those sums were paid out as damages for breach of contract.'[24] Thus workers did not receive the promised houses, but developers received their fees.

Liberal Prime Minister David Lloyd George's similarly themed Land Settlement Act (1919) also faltered. This offered rented smallholdings to returning soldiers on land provided by councils. The British man, Lloyd George believed, would hold out against Bolshevism and see an improvement in well-being if he were given soil to root in and the confidence that something was being done for him.[25] The government also hoped it might mitigate rural depopulation. The targeted beneficiaries of the scheme were only men, of course; the more than a million women mobilised to work in auxiliary services, war industries, and the public sector were conspicuously absent from entitlements.[26]

Nonetheless, there was no real meaningful housing policy in this gifted land scheme anyway. While the veterans were not necessarily expected to make the land productive, many were still subject to paternalistic scrutiny over their living arrangements and work ethic. One man in Hertfordshire was reported to the Ministry of Agriculture and Fisheries for not manuring his land frequently enough and repeatedly producing inferior crops.[27] Rather than reimagining tenancies and giving returning soldiers more security and agency over their homes, county councils simply replicated the private landlord–tenant relationship, regulating their stay with tight building contracts, loan agreements, and eviction notices should terms be broken.[28] In the end, the scheme proved a financial loss, serving only 22,000 men across England and Wales; some 10–12 per cent of those smallholdings were recorded as complete failures, with even fewer remaining productive and sustainable over the longer term.

The national housing crisis grew, and by the early 1920s there was a clash of ideas about how to address it in the face of ever-declining private and public investment. Conservative politicians were increasingly pushing an austerity agenda as they were concerned about spiralling social spending – even though public housing still only made up less than 10 per cent of the overall housing sector. Landlords refused to invest in repairing their crumbling properties, blaming rent freezes. Space standards and subsidies were reduced in the Conservatives' 1923 Housing Act (though at least the government kept the standard that houses should come with a toilet). This act was primarily introduced to encourage private housebuilding, in a reversal of the 1919 commitment to local authority construction. Government subsidies for public housing then moved away from funding occasional cottage-style houses, as preferred by the general population, towards building flats, in an effort to get more homes for the same money.

Councils were particularly keen to increase dwelling numbers in their industrialised urban centres, and sought to gain construction space by accelerating slum clearances. Many serviceable or reparable homes were demolished in these schemes – sometimes simply because these requisitioned properties came with garden space, and therefore more square footage to construct flat blocks.[29] Others were torn down because they were in prime locations for factories or new office developments. Urban tenants living in these condemned properties were yet again subject to the cycle of eviction and dispersal for public redevelopment.

One local newspaper in Bristol highlighted a catch-22 situation for the evicted. In a Bristol Council housing committee meeting in October 1927, the local council alderman noted that 'none of the houses now being built at St Anne's would be apportioned to people who would be removed from the slums' – destined, as they were, for a higher class of tenant. Yet the alternative of building and offering evicted slum dwellers 'cheaper rate' houses on the outskirts of the city meant that the tenants 'must pay ... high charges in the shape of tram fares' to get back into the city for work.

The solution to this problem of affordable rent rates versus distance to work? Pile them high in blocks of flats. The alderman apparently 'did not care very much for tenements or flats, but one advantage they offered was that they could be erected to accommodate a large number of people near roads that were made already'.[30] All's well that ends well, as long as he didn't have to live in them. Moreover, as these slum clearances and redevelopments were small in scale and done on a shoestring budget (with subsidies ending in 1933), it was determined that the new blocks should only house the poorest of the poor – deepening associations of public housing with destitution and social breakdown (a process termed *residualisation* in academic-speak).

Occupants, of course, had no say in their displacement, the replacement dwelling type, or new rent rates. The Labour government's 1930 Housing Act offered further subsidies to local authorities to rehouse those forced out by slum clearances and keep rents affordable, but tenants still had little say in the alternative accommodation. A 1939 report from the government's Central Housing Advisory Committee exposed the moralising attitude of the political establishment towards evicted occupants of demolished slums, stating that

> A number [of tenants] will adapt themselves quickly to their new surroundings; some will not react to the change in their condition quite so readily and will need initial guidance. Others without continuous supervision will create a slum atmosphere wherever they are sent.[31]

The government was so concerned about that latter type of undesirable slummy tenant, that the Committee also recommended 'separating unsatisfactory families from one another, so far as this is possible, and interspersing them among [poor] families of a good type'.

The idea of a feckless underclass of the poor population was already entrenched among many members of the establishment who doggedly held on to the paternalistic Victorian belief that poverty was the fault of the poor, who demonstrably did not work hard enough to get out of it. Slum clearances and the dispersal of unruly tenants among 'good' tenants highlights no fundamental challenge to that attitude, despite the interventionist veneer.

Troublesome tenants

Yet, while the country was on the cliff-edge of a serious housing crisis at the end of the 1930s, some things had changed considerably since the mid-nineteenth century. Yes, overcrowding remained a significant social and health concern, and eviction was commonplace. Yes, the private market was still failing to meet the needs of the poorest workers. And yes, state intervention in the provision or subsidy of rented housing remained minimal, while a Victorian attitude towards the poor as deserving or undeserving prevailed. The difference was that the small-scale tenant housing gains made in each of these areas were driven by an increasingly mobilised working renter class, and the growing involvement of women activists.

One of the most influential mass tenant movements of the period was that of the women who led the rent strikes in Glasgow in 1915. As noted earlier, profiteering landlords made life unbearable for renters in wartime Glasgow; landlords took advantage of the housing shortage and deliberately overcrowded dwellings while hiking rents to unmanageable rates. Where tenants refused to pay, they were evicted and replaced. Resistance grew, and women workers and residents, whose male family members were often out fighting or working elsewhere in war industries, led the protests. The Independent Labour Party and the Women's Labour League supported the establishment of the Glasgow Women's Housing Association in early 1915, which in turn supported the formation of local committees. As well as individually refusing to pay rents, many of these mobilised women established neighbourhood lookouts for bailiffs doing the eviction rounds and often pelted these unwelcome visitors with flour, wet washing, and other 'missiles' to prevent them from evicting anyone.[32]

Activists including Mary Barbour, Helen Crawfurd, and other women organised protests through meetings with other women in kitchens, across laundry, and out on the streets.

They mobilised women and men in larger-scale rent protests and became household names through their resistance activities. Then in late 1915, when a landlord attempted to take eighteen tenants to court to get rent taken directly out of their wages, thousands gathered outside the courthouse to protest, led by Barbour and her supporters – nicknamed 'Mrs Barbour's Army'. The rent court case was ultimately dropped as a result of the public pressure, but the mass strike continued, and other strikes made their mark across the country as tenants watched and learned from each other, ultimately forcing the government's hand. The Rent Act was passed that year, and rent rates were frozen at pre-war levels – a victory for those tenants, though ultimately no fix for a broken market.

In their fight, these Glasgow women protestors were pulling against social norms of the period. Their homes were feminised spaces where women took the lion's share of domestic work, caring, and raising families. In literature and rhetoric of the day, the home was the woman's sphere, distinctly and deliberately contrasted with the masculine space of the workplace, which was associated with economic production and public action. Women were of course recruited to work (in especially large numbers) during the First World War, yet they were still responsible for most of the cooking, cleaning, and caring at home.

Politically, a lot of trade union–led mobilisation and resistance centred on male workplaces, with labour activists viewing homes and housing issues 'as merely secondary to workplace struggles'.[33] Yet as these home spaces became increasingly overcrowded, unhygienic, and unaffordable for working families in Glasgow and across Britain, the escalating rent rates provided an urgent focus for collective tenant resistance – not least because, while men might have been the main breadwinners, the management of household rents and expenses often fell to women.[34] This put women on the front lines of this very working-class fight – and fight they did. Historian Quintin Bradley writes that, during the 1914 rent strikes in Leeds, housewives refused to produce rent books to rent collectors and prevented them from entering their homes. One housewife 'tossed the poor man out of the house'.[35]

The conditions of a house bleed over into every other aspect of life, too – whether through poverty-induced hunger and threadbare clothing, or strained social relations and domestic violence in an unmanageable environment. As conditions worsened and families reached the end of their tether in Glasgow in 1915, something had to give. Women's voices had to be heard.

The physical make-up of Glasgow's tightly packed and overcrowded tenements also provided the means and momentum for political action. As activist and academic Pam Currie writes: 'The forced proximity of the tenements reinforced opportunities for collective action, facilitating contact between women and overcoming the isolation of the housewife to create a collective identity in struggle.' Political meetings took place in people's homes and communal domestic areas, as well as on the streets and in public houses. This collective action was about 'mutual aid and "survival networks" at a time of crisis'.[36]

Successive interwar governments were not oblivious to the potential power of collective working-class mobilisation. After all, a Marxist–Leninist revolution had taken place in Russia in 1917 and cast a brief shadow over post-war policy-making. Moreover, the 1918 extension of the vote to all men over twenty-one years old – renters and property owners alike – (and women over thirty who met property qualifications) meant that politicians were now motivated to consider working-class renter concerns. Ultimately, though, interwar governments managed to tread a line where they provided titbits (such as a rent freeze and 'homes fit for heroes') while failing to change anything fundamental in the housing status of the working masses. The attitude of government continued to be that rented housing is at the grace and favour of a landlord, and displacement of the poorest in the name of progress cannot be avoided.

Thus, rent hikes and evictions might have stalled in the interwar years – yet so, too, had landlord investment in basic maintenance. Households shelled out less than they might have for rents, but conditions for cleaning, cooking, and caring – a woman's responsibilities – continued to deteriorate. And for those households that fell under the attention of a socially minded state through slum clearances, tenant dispersal not only locked in higher rent rates for whatever development replaced the slums, but clearance operations ensured the break-up of mutual aid networks – the last safety net in a time of crisis. And another huge crisis was, of course, round the corner. As a new world war broke out in 1939, successive governments were forced to rethink how to manage housing shortages. A prefabrication revolution was on the way.

2

Public money for private contracts

Lynn Abbott was born in the early 1950s and moved onto Oulton's Coal Board estate when she was around eighteen months old, back when the houses were shiny new. Family was everything to her back then, as it is now, and family life for a long time revolved around the coal pits and life on a Coal Board estate. Lynn is warm and generous when I ask if we can meet to talk about her memories of those years. She invites me to her home, a beautifully kept bungalow just a few minutes' drive from Cardboard City, and brings her sister Diane and three other long-time friends and Coal Boarders – Gill, Janet, and Angela – to share their reminiscences about growing up in mining families. Memories flow and the five of them together were hard to keep up with, adding to each other's stories, punctuating anecdotes with hoarse laughter, and dropping names only hardcore Coal Boarders would recognise. As daughters of miners, chat often veered from life in the estate's new prefab homes, to what their dads went through to put food on the table, and back again.

'I always felt for me dad you know,' shares Lynn, at one point in our conversation. 'We went to that place, me and our Rachel [her daughter], up in Durham – Beamish [open air museum], and you can go down the pit. They gave us a hat. "Now get on your hands and knees because you'll be going down as you go in" [the guide said]. And there's this bloody fella with a big lantern, there's me behind him crawling on my hands and knees. I got right claustrophobic. When we did get to the bottom, there was like a levelled bit and a coal face. And then there were dynamite sticks. And after that, I thought, what my dad had to do to make us OK, to keep us six fed and clothed! And getting his body like that.'

Lynn and Diane's father, Mac Dickinson, ended up with ailments familiar to miners up and down the country: vibration white finger; pneumoconiosis; deafness. Lung cancer was a common cause of death for miners in the end. All of Cardboard City's original residents were coal-mining families, with the men working in dangerous conditions to maintain the country's post-war energy supply. Because of this, there was huge pride in the work, too.

As the mines closed, Oulton's miner residents dispersed, often in search of new pits to work at. From the 1980s to the present, the estate inevitably diversified but it retained a low-income, working-class character through its ex-miner pensioner residents and new low-wage or welfare-recipient arrivals. Many recent residents were public sector workers, fulfilling the country's changing needs just like the miners. My mum is an NHS administrator; Dad – previously a factory worker and caretaker – found a job as an NHS driver while living at Wordsworth Drive. My brother's a mail sorter with Royal Mail. Cindy is a teaching assistant in a local primary school, and Susan worked in NHS administration until she retired.

The low-income character of Cardboard City's community featured as a big part of eviction discussions – in our campaign and around the council's table. Not least because it can't be taken for granted that low-income renting families can continue to afford private rents, generation after generation. When Pemberstone's planning application was being considered by Leeds City Council's planning panel, one of the Labour councillors remarked that she was particularly concerned about the loss in affordable housing for the country's key workers. 'We support affordable housing for public sector workers,' she said. That was, after all, who the estate was built for in the 1950s. It turns out the support was in spirit, rather than practice. When the collieries closed in the late twentieth century, many miners lost their homes. When Pemberstone won its redevelopment application at appeal some four decades later, all shorthold tenants were swiftly thrown to the mercy of the private rental market.

Citizens working in public service have always been politically expedient – heroes when their efforts are needed to keep things going (as during the pandemic), villains or scroungers when they ask for help or compensation (as when they strike for better pay and conditions). Or they are simply nonentities, easily forgotten when no platform can be made of their needs. Even after the Second World War, political promises for better living and working conditions fell by the wayside when the crisis was far enough in the rear-view mirror.

The Second World War impacted all areas of British life, with housing proving to be critical. As well as rising demand for new houses due to bomb destruction, lingering slum conditions, and increasing birth rates, the country was faced with squeezes at the supply end. Labour and material shortages were chronic. Politicians had to think creatively about solutions – and advancements in construction technology coupled with the wartime expansion of manufacturing seemed to open a world of possibilities. Moreover, wartime leaders were a politically diverse bunch, which helped to propel momentum for change. A coalition government – led by Conservative Prime Minister Winston Churchill but also featuring significant figures from Labour – meant that voices championing workers' concerns had a platform. Of course, Britain's workers had doubled up as the soldiers that brought the country victory, so, as in 1918, gratitude and reward once more became watchwords of the day. Yet there was pressure this time to do it right. Capturing the mood of the moment, the Earl of Dudley entreated his fellow lords and elected politicians to learn from past mistakes, declaring in 1943 that:

> They [the British population] have all been proved heroes in the fierce fire of war. The courage shown by this country and the cheerful sacrifices made exceed all reckoning ... If the people of this country are let down again the consequences will, I believe, be fatal. Therefore let all those responsible for their welfare spare no effort to give them that one thing without which their happiness cannot be assured – namely, decent and adequate homes to live in, with a standard which they themselves regard, and regard rightly, as the very minimum.[1]

When Labour won an election victory towards the end of the war in 1945, the party was able to plough ahead with housing and other social reforms. It heralded a period of significant change in the composition of the housing sector, and tenants were both beneficiaries and victims of the ebbs and flows of housing policy changes.

Wartime planning and debates in the Lords and Commons chambers focused on how many houses to build and out of what materials. While one Labour MP predicted an urgent need for 2 million to be built *per year* immediately after the war, the coalition government White Paper published in March 1945 calculated the short-term supply should be around 750,000 new homes plus 500,000 from slum clearances.[2] Once in power, the new Labour government settled for less ambitious, though perhaps more feasible, targets. Grappling with material shortages, target figures began at 240,000 per year, but were gradually adjusted downwards, dropping to 200,000 by 1951.[3] While this was the largest government intervention in housing up to that point, at those rates it would have taken years for the bomb-damaged houses to be replaced, without even beginning to address the additional needs caused by increased marriages and births.

In any case, the Labour government didn't manage to meet even the adjusted targets – building just over a million by 1951.[4] The housing programme fell well short of expectations – half a million houses short. Discontentment with slow progress was part of the reason Labour was booted out of government at the next election, when the Conservatives used housing as their trump card and won. The new Conservative government then smashed earlier records (for a few years at least), building a promised 319,000 in 1953 and 348,000 in 1954, with numbers and commitment to building declining thereafter.

With these significant building sprees, the make-up of the housing sector was changing rapidly. By 1951, local authority housing made up around 18 per cent of the sector; private lets still made up the majority at about 50 per cent, and the rest were owner-occupied dwellings.[5] The private-landlord share of the sector was in fairly rapid decline, while both council housing rates and owner-occupation were on the rise – especially after the 1953–54 building boom. By 1961, private lets had decreased to less than 30 per cent of all tenures.[6]

Having the council as a landlord made a qualitative difference to living standards for many. In the private sector, countless slum properties continued to stand as demolition interventions were paused during the war. Moreover, rent controls had been reintroduced during the war, which weakened eviction powers and set private rent rates at 1939 levels so as not to aggravate the housing shortage. Rent yields decreased year on year against rising wages and inflation, so landlords skimped even further on maintenance. Scholar Peter Malpass notes that 10 million households in England and Wales alone lived in properties that, at best, lacked basic amenities, or at worst were totally unfit for human habitation.[7] Dismal conditions and overcrowding continued to be chronic across the country.

Take the situation of 'Mrs F.' and her family in Leeds, recounted in the *Yorkshire Evening Post* in 1948:

> Mrs. F and her husband lie awake every night ... listening to rats and mice chasing about the floor. There are so many

> of them. For this 'home' for herself, husband, five-year-old daughter and three-year-old son, Mrs. F. pays 10.s. a week. The bedroom ceiling was so low that ... [she] is afraid it will collapse on her and the family. Both rooms are musty with dampness. The outside wall is insecure in places. From the inside daylight can be seen through spaces between the bricks. The house is draughty. The kitchen fireplace is loose. There are gashes in the floor boards. Window panes are broken.[8]

Mrs F. was expecting her third child later that year but was told to make arrangements for it to be born in that mouldering apartment as there were no vacant hospital beds. In another case shared by the newspaper, a 'Mrs X.' lived in one cellar room with her husband and baby. The journalist described the cellar as rat-infested, with rotten wood floating in 'pools of thick black water nearby'. The room had no lighting and broken cellar windows. Above them lived eighteen people sharing seven rooms. In response to these sorry tales, Edwin Booth of the Leeds Property Owners Association (the organisation introduced in Chapter 1, which provoked strikes in Leeds with its 1914 rent hikes) trotted out the same old defence landlords had been using for nearly half a century already, stating that 'there is no incentive for landlords to repair houses ... [as they] are unable to raise their rents under the Rents Restrictions Act'. Funnily enough, most landlords hadn't invested when rent yields were high, either.

In order to tackle these horrific slum conditions, both Labour and Conservative governments up to the mid-1950s prioritised building new houses first, and advancing slum clearance second, although they sometimes went hand in hand. Government-funded housebuilding then accelerated along two tracks: the first, well-documented track was the construction of municipal houses directly through the local authorities. The second was the construction of state-owned houses by nationalised industries to serve their workers.

With coal emerging as one of the biggest post-war nationalised industries, the National Coal Board became one of the country's biggest landlords, managing more than 160,000 houses and upwards of half a million tenants.[9] These NCB homes were on the state's books through nationalisation, and rents were deliberately pegged to local authority rates. In that sense, they were public housing comparable with municipal houses. Yet NCB homes were ultimately run by a separate entity to local councils and were tied to the operations of the national coal industry.

As such, their location, management, and, ultimately, their sale were shaped by a set of forces quite distinct from the local authority house; in other words, these weren't simply 'homes for heroes', they were worker houses serving an industry. This industry-shaped side of the 1950s' public housing boom reveals early cracks in the government's plan for public housing security: tenants came last. To tell this aspect of the story requires a short detour to the origins of the National Coal Board and the state of its housing stock in 1947.

Feudal beginnings

Coal was in short supply as a result of the war, and shortages were exacerbated by poor weather conditions in the immediate post-war years. Demand grew as the country sought to get itself back on its feet, forcing coal rationing and threatening a wider energy crisis. Keen to ramp up production, Labour Prime Minister Clement Attlee nationalised the coal industry in 1947, with the National Coal Board as the industry's public managing body. It acquired 958 mines in its first year – including Water Haigh in Woodlesford, Fanny Pit at Rothwell, and Newmarket and Savile at Methley, the four closest to Oulton.

Coal mining was set to be one of the largest post-war industries in Britain, employing some 850,000 people in the late

1940s. While the National Coal Board was able to acquire nearly a thousand mines to boost production, what it lacked was accommodation for the miners and their families. The return of issues dating from the 1910s – nationwide house shortages and persistent slum conditions – was not just a social concern, but one that risked stunting a post-war industry vital to Britain's economic recovery.

The first tranche of NCB housing stock – around 140,000 dwellings – was inherited, as some of the acquired collieries already came with worker accommodation. Prior to nationalisation, privately owned collieries and other industries such as agriculture operated a tied cottage system, whereby workers were given dwellings for as long as they worked in the role and could be evicted when the job ended. This feudal practice placed the tenant worker in an insecure position because there was no recourse against eviction upon termination of employment, which could be for ill health and redundancy as well as a worker quitting or being fired.

Colliery and farm owners and managers reigned supreme in these arrangements. In the agriculture sector, for example, a farm owner was able to purchase houses in a local village, gain a certificate from the authorities to state that this was now farm accommodation for farm workers, and promptly evict whoever was living within it – no matter how long the families had been living in the homes or what their connections to the local area were. Tenant farm workers would then move in, but were subject to eviction should they leave or lose their farm role. While the Rent Restrictions Act of 1939 prevented eviction in the absence of alternative accommodation in many types of rentals, tied cottages were not included in its provisions.

In one case reported by the *Lincolnshire Echo* in May 1946, tenant farm worker Charles Thompson tried to stay in his tied cottage after leaving the farm's employment because, as he said to the landlord, 'I do not know where to go'.[10] The dispute reached local magistrates and Thompson was given twenty-eight days to vacate his home and return possession to the landlord. In 1947 in Chislehurst, the local MP brought to the House of Commons a case of an ex-serviceman in his constituency whose 'health gave out working on the land, [so] he was evicted five days before Christmas along with his wife and seven children'.[11]

Some landlords were not even evicting to get new workers in; they were aiming to sell the houses for profit. While local authorities were technically obliged to rehouse an evicted tenant, it did not have to be in the immediate vicinity of the original home and so families and social networks were broken up anyway. Thus, for many across the country, housing conditions remained feudal and extended family/neighbour safety nets were broken without a second thought.

Rents for tied cottages were either deducted from wages or essentially cancelled out through downwards wage adjustment; as such, many tied-cottage tenants found themselves economically trapped. They were priced out of local owner-occupation and private rentals due to their low wages, and local authority housing outside of urban areas was relatively scarce – leaving tenants trapped in insecure work accommodation. In agriculture, the proportion of farm workers living in tied cottages was 34 per cent in 1948 – around 300,000 – increasing to 53 per cent by 1976, even though the total labour force declined.[12] That relatively high proportion might have been because these tied homes were often, as one Warwickshire newspaper stated in 1955, 'the only inducement for a man to enter agriculture', at least for the very poorest of workers. Housing costs and scarcity were such that they couldn't get a roof over their head in any other way. It was not until 1976 that the law changed to give farm workers a bit more tenure security.

For the mining sector, there were a few examples of colliery owners setting up housing schemes for workers that were not so brutally insecure.[13] However, for the majority of collieries, business needs came above providing housing quality and security. The situation then changed with post-war nationalisation, as colliery-tied dwellings were mostly subsumed within the NCB's soon-to-grow housing stock. Of the 140,000 houses inherited from private collieries after 1947, most were brick terraced properties in an appalling state of repair. Many housed tenants were not even linked to the mines – who themselves would have been turfed out by the government to make way for new coal workers. The new Labour government promised that these transferred houses were to have 'far greater security' of tenure than they did under private collieries (and certainly better than agriculture workers experienced for many decades longer).[14] They couldn't have been much worse. Either way, the transferred stock was never going to be sufficient for the expanding coal sector, and so the next step for the NCB was to build, build, build.

The NCB as landlord

The expansion of NCB housing in the 1940s and 1950s was shaped by the growing role of the state in other areas of welfare and the economy. Labour won the 1945 election off the back of a promise for radical reforms, the most famous of which was the creation of the National Health Service (inaugurated in 1948). The blueprint for an expanded welfare state came from the 1942 Beveridge 'Social Insurance and Allied Services' report, which gave a great many recommendations for tackling the five 'giants' that the author, Sir William Beveridge, argued were holding Britain back: idleness; ignorance; disease; squalor; and want. Post-war Labour Prime Minister Attlee and, in particular, Minister for Health Nye Bevan, took Beveridge's 'cradle to the grave' welfare recommendations and turned many of them into policy. This radical expansion of the state signalled a party that was riding the wave of working-class voter aspiration; after all, the British population had voted for access and fairness to characterise work, health, and education.[15]

Left out of this mix, though, was a long-term solution to the general housing supply crisis and costly private rents. Beveridge dedicated several pages to 'the problem of rent' in the 1942 report, but failed to come up with a meaningful solution to the terrible living conditions and high charges facing renters in 1940s Britain.[16] Part of the problem was the unevenness of rent rates across the country and the apparent difficulty in working out whether this was a result of *actual* costs to landlords of running a house, or landlords' desires to charge more for whatever reason (typically profit).[17] Attlee's Labour, and successive governments of all stripes, seemingly couldn't solve the problem either.

Scholar Peter Malpass notes that, though nationalisation was front and centre of Labour policy for the decade before the party's 1945 victory, construction was never a target for nationalisation – despite frequent criticism of speculative builders and poor-quality housing.[18] Moreover, Nye Bevan was personally strongly opposed to any centralisation of housebuilding, preferring – in line with the 1918 Tudor Walters recommendations – local authorities to retain control. Thus, where health, education, and other key services were soon to be state-run, there was to be no National Housing Corporation or National Building Industry. In fact, there was not even a dedicated housing ministry for quite some time.

In the post-war wave of welfare reforms, the Labour government attempted to find a middle ground, meeting public provision and the housing market halfway. The spirit was certainly public: Bevan believed housing should be available to all and not means-tested. Moreover, the accommodation had to be high quality, with plans for everyone to benefit from the same high space standards, again set by the Tudor Walters Report – including the rural cottage aesthetic, at least as far as materials would allow.

The government also established the principle of 'mixed communities' through the 1949 Housing Act, by removing the requirement for municipal housing to be kept only for the poorest. In other words, Labour sought to avoid ghettoising the poorest in council housing, and instead aimed to provide inexpensive rented homes for all types of people who needed and wanted accommodation after the war. This meant in theory that miners, shopkeepers, housewives, teachers, lawyers, factory workers, the unemployed, and others, would all live as neighbours in affordable rented council housing with secure tenancies.

In a speech in Parliament, Bevan argued that it is 'entirely undesirable that on modern housing estates only one type of citizen should live ... If we are to enable citizens to lead a full life, if they are each to be aware of the problems of their neighbours, then they should be all drawn from the different sections of the community.'[19] In many ways, this was a recognition of the interdependence of neighbours and the importance of that network and of social mixing in wider societal well-being. Bevan was concerned about the quality of utilities, too, offering larger rooms with fitted kitchens and inside toilets. The approach represented a dramatic break with the slum housing of the recent past.

With local authorities in charge of delivering Labour's housing vision, the project looked truly revolutionary on paper – but the level of expertise and capacity required to make it work seemed to be taken for granted. Most local authorities were ill-equipped to manage such a large programme of new and urgent construction alongside slum clearance and redevelopment. Responsibility for development within each council was often split between different departments, compounding the administrative problems caused by housing policy's fragmentation at the national level. And the newbuilds' rents were often still too high for the poorest workers to afford.[20] Council tenants then tended to be in skilled or clerical working-class positions.

Another problem was that the provision of housing on the basis of general needs was a political principle that accompanied building targets, rather than a protection enshrined over the longer term in law with consensus across Parliament. That meant that when government budgets tightened, or when the political winds changed direction with a new party in power, housing targets were at risk of contraction, mixed communities could become expendable, and housing quality could be reduced (as happened from the mid-1950s). Moreover, the multiple economic and welfare plates that the Labour government was spinning in the early post-war years inevitably meant some policy pragmatism and compromise were sought from the outset.

One of those spinning plates was how exactly to get enough houses built, considering nationwide shortages of labour and materials. The Labour government failed to create a new Ministry of Housing to focus on the challenge – what some critics refer to as Attlee's greatest administrative error.[21] Instead, Bevan built a national housing programme partly on a foundation of thinking that came from the coalition government in the war years. Enter the private sector.

The cross-party (though Conservative-dominated) view during the 1940s was that in the longer term, the private sector should ultimately be responsible for the bulk of new housing; any state programme of mass housing in the interim was only temporary, to plug the gaping hole.[22] While Bevan favoured a more municipal solution to the problem of decent and secure rented housing, his party failed to implement policies that ensured and protected municipal dominance into the future – and the Conservatives had little interest in making housing a long-term public responsibility in the first place.

In their book *Squalor*, writers Daniel Renwick and Robbie Shilliam challenge a widely held assumption that there was a post-war consensus in favour of an expansive welfare regime that included housing. The reality of the British housing context – inequitable land allocation across the country, high building costs, rent controls, moral judgements around housing, and uneven rent rates – fomented dissenting views around construction and who should manage the properties. While Bevan and key Labour figures might have philosophically supported a state-controlled provision of housing needs, the political terrain leant more towards the state accommodating private interests.[23]

For example, local authorities relied on private contractors to build their houses.[24] Housing was seen as an important social duty, a Ministry of Housing undersecretary remarked in 1953, but the priority was to reduce the 'burden' on the Exchequer 'by encouraging private enterprise to do more'.[25] When Bevan needed to meet building targets in 1950, he agreed to increase private sector housebuilding from 10 per cent in each district to 20 per cent – with some districts permitted to exceed even that number.[26] These state contracts and bulging targets bolstered market prices and gave property developers a shot in the arm to kickstart their long-term post-war commercial dominance – sustaining their political influence (to which I'll return shortly). It wasn't a conspiracy of profiteers, just the familiar outcome of political power and desires for expediency meeting vested interests.

Another spinning plate was the nationalisation of the coal industry and the sector's urgent need for mining labour, primarily across the north of the country – and for those miners to live near their places of work. Local authority resources were wholly inadequate for the demands for miner housing, not least because the private sector could pick and choose their construction jobs. Profit-conscious private enterprises were reluctant to build in mining areas (largely in the North and Midlands) due to the risk of subsidence. The majority of building licences for private companies were then issued in the South – creating a North–South divide in public housing provision from the beginning.[27]

Local authorities had to pick up the slack and said they couldn't meet Coal Board demand, so the Board had to build its own houses. While coal was a public industry, the NCB enjoyed a lot of autonomy from central government and little direct interference from ministers.[28] As such, the Board's parallel programme of house construction ended up being quite distinct from local authorities'.

On paper, the NCB was to fit within the norms of local authority provision. In the first instance, councils were required to assess whether they could meet the demands for coal-mine housing. Some 12,000 colliery homes were built this way. Then, between 1951 and 1953, the NCB committed to building an additional 20,000 houses in manpower-deficient areas.

To manage this housing expansion and other land issues, the NCB set up an Estates branch. Estates management was a mighty task, as the NCB had become one of the largest landowners in the country, as well as one of the biggest landlords. As housing needs increased, the Board established the Coal Industry Housing Association (CIHA) in 1952, under the directorship of civil servant Miles Hudson, who had been the principal surveyor with the Ministry of Housing and Local Government and was seconded to the CIHA role. A newspaper piece described Hudson as forty-three years old, with 'a special interest in non-traditional housing'.[29] The CIHA was to manage housebuilding targets, contracts, construction, tenancies, and rents for Coal Boarders.

From the get-go, collieries across the country were organised into geographical areas and some had an acute housing need for their ballooning labour force. Out of the nearly 20,000 houses proposed by the NCB by 1953, some 9,000 were needed in the North Eastern Area alone, which included the pits near Oulton in Yorkshire – the soon-to-be home of Cardboard City.[30]

The local councils took absolute precedence in public housing development for a time. Even though the two teams – councils and the NCB – were ostensibly working towards the same ends, competition and frustration was evident. For example, the CIHA was prohibited from using local labour and materials to build Coal Board houses, so as not to impinge on local authority construction. As a result, the CIHA's building contractors had to bus in labour at a higher cost. Miles Hudson complained that this practice amounted to a racket, as local men were apparently moving to neighbouring areas 'so as to be paid for playing cards in luxury coaches'.[31] Hudson and the Board felt that local authorities were 'blackmailing' them at times, forcing the Board to pay additional water-connection fees on pain of stalling utility agreements. 'They knew we had an urgent need for houses', Hudson wrote in 1956, 'and could not work without the Agreement, so the Board had to pay.'[32]

Local authorities were also keen to ensure that rent rates for the mining houses should not 'under-cut' council house rent rates, perhaps fearing that lower rents might drain local labour into the mines at the expense of other industries.[33] For their part, the NCB did not want non-miner residents living in miner housing. Whatever the reasons for pegging NCB rent to that of local authority housing, it highlights the emergence of a rent-rates structure that didn't necessarily cater to the poorest tenants.

The needs of the pits did not always converge with government aspirations for mixed communities, either. While discussions between the NCB and local authorities included the paper commitment that 'all possible steps should be taken to avoid the segregation of miners into separate mining communities', the realities of pit location and high labour requirements meant that the opposite often occurred.[34] Where large estates such as Cardboard City were built for NCB housing, the tenants were entirely linked to the mines because the stock was only for mineworkers.

The construction materials of many of these houses differed from the mainly brick houses being put up by local authorities, too. The NCB was able to outpace local authority construction in many areas by utilising modern materials. No need to wait for the brick industry to recover from the war when there were new and exciting ways to build houses more quickly. In fact, the NCB seemed to be at the vanguard of the prefabrication revolution that had captivated Parliament for the best part of a decade. Yet silver bullets are what they seem: a simple solution to a complicated problem. Forgive the pun, but cracks soon appeared.

Windscreen wipers for the windows

As mentioned in the introduction, prefabrication did not entail just one design; rather, it was 'a series of different methods of framing and classing a basic set of accommodation', which included steel-frame construction, as well as cast-in-situ concrete and pre-reinforced concrete – in other words, housing with pre-made components that was not a conventional brick masonry structure.[35] This isn't a book about technical specifications, but it's important to outline some of the details, as the construction materials were soon to become the problem.

Prefab houses could be temporary, with a very short lifespan of a decade, or supposedly permanent (although ending up as anything but). Since the early 1940s, politicians in Parliament had been engrossed in a series of debates around prefabrication and non-traditional housing. The wartime Burt Committee, set up by the minister of health, the secretary of state for Scotland, and the minister of works in 1942, recommended prefabricated housing as a solution to a housing crisis that was expected to worsen after the war. Although discussion of prefabrication didn't start there (prefabricated houses had existed in some form since the fourteenth century), the Burt Committee report certainly provided a focal point for political attention and the war gave the discussions further momentum.[36]

As part of his building remit, Minister of Works Lord Portal commissioned a series of investigations into suitable designs that he hoped could 'solve' the post-war housing problem. He even had one design named after him: the Portal Bungalow (exhibited in 1944). Conservative peer Lord Barnby was another champion, speaking time and again of a prefab building's utility. Highlighting their 'scope for artistry', Barnby waxed lyrical about how prefab houses would be the new automobiles: no longer scorned for ugliness, because advancements in technology meant that houses needn't forgo comfort or visual appeal.[37]

The general public was more comfortable with mass production techniques by that point, too, following their use in war munitions and military infrastructure. During this time, around the mid-1940s, prefabs were frequently spoken about in Parliament as the ideal solution to the acute housing crisis in agriculture, as some of the designs vaguely resembled rural cottages. In fact, the two-storey pebble-dashed Airey prefab house was the leading prototype for this purpose. However, as the post-war housing crisis became more apparent, prefabs were increasingly raised as a potential solution to all the country's housing ills.

The most famous prefabricated houses were the temporary bungalows built after the 1944 Housing (Temporary Accommodation) Act. Prime Minister Winston Churchill was a particular fan of this scheme, having frequently spoken enthusiastically of non-traditional housing – most famously in his March 1944 speech, 'Our Greatest Effort Is Coming'. Promising at that point around half a million temporary prefabs to satiate need, Churchill declared his hope that with such homes, 'several hundred thousand of our young men will be able to marry several hundred thousand of our young women and make their own four-year plan'.[38]

In the end, 156,623 temporary homes were built, each designed to last ten years – better than four, but hardly the foundation for a lifetime of housing security. These bungalows (steel-framed, timber-framed, cement-clad or concrete-reinforced) mitigated labour and material shortages by making more use of available materials, and through prefabrication in factories they required less labour and time than a traditional masonry house. The war, of course, meant that factories were in a better position to scale this up than they might otherwise have been. In fact, a car factory was behind the production of the first steel Portal bungalow prototype, and people joked that the windows should have windscreen wipers.[39]

Prefab historian Greg Stevenson writes that such housing was described as temporary because of people's concerns that the construction materials were too lightweight to live in for too long.[40] The government was essentially saying: 'Don't worry, we'll build you proper houses soon.' If there were worries about the exterior, tenants were soon won over by the bungalows' internal fixtures and fittings, including built-in cookers, sinks, and fridges that were far superior to what these poorer renters had seen before in their cramped terraced houses or slum apartments. These homes often came with garden space, too – a feature that has consistently been an aspiration for renters and homeowners in Britain for more than a century. The Temporary Housing Programme was also designed to appease industry and the construction trade unions, which feared post-war job losses once the need for munitions and war infrastructure decreased. These workers could be redirected straight to housebuilding. Win–win?

Sadly not. Even before its mass roll-out, temporary housing clearly presented numerous problems. According to scholar Nick Hayes, experiments with prefab housing up to that point had repeatedly failed: the structures were costly to put up, unpopular among tenants, and characterised by defects.[41] Then there was the concern that temporary is rarely as temporary as promised; deterioration sets in, yet no one wants to pay for refurbishment. Lord Latham, leader of London County Council, remarked from the Labour benches of the House of Lords in May 1943:

> I should hesitate myself before contemplating any wide use in normal circumstances of pre-fabricated buildings for houses and cottages. Some of us are not without experience of the experimental dwellings put up after the last war. Some of them have stood up very well, but others have manifested defects which must not be allowed to recur.[42]

From the Conservative benches, Sir Jonah Walker-Smith, added:

> I was induced under the conditions of the last war to secure the erection in Scotland of a considerable number of [temporary] houses, which were intended to last only two years, but I regret to say that once they were up they remained, and continued to exist as slums for the following 20 years.[43]

Walker-Smith was right to be concerned. Tens of thousands of those original prefab temporary bungalows created after the 1944 Act remained standing well into the 1970s, and thousands were occupied well into the 2010s. One of the longest surviving of those estates was Excalibur in Lewisham, where 187 Uni-Seco timber-framed bungalows still housed families until very recently. These two-bed council bungalows had built-in cupboards, an immersion heater, an indoor toilet, and a garden. Mr O'Mahony, a resident who lived on the estate from the end of the war until recently, told historian Elisabeth Blanchet what it was like to move in: 'To find a bathroom inside was magic … and a refrigerator! Ordinary people didn't have them.'[44]

More than a decade ago, Lewisham Council approved plans to redevelop the estate. Excalibur's tenants fought fiercely to save it from demolition because they were well-kept and beloved homes, with memories and long-standing neighbourly relationships. Residents had ploughed money and time into making these homes their own over the years, undoubtedly saving the council money. But the tenants ultimately lost their homes; the council evicted and relocated everyone, and is in the process of constructing 371 new houses on the site. Just six prefabs have been listed and saved for heritage purposes.

Similar stories of resistance to prefab redevelopment can be heard in Bristol, Newport, and elsewhere across the country. Yet demolition was long written into the DNA of these homes, which were designed to be past their useful life by 1955 at the latest. It was a planned obsolescence of these families' lives. Eviction may have been kicked down the road by an extra sixty years, but it was going to happen at some point because the houses were simply not built to last.

Beyond the 156,623 bungalows built in the Temporary Housing Programme, prefabrication took off for what were considered more permanent prefabricated housing – which came with around a sixty-year 'technical guarantee' – essentially a projected lifespan. Several of these prefab designs were taken up by the National Coal Board for construction on colliery estates in the 1940s and 1950s, including: Easiform; Reema; Wimpey No-Fines, Cornish Units, and – of course – Airey (the model populating Cardboard City). These non-traditional house designs could be part-constructed in factories and put up on site by unskilled labour rather than professional builders. In that sense, their use promised to mitigate another post-war crisis: unemployment. Returning soldiers, the unemployed, and men who had worked elsewhere in the war machine could be diverted to construction without barriers to entry or the usual time lag of training.

Churchill was certainly sold on prefab promises, and the press associated him with these developments, too – dubbing one of the first publicly exhibited prefab prototypes the 'Churchill Steel House'.[45] The technology involved in this type of building method seemed to capture the imagination of many other political leaders at the time, who likened these houses to the factory line of cars, furniture, clothing, and other consumer goods. The wartime Committee for the Industrial and Scientific Provision of Housing championed the idea of prefab homes as another consumer good which could be discarded and replaced when no longer needed.[46] While that sounds wasteful to an environmentally conscious population today, back in the 1950s mass consumption was very much in vogue – particularly among those who could afford it.

Just like corporations producing consumer goods such as cars and coats, private building companies stood to benefit from a sudden surge of interest in mass-produced housing, too. Each prefabrication design was developed by a different company, many of which had fostered strong relationships with the Ministry of Works and other government departments through their roles in military-related manufacturing during the First and Second World Wars. The political decision not to centralise house planning or nationalise the building industry after 1945 meant that these businesses were all well primed to take a slice of the post-war building pie. The beneficiaries included Sir Edwin Airey, the building entrepreneur behind the Airey homes of Cardboard City; his story is characteristic of many of the big construction magnates of the period.

Retooling armaments to abodes

Edwin Airey was a bespectacled chap with a long face, receding hairline, and – as was fashionable at the time – a cropped moustache with cleanshaven chin. A civil engineer and industrialist, Airey had developed an enterprising construction business model long before the housing crisis of the 1940s. In 1905, he took charge of the business his stonemason-turned-builder father had built in Leeds, William Airey & Son, and signed numerous contracts across Yorkshire to expand the company's construction works. During the First World War, Airey won government transport and building contracts for gun-ranges, factories, and hangars for Britain's Air Force. He also stepped up as chief technical officer on transport and cold storage for the Ministry of Food, making him a trusted industry voice. According to historian Eveleigh Bradford, 'this work brought him influential contacts and powerful connections'.[47] Airey's wartime relationship with the Ministry of Munitions and the Ministry of Health brought him a knighthood in 1922, and set him in good stead for the next war on the horizon.

During the interwar years, Airey became interested in non-traditional building methods and developed the Duo Slab prefab house prototype. Around 1,600 of these were commissioned and built for Leeds workers in 1920. The Duo Slab method used concrete blocks and cast-in-situ concrete columns as an alternative to brickwork. By the Second World War, Airey had served as lord mayor of Leeds and overseen the development of a range of different iconic buildings, including the Queen's Hotel in Leeds City Square.[48] He also expanded on his non-traditional housing designs, convinced that bricks would soon be obsolete in housebuilding.

Despite his first Duo Slab designs being criticised by 1920s' tenants as damp, cold, and cracked, Airey went on to design his permanent concrete prefabricated house along similar lines. As an update to the Duo Slab, the new design involved fixing concrete-clad slabs to posts, and the house had a pebble-dashed finish meant to give it a cottage-style feel. Yet complaints of cold and dampness plagued the new houses, too.

The design was a contract winner. In 1946, Airey managed to secure a government deal – reportedly for more than £2 million – for the construction of 26,000 Airey houses across the country.[49] He went on to promote these houses to councils in England and Wales, appearing at the London Conference of the Rural and District Councils Association in 1946 – where he shared a platform with Nye Bevan, newly in charge of health and housing.

While Bevan criticised the temporary prefab programme – which remains the only national housing programme to have been centrally rolled out – he did praise the permanent prefabs. According to his biographer Michael Foot, Bevan personally encouraged the various prefab-housing inventors and reportedly told Airey contractors that they would get the government order 'when they had devised a decent sliding roof'. The Cornish Unit, designed by local mining firm the English China Clay Company, won Bevan's wholehearted approval, as it was the non-traditional design that seemed closest to the rural cottage so sought after in British housing planning.[50]

Airey's path to 1940s mass prefab housebuilding contracts had been well trodden by many others. The steel-framed Arcon bungalow that formed part of the 1944 Temporary Housing Programme was designed by a team of architects funded by building and civil engineering company Taylor Woodrow, which had constructed gunnery camps, land and sea defence works, hospitals, factories, caissons, and other military infrastructure throughout the Second World War. The organisation had expanded massively to meet war need and was concerned about a contraction of steel demand as the war was coming to an end, lobbying the government for some longer-term security. They needn't have worried. In 1944, the government contracted Taylor Woodrow to build around 40,000 temporary bungalows, and the company went on to expand their civil engineering work massively overseas. Taylor Woodrow merged with fellow prefab house contractor George Wimpey to make the housebuilding megacorporation Taylor Wimpey in 2007.

George Wimpey was itself a major builder of military infrastructure during the Second World War. It began life in the late nineteenth century as a public-works contractor, moved into housebuilding and then, during the war, won many contracts to build concrete storage tanks and aerodromes. In fact, Wimpey was so successful at winning government contracts in the war's early years that there were rumblings of corruption, and even accusations that Winston Churchill might have a stake in the company.[51] Some 300,000 prefab Wimpey No-Fines (constructed using concrete with no fine aggregates) went on to be commissioned after the war, dwarfing by some margin the number of Airey houses built.[52]

The contractors commissioned to install these hundreds of thousands of local authority and NCB units were often different companies again. Peter Malpass notes that little is recorded about who actually built local authority housing stock, but it must have been private contractors because councils lacked the means.[53] Newspaper reports from 1946 detail how the Ministry for Health instructed councils to commission Airey prefabs after the rural housing deal was given to William Airey & Son:

> The [pre-fabricated] houses should be put up by local builders with whom the local authority would place contracts in the ordinary way. The contractor would be provided with the necessary wall and floor components for the houses from government sources at a fixed price. The price, the Minister explained, was higher than the present cost of corresponding material for a house of the traditional type, but this should be partly offset by a reduction in the cost of erection.[54]

The devil, as always, is in the detail. These prefabricated houses were more expensive to build than their traditional counterparts, and the beneficiaries in this instance were private contractors. Landowners may not have made the profits they hoped for with these developments, because the government's compulsory purchase powers compensated landowners at existing use value rather than speculative market value (a principle, notably, not followed today).[55] Nonetheless, once the state requisitioned the land, local authorities had to pay someone to build the houses, as well as shelling out high set prices for materials – and it was to private building contractors that these monies flowed. Where extra construction costs were incurred by councils, the government provided subsidy grants.

Moreover, in the 1950s, local authorities that permitted the construction of prefab housing in their area were entitled to a bonus funding allocation from the government as a reward for labour saving.[56] This may have incentivised further contracting of prefab specialist companies such as Wimpey and Airey. For NCB housebuilding, records show that contracts went to a range of different private construction organisations, including George Wimpey & Co. Ltd, William Airey & Son Ltd, Henry Boot & Sons Ltd, John Laing Ltd, and Butterley Construction Co., among others.[57] Some of these companies continue to dominate Britain's building landscape today. Their ongoing financial success is due in no small part to the state funding poured into their coffers as Britain sought to rebuild itself after the war.

Thus, while the National Health Service offered a clear shift to public ownership, the state housing sector continued to be a mix of private and public provision, with the former never losing a foothold on what remained a commercial market. A mixed approach to housebuilding for rent is not inherently wrong, but in the case of the post-war housing emergency, life-changing policy decisions about shelter and living conditions were clearly shaped by expediency and networks of contacts at the top, rather than a long-term vision of sustainable and secure homes for renters.

The situation can be likened to government contracts issued across 2020–21 amid the COVID-19 pandemic. Companies tenuously linked to public health manufacturing retooled their businesses and supplied products (often of shoddy quality) to the government on multimillion-pound contracts won through networks. As with COVID contracts, this expediency model for housing in the 1940s was at the public's expense in more ways than one.

First, public money went into commissioning designs from competing architects, rather than having them all work together towards a cost-effective design that could be produced at any factory across the country. During the war, prefabricated and non-traditional construction methods were the only ones licensed and so they quickly became the only options. Influential post-war figures such as Bevan thought that building-industry growth could only come from stimulating new techniques, so they put resources into encouraging inventors to competitively work on this. Such incentives encouraged private architects – or the private builders sponsoring architects – to churn out mediocre proposals (that still received contracts). The winning designs also contained unique features, which meant sourcing parts for repairs became an issue across subsequent decades.[58]

Second, public money was poured into the pockets of private contractors but the public got little value for money in return.[59] More than £200 million was spent on the 1944 Temporary Housing Programme alone (exceeding its budget by some £50 million), but the scheme ultimately produced fewer than 160,000 houses. Airey houses, like other supposedly permanent prefabs, weren't cheaper to build than traditional houses, either. Expensive parts meant they cost more than their brick counterparts in the short term, as well as in the longer term due to their need to be demolished and rebuilt.[60]

Building companies also sought to price fix, until they were exposed in the early 1950s. A scandal erupted in 1952 when it was brought to the attention of Parliament and the government's Monopolies Commission that, for at least eighteen years, an outfit called the London Builders' Conference was operating a pricing racket in building contracts across London, with similar groups existing across the country.[61] Members of the Conference, including large construction firms such as Laing (the founder), as well as many non-member firms, agreed to tender contracts at a so-called 'fair price' agreed within the group. This collusion ensured that the lowest quote would still be significantly above the cost of doing a job. When a member company won, it would compensate other members the difference between the so-called 'fair price' rate and a genuinely competitive low tender, artificially inflating prices.[62] Of course at this point, most building work across the country was funded by the government for post-war reconstruction and municipal housebuilding. Uncompetitive pricing was costing the government, and therefore taxpayers, dearly. And where houses are more costly to build, tenants always end up paying higher rent rates.

The Monopolies Commission launched an investigation in 1953 and found that Conference members and co-operating non-members were responsible for around 73 per cent of the total contracts in the Greater London area in January 1953 – a portion the Conference admitted was fairly typical.[63] In fact, price-fixing had become easier after the war because the government switched from advertising for tenders to operating on an invited-tender basis. The list of approved contractors in each locality was relatively small, making collusion easier.[64]

The Conference's chairman, Sir Alfred Hurst, tried to defend the scheme, arguing that it covered overheads and stabilised prices in a way that was fairer to the industry. He also pointed out that other professionals like architects and surveyors determined fees without price competition (which, again, would have inflated overall building costs). Nonetheless, the practice was roundly criticised by the Royal Institute of British Architects, by the leading industry publication the *Builder*, by politicians and the public – and, ultimately, by the government's independent investigations. Price-fixing was, the Monopolies Commission concluded, 'not in the public interest' and was ordered to end.

This racket may explain building delays in areas such as Barry, Wales, in 1950. The Labour MP for Barry, Dorothy Rees, told Parliament that in the previous December:

> The Welsh Board of Health approved a scheme of building some 90 houses by private builders, but the tenders were too high. Negotiations have been prolonged, and up to the present not a trench has been dug nor a brick laid. When a letter was sent to the builders, which asked them to come to some finality about the negotiations, a reply was received from the Federation of Master Builders. The letter ... reads: ... 'Unfortunately, activity over the General Election has prevented the builders who tendered from meeting. I am hoping they will be able to meet early next week, and I will then write you further.' The letter is signed by the secretary of the Master Builders' Federation. They were not building polling stations, and, apparently, neither were they building houses.[65]

Rees was clearly concerned about the political aspect of these delays; it seemed that the builders were more concerned with future contracts under a new government than the pressing housing matters of the day (for which they would be paid!). Yet her point also underscores the financial challenges local authorities faced getting reasonable tenders for housebuilding programmes.

While reports from the time state that some of the largest, longest-established, and well-respected building contractors were part of the London Builders' Conference, it is unclear if one of those was William Airey & Son. Either way, the building market – and Airey's possible tender range – would have been inflated by this artificial price fixing. The Conference's constitution made clear that both members and non-members stood to benefit.[66] In the end, the Conference wound up the so-called fair price scheme, dropped 'London' from its name, and continues to operate as the member organisation the Builders' Conference.

The high costs for a relatively small number of houses might never have been a problem, had the housing units been fit for purpose – that is, providing decent homes for families to live in at affordable rents for their rest of their lives. The non-traditional housebuilding programme reportedly saved money elsewhere from reductions in required site 'man-hours', building time, and coal use.[67] However, these short-term savings were never weighed up against longer-term costs on the public purse.

The Temporary Housing Programme bungalows had a lifespan of little over a decade and the houses were always going to have to be rebuilt – with the additional labour, time, and energy costs that incurred. But, as I will pick up again later, many of the supposedly permanent prefabricated homes were also soon to be declared defective and fit neither to mortgage nor to live in just a few decades after their construction. Like the private landlords of the nineteenth and early twentieth centuries, the government and these private companies were yet again creating a condition of insecurity in worker housing – a new version of slums, even, as their maintenance proved to be difficult and costly.

The government and NCB were not considering these issues in the 1940s, of course. Their absolute priority was to meet urgent labour housing needs, and prefabs seemed to be the silver bullet. They rolled out their accelerated building programme across the country, and, in a small Leeds suburb in West Yorkshire, Cardboard City was soon to be born. As the next chapter will show, some of Bevan's vision for decent housing was realised in these developments, for a time at least. Airey homes were spacious, with modern conveniences and gardens. They were homes cherished by the thousands of tenants who lived in Oulton over the decades. Yet, these houses not only had a material lifespan, they also had an economic one tied to the productivity and longevity of the mines. In that sense, they were far from secure.

PART II

THE RISE AND FALL OF A CARDBOARD CITY

3

My own cupboard

Airey houses came in two models: urban, with a hip roof, or four sloping roof sides; and rural, with a gabled roof, or two sloping sides. Cardboard City had a mix of both types. These prefabs were constructed in semi-detached pairs put together by fixing concrete slabs to posts, creating a panelled look with a pebble-dash finish. The 1947 Airey builders' handbook advised that construction of a unit required just six men, none of whom were required to have previous building experience.[1] It was possible, the handbook stated, to erect a pair of semi-detached Airey houses in 410 manpower hours. In other words, it could take an unskilled team of six people less than two working weeks. While materials might have been costly, the savings in labour and time were clear – and those post-war years were ones of urgency and pragmatism.

The average citizen had little say in this design-and-development process. Tenant views were never actively sought.[2] Yet they and their families were often evoked during policy making and design. Wartime and post-war planners were keenly imagining the needs of workers, and particularly housewives, in the housing of the future. A coalition government report from the mid-1940s noted that women, who had mobilised massively for the war effort, would now be intolerant of poor conditions in their homes.[3]

When debating the issue of post-war agricultural housing in the Lords in 1943, Labour peer Lord Addison (architect of the 1919 Housing Act) remarked: 'The farm labourer's wife wants a decent kitchen and plenty of room for the wash-up and that sort of thing. The kitchen is the centre of her home.'[4]

Responding to Addison, the Earl of Dudley – a Conservative – disagreed and shared his own view: 'As a matter of fact the current trend of demand which came out very clearly in our evidence was for a smaller kitchen and a larger living-room. That is what the modern up-to-date housewife wants and we have to plan for the young generation.'

Even William Beveridge, architect of the 1942 Beveridge social services report, had housewives on his mind when imagining the future of town planning. In 1948, just appointed as chair of Newton Aycliffe New Town, Lord Beveridge argued that new towns should be a 'housewife's paradise' – somewhere beautiful to live that was equipped with all housewifely amenities in walking distance.

It is unclear how many women these lords and decision-makers spoke to in the course of their considerations. As historian John Boughton points out, these visions reflected the gendered roles of the time.[5] Whatever the case, it was clear in the minds of these political leaders that the post-war housewife wanted and deserved more domestic space and better amenities. Laudable developments, certainly – but not without baggage.

This increasingly prevalent image of a modern housewife was one of motherhood but also of competent household management – a form of respectable work, particularly for conservative (with a lower-case c) women. Housewives had existed for centuries. But the *modern* housewife emerged as a distinct social category in the early twentieth century, not least because the paternal state was constantly concerned about the physical and moral health of the family. An effective, upstanding housewife was seen as the foundation of those things, part and parcel with decent accommodation.

The modern housewife also found clearer definition in this time, as technological advancements like washing machines individualised household labour and shifted it inside the home.[6] Adding to that shift, the Second World War caused a shortage of domestic help as women turned to wartime employment and then found better wages and opportunities elsewhere after the war's end – pushing a wider range of women into their own kitchens. The increasing influence of consumerism helped, too. The marketing arms of domestic consumer-goods producers spotted an underserved and growing audience to target. After all, it was women who often controlled the household purse strings.

Scholar Judy Giles has highlighted how many working-class women in the interwar years, far from feeling boxed in, sought rather to embrace this societal role – when and where they could afford to.[7] For these working-class women, being a modern housewife offered a break from the drudgery and danger of low-paid manual work while giving legitimacy to gendered domestic and care roles for which they were responsible anyway. Though political leaders may not have imagined it at the time, expanded domestic spaces also served as useful rallying locations for housing activism in the decades to come.

Gendered assumptions about care and unpaid domestic labour notwithstanding, there was much that was revolutionary in the spacious design of municipal and NCB housing at the time, prefab or traditional. Each design was generous in its apportionment of space for living, storage, and all mod cons. The provision of electricity and plumbed water in prefabs was also a revelation, as in 1951 around a third of households across the country still didn't have plumbed-in baths and a quarter didn't have electricity.[8]

The interiors of prefabs were of a similar standard to brick local authority houses: two or three bedrooms; an indoor private toilet and bath; a kitchen and living room; heating with a stove; and electricity. This was a considerable upgrade compared to the poorly equipped pre-war working-class housing norms. For scholar Neil Gray, such a drastic change was born less out of a feeling that the working classes *deserved* better, and more as a result of political *fear* over direct housing action (with memories of 1915 rent strikes still lingering).[9] Whatever the motivations of the political establishment, Britain's rapidly expanding families enthusiastically welcomed additional rooms for children, pram space, and general storage space.[10] Moreover, survey after survey highlighted that tenants wanted at least a bit of outdoor garden space to grow vegetables and make their home their own.

Airey houses checked all the boxes.

'My own cupboard'

My dad, Mark, recalls moving into his first Airey house on Brow Bottom Lane in Mixenden, Halifax, in the mid-1960s. He was of primary school age, and this new home made a big impression. Like Dad's later Airey home in Cardboard City, his Mixenden home was a three-bedroomed semi-detached house, though this one was the right-hand side of the pair. Prior to Brow Bottom, he had lived with two younger sisters and his parents in a brick one-bedroom house in Claremount. In that end-of-terrace back-to-back property, his family all slept in the same bedroom, bathed in the kitchen, and toileted in an outhouse shared with other houses. There wasn't a patch of green on the whole street, let alone a private garden. So their new Airey home seemed the height of luxury.

The Mixenden house was a council property and, as part of the standardised Airey design, it had three doors – front, side, and back – as well as a spacious kitchen and living room downstairs. Dad recalls that the kitchen had a sort of utility space for storage and the back door opened out to the garden. The living room connected to a hallway, which opened onto stairs. Upstairs, there was a small, separate water closet (toilet room), a bathroom with a bath and a sink, and three bedrooms – one large, one medium, and one very small 'box' bedroom that had a built-in cupboard over the stairs. Being

The smaller two-bedroom variety of Airey house on the Oulton NCB estate, under construction in the early 1950s. Image by kind permission of the E. R. Manley Collection, leodis.net.

the only boy child in the family, Dad got his own room, the box room, and 'my own cupboard', as he still calls it with a sense of pride and protectiveness. (I would get the equivalent room and cupboard in Wordsworth Drive several decades later.) Each Airey home had a driveway garden at the front, and a garden to play in and hang washing at the back. Edging the garden was a low concrete wall with wire fencing to mark boundaries.

The Airey houses of Oulton looked much the same, though there were some two-beds as well as three. Laid out in pairs in quiet, curving streets and cul-de-sacs, their front gardens and driveways have since been marked out with hedges and small fences for decoration and privacy. Between Wordsworth Drive and Sugar Hill Close there was also a large green space with a little beck (which probably prevented the building of more houses, though it also provided a fun playing spot for kids on the estate). Round the back of the houses were expansive fields and trees.

The development of the Cardboard City estate began around the winter of 1952. A few months earlier, the local council had rejected the use of *any* non-traditional houses in the vicinity; then something must have changed their minds.[11] Across 1953, 210 Airey houses were built on these Oulton fields and would initially serve several local collieries. These houses weren't so much built *in* the village of Oulton as they formed something of a satellite estate: a series of streets on their own, they were isolated by surrounding fields. It was a fifteen-minute walk to the nearest shops in the main part of the village. The nearest primary school was two miles away and, while the local secondary school Rothwell Secondary Modern (later renamed Royds, and now Oulton Academy) would be just a ten-minute walk, it wasn't built until a few years after the construction of Cardboard City began. Miners had long been settled in isolated communities. 'Meanly laid-out villages of flimsy houses where everyone knew each other's business', to quote Jeremy Paxman in his history of the coal industry.[12]

As Oulton village adjoins the town of Rothwell and the village of Woodlesford, they're often considered as three parts of a local whole (or at least, that's how my school classmates and I saw it, with many of us hailing from one of those three places). In fact, until 1974, Oulton, Woodlesford, and other nearby areas were part of the Rothwell Urban District Council. The council was then abolished, and the district absorbed into an enlarged Leeds metropolitan council until a further reorganisation in 1986.

The area has a long and rich history of quarrying and mining, industries shaped by a handful of individuals and companies. Across the eighteenth and nineteenth centuries, the Calverley family dominated – a dynasty of coal barons and bankers. They inherited their initial wealth from a distant relation, a Leeds wool merchant and banker called John Blayds, who acquired many plots of land to establish a country estate in Oulton from the 1780s.[13] The Calverleys were the original

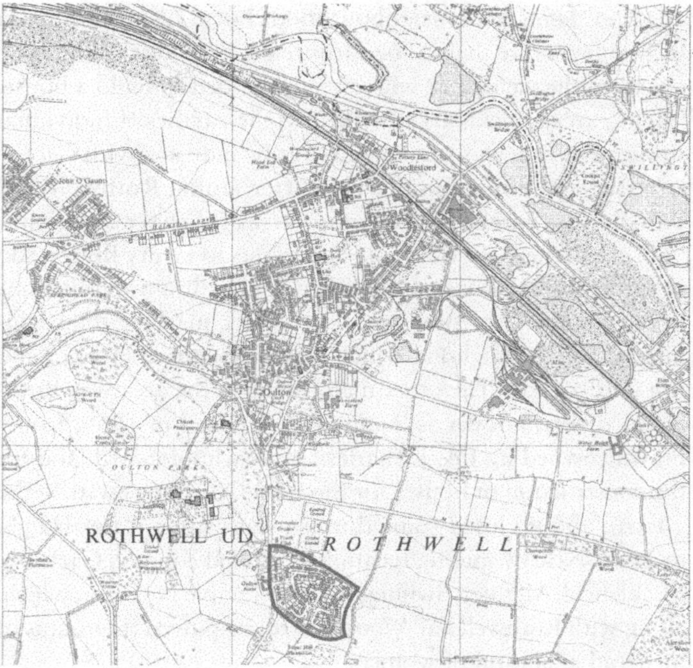

The new Coal Board estate, outlined at the bottom. Oulton is directly above, Woodlesford around the railway track, and the edge of Rothwell town is visible on the left edge of the image. Reproduced from the 1965 Ordnance Survey map. Outline by the author.

designers and residents of Oulton Hall, a large stately home with an expansive estate about ten minutes' walk from Cardboard City. (After serving as a psychiatric hospital from the end of the First World War to the 1970s, and then falling derelict for many years, Oulton Hall is now a tired-looking spa hotel with golf course; it is one of two major employers of teenagers in the village, the other being a Toby Carvery).

The Calverleys owned much of the freehold land in Oulton, Woodlesford and Rothwell – and it was certainly productive. Sandstone had been quarried locally for more than 200 years by the turn of the twentieth century, and for a long time the quarries defined the neighbourhood. Local historian Edwin R. Manley wrote that in the early years, individuals dug stone out from the vicinity of where they intended to build a house, leaving areas pockmarked with curious cavities.[14] Individual stone quarrying was soon taken over by industry, with George Armitage & Sons dominating. After stone, Rothwell and Woodlesford turned out to be ripe areas for coal extraction.

In 1908, the Calverleys sold land rights to Henry Briggs, Son & Company Ltd, a long-established mining firm with other pits in the county. They sunk two deep shafts, marking the beginning of Water Haigh Pit, which was nationalised in 1947 and ran until 1970.[15] The other major mine in the area was Rothwell Colliery, known as 'Fanny Pit'. Opened in 1867, Fanny Pit was owned by J & J Charlesworth (who donated land for the construction of houses for the John O'Gaunts estate in the 1920s), and it closed some thirteen years after Water Haigh, in 1983. Nearby mining locations included Kippax, Garforth, Micklefield, Methley, Swillington, and Temple Newsam, which, along with Rothwell and Woodlesford, employed thousands of men and a handful of women.

Workers diversified from predominantly white British and Irish after the Second World War, with recruits coming in from Poland and other European countries via the European Voluntary Workers scheme. The mines also recruited a handful of newcomers from Commonwealth countries, namely the Caribbean and India. Howard Benson writes that Water Haigh was a friendly pit and gained the nickname 'The League of Nations' because of its relative diversity of nationalities.[16] Although these migrants lived and settled within commuting distance of the local pits, Cardboard City's residents remained mainly white British throughout the estate's years as Coal Board housing, though there are some records and recollections of Polish workers living there with their families.

In 1953, Cardboard City's construction in Oulton's rolling green fields was apparently met with consternation from locals, who opposed the loss of land as well as the 'form' of construction (a euphemism for ugliness, I suspect).[17] The new miner residents might well have had louder complaints about lack of amenities for this isolated estate. When the Calverley family transferred land rights to the National Coal Board in 1955, the covenant dictated that the purchasers should 'not use the property hereby conveyed for any purpose other than the erection of private dwellinghouses and two shops'.[18] While a tender was put out for two stores, no shop appeared in the site's seventy-plus year history.

This geographic isolation had two clear implications – first, it signalled the paramountcy of industry when it came to housing workers after the war. Many of the 'homes for heroes' were little more than roofs over heads to enable productive work, rather than the infrastructural seeds of community. Elsewhere, predominantly in the South East, New Towns aspired to have shared village greens, walkable shops, and communal facilities – all part of a post-war vision for neighbourliness and self-sufficiency.[19] This was not a vision for Rothwell's miners, it seemed.

Second, the Coal Board estate's singular purpose as worker housing hinted from the outset that the community might struggle to be sustainable beyond the existence of the mines. While few miners imagined the pits might close less than three decades after the housing was built, there should have been red flags when a factory-made estate was hastily assembled without shops and ready access to other basic services. Yet a community did emerge.

The Coal Boarders

Thousands of people have called these streets home over the decades, and many remain connected to the area long after leaving the estate. There's a chat group on social media for former 'Coalboarders' where memories and pictures are regularly shared. According to recollections of the early days, from around 1953 each colliery was allocated a certain number of houses and, as they were finished, people moved in. At the time, the estate was a still a bit of a building site as pavements had not yet been tarmacked. Some families moved into homes that did not yet have windowpanes fitted.

Lynn Abbott (née Dickinson) was one of the early residents, moving in as a child before everything was completed. She recalls her dad explaining the 'shocking' waiting list for available houses: 'My dad said that every Friday, when they used to go get their wage at the little office at the pit, as a house was finished, they'd ... look down the list to see who were waiting for one, and my dad was asking every week. And then all at once he went for his wage and they said, "Mac! Keys!" And that was it. And because my mam lived up in Leeds in the back-to-backs up York Road, she wasn't sure she wanted to be in the middle of fields. It were too open for my mam, she said, "Ooh, you don't know what you're gonna get, like burglars."'

When the Dickinson family grew too big for their home at number 20, they moved a stone's throw away, to number 25 Oulton Drive.

Because mining was a way of life in the area, many families – including the Dickinsons – had close and extended family networks on the estate itself. Many kids were even born in the houses. Angela Kellett's sister Maureen was born in the front room of 10 Wordsworth Drive when Angela was six years old. Another Coal Boarder, Mick Wagstaff, recalled:

> I was born in number 10 Sugar Hill Close, and my wife Jenice was brought up in number 3 Sugar Hill Close with her grandparents George and Ethel Ansen. My dad was Deputy and Overman at Rothwell Fanny Pit. My mum used to work in the Miners' welfare. Grandad Arthur and Grandma Flo Bradley lived on Wordsworth Drive, Auntie and Uncle Bob and Yvonne

Oulton Drive and the Dickinson family's first house. From left to right, Amy Dickinson, her toddler Lynn, and husband, Mac Dickinson. Image courtesy of Lynn Abbott.

> Tonks lived on Shelley Crescent ... I remember all the kids from Sugar Hill playing kick-out can every night, and playing marbles next to the phone box on Shelley Crescent.[20]

The estate was green and leafy, and people mostly kept their gardens and hedges nice. Residents recall spending a lot of their time outside when they were children, playing with friends on the estate and in the nearby woods and fields. As adults, too, they would catch up on local news and assist each other with errands. A youth club opened in 1955, just a five-minute walk away. Angela remembers going to the club with friends during their early teens and seeing local band Johnny Dawn and the Electrons practising, as the band's guitarist also lived in Cardboard City. 'They were big down there,' even if the band didn't become a national hit.

Soon enough, the estate became a village. Most amenities were not close and, as Diane Lilley (Lynn's sister) explained, it was 'a bit of a walk into the village to the nearest shops' – so the gap was filled by visiting traders. Memories of early entrepreneurial residents and other visiting locals include George Crossland, who used to pass through the town on a Saturday morning with his horse Nobby, selling hardware. Residents also recall a door-to-door BetterWare salesman who lived locally and had been badly burned in the war.

From early on, around the mid-1950s, Jack – or Jackie – Bramble used to park his mobile veg shop on Wordsworth drive every day. In a broad Yorkshire accent, he used to announce his arrival shouting things like 'REYT RIPE BANANAS!' Jack Bramble also sold penny sweets and occasional single cigarettes to local youths. His grocery service was essential to the estate where accessible shops were lacking. Few households had access to a car. According to Diane, 'Jack Bramble kept everyone on the estate going. He used to have a little book, you know, and he took note of the money all week and they'd pay up on a Friday.'

Other essential and non-essential services popped up for and by residents, too. Coal Boarder Ted Sparks used to cut the hair of local boys and men in a makeshift barbershop in his garden shed. At various points over the past seven decades, these busy streets were also regularly serviced by Anthony Fell the ice cream man, a fish and chip van, and a range of other mobile traders. Residents grew fruit, vegetables, and flowers that they would sell to each other.

Families within and across houses used to support each other and doors were rarely locked. As kids grew up, some married and moved around on the estate, keeping employment with the mines and connections with their relatives and friends. Inside the homes, families made their own adjustments and renovations, investing money and care in their long-term affordable lets.

Neighbouring land – also sold by the Calverley family – was covenanted to be used for sports and recreational purposes.

As well as a youth club, the area housed the Miners' Welfare bar and other facilities in an old mansion, which was later demolished and the land transferred to Leeds City Council. The cricket ground and other sports pitches remain at the centre of a thriving club adjacent to a modern leisure centre and swimming pool.

Snobbery

It's easy to romanticise the isolation of the estate, particularly as close friendships and relationships developed and cemented such an interdependent community. But the Coal Boarders thrived despite their isolation, not just because of it. The proximity of the secondary school and the sociality of children certainly helped. John Readman didn't move to the estate with his wife Cindy (Save Our Homes LS26 Chair) and their children until around 2006, but he already knew the estate well by that point. As a local schoolkid, he'd visit the estate to play with some of the other resident children, his fellow classmates. He remembers a playground with swings and a roundabout situated in a grassy area round the back of 46 Wordsworth Drive – which would become his home several decades later. The council took the playground away, supposedly to be repaired, at some point in the 1970s or 1980s, but it was never returned, and only a metal pole is left to mark its existence. At sixteen, John went on to join Rothwell Colliery in haulage and was soon working alongside Cardboard City residents and future neighbours, including Chris Shires and Barry Abbey (who's still living there today with his wife, Mavis).

Not all Oulton locals were friendly to residents though, especially those without connections to the mines. Lynn and Diane remember that their mum, Amy Dickinson, was distressed by vocal snobbery as she was queueing for bread at a Woodlesford bakery during the 1977 bread strikes. 'What's *she* doing in the queue?' she heard people whispering as they glared. Even though a bakery employee vouched for Amy as a regular, she was hurt and started using a different bakery after that. Diane explained that the rest of Oulton and Woodlesford 'didn't like us because we lived on the estate. I don't know why, they all looked down on us. Because they called it Cardboard City. What they didn't realise was that there was a community up there, it was brilliant.'

The term Cardboard City, adopted by other locals, was a dig at the quality of the housing. I don't know exactly when the derogatory nickname first emerged, but cardboard has long had an association with poverty and homelessness. Scholar Maria Rentetzi writes that the 1960s boom in consumerism and associations with the cardboard box as shelter went hand in hand.[21] Shops churned through disposable goods that were packaged and shipped to shelves in cardboard. The packaging was then tossed to the street as rubbish and picked up by passing homeless people in search of a makeshift shelter. Cardboard might have been rubbish, but it was sturdy, warm, and light – and consumerism made it ubiquitous.

Though Rentetzi was writing about the United States, the same pattern emerged in the UK over the period. Homelessness was on the rise in Britain across the 1960s to 1990s, by tenfold or twentyfold in some areas (the cause, after relationship breakdown, being largely eviction-related).[22] From the late 1970s, there was a famous 'cardboard city' in London: an occupied underpass between Waterloo station and South Bank that housed hundreds of homeless people – all sleeping in cardboard boxes – for two decades. Perhaps Oulton village residents were invoking a similar kind of imagery in their sneers about the Coal Board estate.

Whatever the case, for many of the residents the 'cardboard' label stung – and still does today. Yes, the houses were freezing in winter and families had to keep two coal fires going all night to keep warm, or wrap up with loads of blankets. Yes, the windows used to freeze on the inside. But as the next chapter will show, these conditions were initially caused by the design, and were exacerbated by inadequate maintenance by the Coal Board and subsequent private landlords. Many poorly insulated brick properties in the period suffered similar conditions under similar landlord neglect. The Oulton estate certainly wasn't a temporary or impoverished community, as the word 'cardboard' insinuates. Looking beyond the draughts, the houses had plumbed-in baths, a separate inside toilet, and good-size rooms, and were up to date for the period.

Yet for this book, the moniker Cardboard City remains relevant. Some ex-residents now use it with affection to capture the uniqueness of the estate compared with the rest of Oulton, arguably turning the snobby dismissal of Oulton villagers into a badge of pride. I understand why Lynn and Diane struggle to see it this way when they and their mother felt rudely alienated by the term. But for me, the label speaks to something bigger still: that houses and estates are homes that people make, through relationships, routines, shared history, and a sense of belonging – just as much as through physical materials. In fact, these houses were, and continue to be, homes that Coal Boarders have made *despite* the poor-quality physical materials provided for them by building companies and the NCB.

Something similar could be said about the other cardboard city in Waterloo, which was emptied and destroyed by authorities in 1998. In the final months of its existence, long-time resident Tom remarked in an interview with the *Independent* newspaper that 'I may not have a house but this is my home ... These people are my family, and I'm not going anywhere.' It was an effort to exert some control over living choices that had previously been out of his hands.

Risk and care

Oulton's Cardboard City came to be a tight and caring community, not just because people had blood relatives living nearby. Camaraderie and care emerged from the working environment in and around the collieries, too. Working in pits was not easy and cost many thousands of men their health or their lives across the country; 468 died per year between 1948 and 1955.[23] Even though pits gradually became safer after nationalisation (with ninety-two deaths a year by 1971), coal mining was still a dangerous profession. Tunnel collapses, flooding, suffocating, and injury from machinery were many of the daily dangers that miners faced, not including lung disease, infections, and degenerative arthritis.

On 12 October 1955, three coalface rippers sustained burn injuries and shock after a small explosion in Water Haigh Pit, Woodlesford. It was presumed that a gas leakage may have been ignited by sparks from their hole-boring work. In another incident, an underground train derailment in nearby Fanny Pit injured eleven men in May 1959; while most injuries were minor, two of the men had their hands crushed and required longer treatment. In 1973, seven miners lost their lives at the nearby Lofthouse Colliery near Wakefield: an inrush of water trapped the seven men, likely killing them instantly.

Residents from Cardboard City played a role in the rescue efforts. Lynn remembered her friend Gill Ward's dad frantically knocking on their door as news of the Lofthouse disaster broke, and the men assembled a local group of rescue volunteers to join the effort. Gill recalls her dad saying, 'We're never going to get them out alive,' as there was just too much water. He was himself buried in a different pit at one point and spent thirteen months in hospital. A subsequent inquiry into the Lofthouse tragedy found that the inrush could have been prevented; the flood water came from an abandoned Victorian mine which the NCB missed because it had not requested additional documentation when developing the Lofthouse pits.

In another incident, Mavis and Barry Abbey remembered moving into their first Cardboard City home of 14 Oulton Drive in 1970. They stripped off the wallpaper to decorate and found the previous tenant's name, John, written on the wall beneath. John had apparently left that house after 'running off with the woman next door'. He stayed working in the mines, though, and was later killed in a local pit after a loose stone fell onto him from a height.

Despite such tragedies, nationalisation significantly improved mine safety through regular inspections, record keeping and the implementation of minimum health and safety standards. But safety was often as much about the people around you as it was policy and procedures. Miners and their families looked out for each other in the job, and outside of the pits through friendship groups, neighbourhood communities, local and national welfare organisations, and the National Union of Mineworkers. The estate helped shape an interdependent way of life for Coal Boarders in Cardboard City.

Care has long been seen as a gendered practice that happened within the home. Women are overwhelmingly the carers of children and relatives with support needs, as well as the main housekeepers – all of which are unpaid labour tasks that remain under-recognised today. But care in the community was just as important. Cardboard City was some distance from doctors' surgeries, shops, and other neighbourhoods. That inevitably fostered closer relations and interdependence between the families who lived here. Mavis remembers that when she and Barry and their infant moved onto Oulton Drive in 1970, they got to know people quickly – especially the local teens. Girls aged between fourteen and fifteen regularly offered to babysit ('There were plenty of babysitters around!' Mavis laughed in our interview), and many teenage boys would come and chat with Barry while admiring his motorbike.

Residents never let the estate suffer from its isolation, either. Gill Ward, an early arrival with her parents in the 1950s, explained that for a long time her dad was the only resident with a car so he used to drive people around whenever they needed it. At some point in the late 1950s or early 1960s, Lynn recalls that two mums, Mrs McNalus and Mrs Nesdon, organised for a local farmer and taxi driver – Freddy Knowles – to provide a regular bus service to Cardboard City, ferrying kids to and from school and getting people to work. The local kids called the bus the 'red devil' because of the wild way it was driven, and Freddy's dad, 'Grandad Knowles', was employed as the conductor collecting the fares.

This closeness and interdependence were further bolstered by the solidarity of miners. The Welfare Club put on an annual bus trip to Bridlington and Scarborough, which was the 'highlight of the year' for a young Janet Street. Then, during the miners' strikes, neighbours did what they could to survive. Barry recalls burning bike tyres at night to keep the house warm, while Diane and Lynn remember the miner dads going picking for coal around the pits and getting in trouble with the NCB. Lynn laughs, 'My dad got caught, the bloody police got my dad. They let him off, but they said: "You're stealing from the NCB."' Like other miners on strike across the country, they had few options. Their homes were coal-fired and everybody was using all the fuel they could to keep going – stolen coal, wood, or tyres.

After the 1970s' strikes, residents recall a new distance in their relations with the NCB – not least because the Coal Board had run out of money for repairs: 'There was no money from the Coal Board at all,' Angela explained. The Coal Board's presence was rarely felt on the estate anyway: 'We were left out on a limb really.' As Angela remembers, 'If you saw the NCB van on the estate, you knew something had gone amiss,' as it was never good news when they turned up. It was neighbours who filled the resource and care gaps. These local support networks had to be increasingly relied upon by generations of NCB tenants (and municipal prefab tenants) up and down the country, as, from the 1970s, security of tenure and attention to maintenance deteriorated, along with the properties.

4

Robbery without violence

One of the early housing problems the NCB grappled with was how to ensure their housing stock continued to serve the needs of the industry. Despite NCB newbuilds being considered and included statistically as general public housing, the reality was that industry interests came first and the NCB needed miners. In the hashing out of tenancy terms and conditions, it was decided that rent agreements would contain two rates: a progressive, lower-level rate contingent on NCB employment, and a standard, higher-level rate that was aligned with (or slightly above) the local authority rate. If a miner was fired or voluntarily resigned, the rent was automatically meant to increase to the higher standard rate.

This may not seem unreasonable, given that the standard rate was roughly aligned to local council house rates. However, the sharp hike was intended to force the tenant out of the property, rather than to make up any difference in rental income (notwithstanding the fact that local authority rates were increasing over the 1950s anyway, just as mining wages began to decline). The assumption behind setting these so-called service-tenancy terms was that, to quote the NCB: 'The increase in rent will induce the mine worker to leave the house. If at the end of the three months he has not left the house he is then served with a Notice to Quit.'[1] Variable rents, exploitative conditions, and forced evictions characterise all rented house types across the mid- to late century.

Through service tenancy agreements and their Notice to Quit, the National Coal Board essentially managed their tenanted houses much as private collieries managed their tied cottages in the decades before the war. Ease and speed of eviction were paramount.

One ex-miner in Widnes, James Francis Hopkins, took the NCB to court over his Notice to Quit in 1955. Hopkins argued that the NCB's hiking of his rent after he left his job constituted a new tenancy agreement – one not linked to his NCB employment. Therefore, he logically concluded, if he was willing to pay the higher rate, he had rights to stay in his Coal Board home and community.[2] Unfortunately, the judge found in the NCB's favour and granted possession. Hopkins had to leave. A few years later in 1961, the National Union of Mineworkers protested at 106 ex-miners being evicted from their Coal Board homes in Derbyshire. These residents no longer worked in the mines and the Board wanted vacant houses to help attract new recruits. The ex-miners were served with just a month's notice to get out.[3]

Dependents of deceased miners faced the same fate in Worksop, which operated a policy of repossessing Coal Board houses if a miner's only survivors were daughters, or if they were sons not in the mining industry (sons in the mining industry were permitted to keep the house).[4] Few women were employed by the collieries, so daughters of deceased miners did not have the option of taking up local pit work to stay in their homes. While Worksop appears to have had the tightest conditions in this regard, other areas had different criteria or considered cases on individual 'merits' – highlighting inconsistency in the security of NCB housing across the country. At best, the male miner – serving, ex, or dead – was at the centre of these considerations, and his family only had tenancy rights in relation to his employment.

In some instances, injured or retired miners, or miners' widows, were permitted to stay in their Coal Board house;

that was as far as the general-provision principle seemed to stretch. Yet in 1950, the *Midland Counties Tribune* reported that two long-serving miners in Arley were threatened with eviction after suffering eye trouble that prevented work.[5] In Cardboard City, too, Gill recalls that a neighbouring family had to leave their home at some point in the 1960s after the husband retired from the pits. The NCB stated in committee meeting minutes from August 1952 that they would rather 'pull down the houses or ... give them away, since they would get no benefit from having non-miners in their houses'.[6]

The National Union of Mineworkers was complicit in this system as it agreed to let the 'tied' nature of the tenancies pass without much protest, 'provided that they [the NUM] were not asked to commit themselves nationally to approving it'.[7] In other words: 'We won't say anything as long as you don't put the spotlight on us.' The NUM's passivity seems incongruous in light of their prominent role defending the employment rights of miners, particularly across the 1970s and 1980s. But, as Neil Gray argued in relation to the Glasgow rent strikes, trade unionists and labour activists have rarely considered housing as part of workplace struggles.[8]

If they did, they might also have protested NCB efforts to take the power of the rent book out of the home and into the hands of the Coal Board. As we saw in Glasgow and Leeds in 1914–15, protests against rent hikes were often enacted through housewives refusing to produce rent books and booting the collectors out of their homes. Perhaps wanting to avoid those dynamics and reduce the power of the homestead (and by extension, the housewife), the NCB made duplicate copies of tenancy agreements so that they could 'establish the terms of a tenancy without needing to rely upon production of the rent book'.[9] This move also fits into a general pattern of removing human contact from the renting process. Any dispute or contention over tenancy would be fought in the courts via paperwork, rather than by dialogue between tenant and property owner.

Maintenance also provided an ongoing sticking point for miner–Coal Board relations. In the drafting of the template tenancy agreement, initial versions included prescriptions that a tenant shall 'from time to time and as often as the decorative condition of any part of the premises so requires paper, paint, whitewash and generally decorate the internal of the premises'. This was then scribbled out and another note in the file states that decoration should not be a part of the tenancy agreement because, should a tenant be referred to a rent tribunal for the calculation of a standard rent rate, 'the determination would be made on the assumption that the tenant actually carried out the interior decorative repairs'.[10]

The NCB was therefore mitigating all the ways that a tenant might secure a rent reduction – not with profit-seeking intent, perhaps, but certainly not in the post-war spirit of tenant-centred public housing. After all, it put the tenant in the position of having to shell out their own money for decoration and maintenance, yet they were not able to see the benefit of that investment in rent rate reduction or security of tenure.

In Cardboard City, Gill and Janet remember their fathers fitting new PVC windows to their houses at their own expense, and in the Dickinson household, mum Amy took charge of the decorating. Residents upgraded fittings and kitchens and even removed internal walls to improve the living spaces. Countless tenants today find themselves in similar circumstances, forking out for decorations, repairs, or furniture replacements to get them done quickly and improve the quality of their home environment, but with no material return from the landlord who would ultimately benefit from this well-kept asset.

'Modern housing management'

For council properties across the country in the 1950s, local authorities were performing similar mental gymnastics around the issue of maintenance, raising (often moralising) concerns about their properties' upkeep while angling to minimise their own responsibility. Government reports and discussions across the late 1940s and early 1950s expressed concerns about tenants and their lack of 'social conscience' (meaning neglect and sometimes vandalism) towards communal property, while also emphasising that local authorities should 'avoid ongoing maintenance' commitments to their properties.[11]

That's not to say the NCB was completely oblivious to the welfare of its tenant workers in their homes as well as down the pits. A 1953 NCB memorandum by Sir Geoffrey Vickers (NCB Board member and previously legal adviser) stated that:

> If the tenants are to reap the full benefit of the new accommodation, the houses must quickly become homes, the neighbours, friends, and the estates communities. Such principles are, of course, part and parcel of modern housing management. e.g. the 'Octavia Hill' system, under which the fundamental aim is, by regular personal contact, to create a sense of mutual responsibility between landlord and tenant.[12]

Yet the NCB failed to implement those principles in any meaningful way. As Vickers himself went on to explain, Octavia Hill's paradigm of personal contact was 'probably' less attainable in NCB properties because the deduction of rent from wages meant there was no rent collector with whom tenants could develop a relationship. Even in council housing across the same period, local authorities were progressively weakening the role of the rent collector – reducing the frequency of their visits and giving them only basic money-collection duties, as opposed to an all-encompassing household management role. Without regular contact with a rent collector who could form a relationship with the tenants, house quality issues (including maintenance and repairs) soon became distanced administrative and financial responsibilities for the NCB and local authorities – and a growing burden, at that.

For the NCB, the 140,000 inherited colliery properties were in a dire condition at the point of nationalisation, not least because of a war-related moratorium on repairs. Post-war maintenance became so expensive that many were kept only just habitable until the miners could be rehoused in new ones promised under the Coal Industry Housing Association construction plan.[13] This arrangement left many NCB tenants in housing conditions akin to those in slums.

Yet, as national slum-clearance policies picked up again after the war, the NCB's national line was to support *fewer* slum clearances by local authorities, rather than more. This was not about preventing tenants from being displaced, nor was it about championing refurbishment over demolition. According to background briefings on the government's policy from 1954, the NCB's priority was seemingly to ensure a 'greater net addition' of houses built by local authorities, as opposed to newbuilds that would replace slums.[14] If NCB properties fell within slum-clearance zones, the NCB planned to request that it be consulted by local authorities: 'The important things are that clearance should be timed to the Board's best advantage from the manpower and welfare aspects and, consequentially, that redevelopment should be sited to the Board's best advantage, also.' Again, the key issue here was maintaining a ready supply of labour for the pits.

In the 1950s, however, Cardboard City was a new estate. While there are always snagging problems with newbuilds, maintenance responsibilities tend to be low at the beginning and then grow over time. Early residents recall a couple of local repairmen who fixed broken fittings and painted. As was the norm for many houses at the time, Airey homes were built with single-glazed windows and wooden frames, so freezing and condensation were common problems, causing rot to set in. Residents recall a chap called Colin who would tear out and replace rotting window frames and the like.

The NCB's commitment to undertaking timely maintenance seemed to wane, though, as the mining industry declined. In April 1983, William Bell 'Billy' Williams, previously the manager at Water Haigh Colliery, wrote to the NCB's area manager for the Oulton estate, Robin Birchall, with an ongoing concern:

> There is too much loose talk in Oulton about the lack of urgency by the 'Board' in its attitude towards repairs on your Oulton estate and some of it has arrived at the local councillors' surgeries ... Does not the topic of an early repair being the most economical still stand? ... I like to think the NCB will be as good a landlord as they are an employer.[15]

In response, Birchall acknowledged a handful of outstanding repairs, such as leaking gutters, and agreed to action some as soon as possible – though stopped short of agreeing there was a backlog.[16]

Managed decline

Throughout its tenure as one of the country's biggest landlords, the NCB often considered whether a property was worth repairing based on administrative and managerial concerns, regardless of who was living in it. If the property was set to be demolished anyway, like some of the dilapidated inherited properties, it could be left as only just habitable with tenants still in place until the CIHA constructed new ones.

In 1955 Water Haigh Colliery managers bemoaned the fact that many of the brand-new family-sized houses on the Oulton estate *still* remained empty some two years after construction because the NCB policy was to give them to transferees – that is, mining labour attracted from elsewhere in the country. Struggling (or 'distressed', as they put it) and inadequately housed colliery employees from slums in the local area were not permitted to move into the empty homes.[17] After all, locally housed miners were already working down Water Haigh Pit, so what was the rush to house them properly when additional labour could be brought in to increase net employee numbers? This housing injustice was felt in collieries across the country. In nearby Doncaster, 2,455 miners working at Markham Main Colliery went on strike in 1954 to protest the outsider-first housing allocation system; this strike cost the Board 3,000 tonnes of coal a day.[18]

There was also an ongoing concern about so-called 'good' and 'bad' tenants that shaped NCB housing manager attitudes to rents and repairs. In minutes from a 1954 meeting of the Colliery Consultative Committee in Woodlesford, the topic of the newly built Oulton estate was raised along with a question about who should make it onto the list of tenants. Water Haigh Pit manager Billy Williams said that 'the Board did not want any dirty tenants on these estates ... Future NCB tenants who were now in such unfortunate circumstances would have to be prepared to accept the action normally taken in dealing with such cases.'[19] It's unclear exactly what that action would entail. If a household came to be considered 'bad' tenants *after* being allotted a house, a strategy that seemed to emerge later was to punish them by withholding maintenance. Returning to the 1983 letter to Robin Birchall about overdue repairs, Williams made the following intimation:

> I know better than most that you have some bad tenants in Wakefield Road, but you also have good ones who think they deserve better treatment [with regards to repairs]. My answer to the political element is that they [the 'good' tenants] are extremely fortunate in not having some of them on the council estate.

Sitting behind this letter was the subtext that, by this point in the mid-1980s, council estates had become bywords for decline and poverty – housing of last resort for those unable or apparently unwilling to provide for themselves.

Williams hints that he has told NCB tenants complaining about long-overdue repairs to be grateful they didn't have council tenants on their estate, or indeed that they were not themselves living in council housing. Either way, the outcome was clear: like it or lump it. He might well have added privately rented housing to his threat, as this shrinking part of the housing sector evaded or resisted efforts to improve housing quality more than any other.

It is worth examining the state of council and private renting across the 1950s to 1980s, to see what options were available to the renting miner who couldn't get into decent NCB housing. While accommodation could be equally shoddy in both the council and private sectors, a clear difference emerged in tenants' ability to fight back. Municipal tenants were much more able to form associations and undertake collective action than their private-renter counterparts. It is important to understand why.

'The landlord usually has his own way in the end'

For many years after the war, private landlords blamed rent controls for proliferating slum conditions in their properties. Low rents, they argued, meant no money for maintenance. The 1954 Housing Act loosened rent restrictions slightly, so landlords were able to raise rent if the house was in a good state of repair. This – as one Labour MP called out at the time – led many landlords simply to whitewash the walls of a property so as to justify hiking rents.[20] Then, the 1957 Rent Act passed by the Conservatives removed almost all controls from private rents for all new tenancies on vacant possession. This resulted in a surge of spurious evictions, rent hikes (even on slum properties), and a further neglect of maintenance.

Thus, from the 1950s, poorer workers in Britain had few decent housing options. Owner occupation was on the rise, but was out of economic reach for those on low incomes. Municipal housebuilding was not keeping up with demand; waiting lists were growing – as were council house rent rates, because the government (Conservative between 1951 and 1964) sought to ensure council rents were 'fair', by which they meant more competitive in relation to the wider private rental market. NCB rent rates were pegged to local authorities and so also rose – at the same time that coal-mining productivity was beginning to falter and wages to decrease in relative terms.

For the poorest renter, some private landlords charged less but offered slum conditions and tight restrictions in return. Any private housing improved as a result of slum clearance and municipalisation was then out of poorer workers' financial reach due to higher rent charges. All three landlord types – private, municipal, and industry – saw housing maintenance as a financial and administrative burden, rather than a responsibility towards their tenants. And with the multitude of ways a private tenant – and sometimes an NCB or council house tenant – could be evicted or 'rehoused' during this time, any personal touches to a rented home or efforts to make roots could leave tenants out of pocket, displaced, and brokenhearted, again and again.

The BBC captured some of this growing crisis in *Cathy Come Home*, a lauded 1966 TV drama written by Jeremy Sandford and directed by Ken Loach. The story followed a fictional young mother and her children as they lost home after home, each dwelling offering worse conditions than the last, until the family is finally homeless and the children forcibly removed from Cathy to be taken into care. Though the hard-hitting film is often discussed in the context of homelessness, it was also about the cruelty of insecure rents and unscrupulous landlords – the precursors to homelessness. The film hit a nerve, highlighting the downward spiral insecurely housed families could easily find themselves on.

Tenants fought rent exploitation and eviction injustices where they could. Tenants' associations proliferated across the country through the 1950s, 1960s, and beyond – usually in response to a specific localised issue and/or council authority. In Westminster in 1950, for example, some 300 tenants gathered in a local school to form an association to fight what they saw as unaffordable council rent hikes. The council argued that rents had to be raised to cover growing maintenance costs, but locals disputed the council's proposed figures as made up.[21] These Westminster renters had learned their organisational tactics from a smaller tenants' association on Thorndike Street, also in Westminster, which had successfully raised concerns about a 'filthy bombed site' near their homes, forcing the council to mount a clean-up operation.

In 1955 in Solihull, a tenants' association took on the local council, fighting a new differential rent scheme set to hit four council estates: a scheme the tenants described as 'robbery without violence'. The proposal was essentially one of residualisation, whereby only the tenants who could prove desperate need would receive a housing subsidy in future. Higher-earning households – which, in poorer families, often included working children – would have their subsidies withdrawn and had to pay 'full economic rent' (likely making it impossible for children ever to stop working, or forcing the family to up sticks and move elsewhere).[22] Newspapers of the 1950s are littered with stories like these: some document small victories and concessions from councils, but many tenant associations had to resign themselves to the higher charges.

Following the decontrol of rent in 1957, and subsequent rate hikes by landlords of all stripes, some tenant protests became radical. One of the largest was in London's St Pancras borough in 1960, where municipal tenants saw their rates double – or even triple in some cases. In protest, between 1,000 and 2,000 tenants withheld the difference between previous rents and the new higher rates.[23] It wasn't a full rent strike, but it provoked the Conservative-led council to threaten evictions for arrears, and the majority of protestors resumed rent payments in fear.

Meanwhile, multiple tenant associations formed to protest these hikes in other ways, some of which ended up becoming militant. An umbrella organisation, the United Tenants Association (UTA), pulled many of the disparate groups together and organised an eight-mile march around the borough in a mass demonstration. Though the leadership was predominantly male, women were at the forefront of the daily protests, with researcher Dave Burn writing that up to sixty women went out nightly, banging on councillors' doors to maintain pressure.[24]

Mass demonstrations of hundreds of tenants were met with the mobilisation of hundreds of police officers, resulting in physical altercations and the banning of mass gatherings in the St Pancras area. The borough issued a tranche of eviction notices for rent arrears. Thinking tactically, the UTA agreed for only three households to face eviction because a handful of flats could be better defended against bailiffs than dozens, so it settled all but three cases. One of the three tenants, Gladys Turner, decided to negotiate an end to her case. The remaining two – Don Cook and Arthur Rowe – barricaded themselves in their flats to prevent the bailiffs kicking them out. Don reportedly used twelve pianos and barbed wire in his efforts to stay in his home. Both men were unable to hold out and were eventually evicted. The UTA was also defeated and the rent rates remained at their new highs – even after Labour won the next local election.

Later that decade, private tenants in Liverpool saw a rare victory after staging a powerful rent strike that dragged in royalty. Tenants of property owned by the University of Liverpool lived in slums in an impoverished ward that was then called Abercromby. Though Liverpool Council was working on slum clearances, the university was not rehousing tenants fast enough or repairing their properties. Tenants were forced to continue to live in condemned conditions with broken doors, buckling floors, leaking roofs, and, according to leaked council reports, lead in their water supply.[25] In protest at the terrible conditions, and to try to expedite rehousing, tenants went on a total rent strike for eight months from October 1968. University of Liverpool students allied with the tenants, providing solidarity, spaces for gatherings, and material support – including testing the water and confirming the lead poisoning. University management reportedly tried to divide the two factions by telling each the other was communist.[26]

The protest came to a head – and national attention – when Princess Alexandra came on a royal visit to open two university buildings in May 1969. Over 1,000 tenants and students assembled outside, holding placards inviting the princess to visit their slums, which she did – much to the university's dismay. Ethel Singleton, resident and secretary of the Abercromby Tenants' Association, spoke directly to the princess, describing to her their appalling living conditions – outside toilets, no hot water. 'It must be awful,' Princess Alexandra sympathised, a statement which garnered national headlines.[27] Kim Singleton describes the activists' invitation and Alexandra's visit as a masterstroke in publicity.[28] In addition to national media coverage of 'Princess Alex in Slumland', the Abercromby protestors watched themselves on US television news. CBS apparently believed it was reporting 'an uprising against the royals'.[29] While the protest connected to a wider tenant movement emerging on Merseyside in the period, with multiple strikes loosely linked into the Amalgamated Tenants Associations Co-ordinating Committee, Abercromby was the one that gained the most attention and a relatively quick resolution. By June 1969, the council had agreed to rehouse the tenants, who never had to pay back their withheld rents.

Liverpool University notwithstanding, large protests at *private* landlord rents, conditions, and evictions were less frequent than those by council tenants, partly because private landlords tended to be smaller in scale and their tenants more distributed, with different households subject to different rent rates and tenancy terms. One tenant's poor living conditions could be completely different to their neighbour's. Scholar John Davis writes that 'creeping' rent decontrol over the 1950s was partial and unpredictable, as were its effects on rent hikes and evictions – making coordination and mass protest more difficult.[30] Perhaps more importantly, localised rent hikes and evictions, and individual protests against them, rarely made news. Where tenants fought back, it was through one-on-one battles hashed out in the courts.

There was some respite for private renters after Labour won the 1964 national election. The new government passed the Protection from Eviction Act as a protection from arbitrary evictions by unscrupulous private landlords, whose incentives to evict had increased with the 1957 deregulations. Arbitrary evictions were made infamous by London landlord Perec (or Peter) Rachman. Rachman would buy up old properties with established tenants, but in order to increase rent charges he needed vacant possession. Rachman's three-step approach to forcing out sitting tenants included, first, offering to buy them off with a pitiful amount of cash; second, making their lives intolerable by harassing them, including by playing loud music next door; and finally, cutting off their water and electricity, and breaking locks and lavatories.

Tellingly, Rachman did not gain infamy as an exploitative landlord. His tactics only came to popular attention because the criminal businessman was swept up in the Profumo affair, which dominated news headlines across 1963. The Secretary of State for War, John Profumo, was discovered to have had an affair with Christine Keeler, a nineteen-year-old aspiring model who had also had sexual relations with a Soviet naval attaché. Profumo lied about his association with Keeler and was found out. The sex scandal, along with concerns that Keeler's link to a Soviet attaché might have undermined national security, damaged the Conservative government and the party went on to be defeated in 1964. When the story made headlines, it was discovered that Rachman (who died in 1962) had also been a friend and lover of Keeler. Labour MP Ben Parkin, who coined the term 'Rachmanism', noted bitterly at the time: 'Rachmanism was exposed not because he intimidated his tenants and fiddled his company returns, but because he slept with a prostitute who had slept with a member of the Government.'[31] (Keeler was not a prostitute, but many labelled her so at the time).

After the 1964 Act, landlords had to go through the courts to evict. Then, through the 1965 Rent Act, the Labour government introduced regulated tenancies for unfurnished private rentals, with improved security of tenure and a new system of fair rents. This tenancy could be passed to a widow or from parents to children, finally acknowledging that a privately rented home can be as multigenerational as an owned one.

Under the 'fair rent' terms of the Act, rent rates had to be determined by independent officers, who would consider the age, location, and condition of the property. Was this progress and protection for the working-class private renter at last? Yes ... and no. While the 1965 Rent Act marked a huge break with the insecure tenancies of the past (and it is only under regulated tenancies that some Coal Boarders remain in Cardboard City today), it signalled a subtle but significant shift in Labour's attitude towards workers-as-tenants and the management of homes: bye-bye to Bevan's vision for quality and affordable homes for all at localised rent rates; hello to a private-landlord sector with market rents, more owner occupation, and houses as assets. This shift was cemented in various ways.

First, the new rent officers were instructed not to consider how much tenants had spent on repairs or refurbishments – ostensibly to prevent tenants from being overcharged for improvements they had already paid for out of their own pocket. But, like NCB housing, this clause also prevented consideration of rent *reductions* after a tenant had forked out their own cash to improve the property. As an injustice, it is perhaps minor – but it speaks of the countless ways tenants have long been discouraged or prevented from making rented houses into homes. From this point onwards, rents began to follow a more market-driven trajectory, as house location and condition superseded public need when determining rates.

Also key is that this act signalled a shift in political consensus to one where private landlords were accepted as a permanent feature. Labour was no longer aiming to municipalise all housing for the benefit of the population. In fact, it had dropped the policy at the 1962 Labour Party Conference, just two years before winning the election. According to scholar Phil Child, with some 600,000 slums still standing by 1961 (after the Conservatives failed to make much progress on clearances), Labour saw full municipalisation as a policy it could no longer afford, financially or politically.[32] Attempts to regulate private rentals were just that – directives to shape private landlordism rather than moves to end it.

Private landlords predictably ducked and weaved around evolving legislation to try to maintain their power to hike rents and evict. The 1965 Rent Act only required unfurnished rentals to have regulated tenancies and court order evictions. Furnished rentals had weaker protections. This differentiation led to a surge in landlords changing their properties from unfurnished to furnished. In other words, landlords proactively forked out for things like sofas and beds because it proved cheaper for them than giving tenants a regulated tenancy.

If furnished-property tenants had any grievances, they could only take their landlords to a furnished rent tribunal, rather than a court. The tribunal only had powers to lower the rent and postpone an eviction order for six months, after which the tenant was required to re-present themselves on a six-monthly basis – a gruelling merry-go-round. As a 1969 Rent Act review committee reported: 'The landlord usually has his own way in the end' – tenants were usually evicted.[33] The committee also revealed that landlords were making more money from furnished properties than unfurnished through charging higher rents, even though conditions and protections were frequently worse. (Those sofas and beds had to be paid for somehow). Furnished tenancies were finally put on a level with unfurnished in 1974.

For NCB tenants, more housing promises were soon to be broken. In January 1972, miners across the country went on strike over pay. Striking miners returned to work after seven weeks in late February 1972 following an improved pay offer, but by this point the NCB was struggling. Many pits had already closed, including Woodlesford's Water Haigh Colliery in 1970. The NCB tried to concentrate on increasing productivity across other mines, but financial losses were mounting. More strikes followed in 1974; but these were nothing compared with those of 1984–85, with Arthur Scargill at the helm of the NUM. The details are beyond the remit of this book, and are covered elsewhere.[34] Suffice to say, these strikes saw the Conservative government, which had regained power in 1979, take extreme measures to break the miners and their union – and with them the place of coal mines in British society. From the late 1970s, the NCB, faced with these economic and political challenges, found maintenance increasingly expensive – and, perhaps, pointless – as its future responsibility as landlord hung in the balance.

Entrenched insecurity

Before moving on to document the fate of Cardboard City from the 1980s in the next chapter, it is worth focusing on a thread that runs through the so-called golden era of post-war public housing: inconsistency. While much housing was indeed built and paid for out of the government's purse, rules over rent rates, maintenance, and rights continually shifted over the shortest of timeframes. Despite ongoing demand, by the late 1950s the Conservatives had convinced themselves that the post-war housing shortage was abating, and so turned to private enterprise, encouraging owner occupation and decontrolling rents. They forced councils to borrow for building from the financial market rather than the government, sending costs upwards overnight. That meant council tenants – who had barely settled into their post-war homes – were suddenly met with steep rises, as costs were passed down to renters.

For NCB tenants, maintenance became a football kicked from side to side depending on whether it was viewed as a cost to the landlord or a potential rent-negotiating tool for the tenant – meaning everyday household repairs could easily escalate into exhausting battles. In the meantime, housing conditions deteriorated. With rents being directly deducted from wages or balanced against lower pay, negotiating power was taken out of their hands. NCB tenants often 'didn't know what power or rights we had', as Cardboard City Coal Boarder Mavis Abbey explained.

Moreover, most battles – and the tenant movements launching them – were limited in scale and spread out across the country, meaning national political gains were nearly impossible. First, such gains were limited by the resources that ordinary tenants had at their disposal: these activists-by-necessity usually pushed back as a last resort; resistance lasted only as long as they could withstand the financial and social hardships that come with protest. Second, these battles were fragmented – popping up in different places and times across the country, targeting different types of landlords, and driven by different, often narrowly local, goals. Scattered fights rarely make headlines.

As individual councils or the NCB exerted localised control over construction and rent rates in the post-war period, protests by tenants inevitably became localised disputes between councils and their tenants rather than part of a national movement against renting instability and dispossession. Labour Party dominance in an area was not a reliable indicator of solidarity either, despite housing being championed as a key public good since the early days of the movement. Quintin Bradley writes of how in 1934 Labour councillors in Leeds implemented intrusive means tests and raised rents for council tenants while allowing slum dwellers to live in the homes for free.[35] Labour councillors viewed the moves as coherent with the party's support for the very poorest of renters, yet differentiation tactics were widely opposed within the Labour movement more generally. Labour councillors had also supported the very same municipal tenants in the previous decades, campaigning against high rents and pushing for council tenant representation in housing policymaking. In the end, the hikes provoked a large rent strike and many of the tenants voted Tory at the next opportunity.

Fragmentation in the struggle against housing insecurity was also exacerbated by the fact that industry unions rarely saw household struggles as part of the fight for fair working conditions and pay. Where trade unions supported tenants, it was again on a local, case-by-case basis. As a result, ordinary tenant protestors were forced to focus their limited energies on fire-fighting the material challenges in front of them rather than the political problems underpinning the system. Whether tenants secured any concessions or lost the battle entirely, there was no way the ordinary renter had much of a chance to effect systemic change. The result: exhaustion.

Dave Burn hints at this when he documents the dejection of the 1960 St Pancras protestors after they lost the battle to keep rent rates affordable.[36] A new Labour Council was elected in 1962, promising to reverse Tory rent hikes, at least partially. But in the end, the new council also failed to do anything. The high rates remained, breaking an election promise and, echoing

Leeds from three decades earlier, undermining solidarity with the tenants' movement. The Labour councillors then declined to give the full reasons as to why they felt their hands tied. Disillusionment set in, the struggle ended, and protestors went their separate ways. The rent hikes were there to stay, and the goalposts for future battles had once again been moved.

Up in Yorkshire and Cardboard City, a similar disillusionment was not far off.

5

Declared defective

The decline in municipal housebuilding throughout the 1970s was a problem for those waiting for a property on the increasingly long waiting lists. It should have been less of a problem for renters already established in council or NCB housing; after all, once you're in, you're in – right? For many sitting council tenants that was the case. From 1980, huge numbers of them experienced a sea change in their housing security, as the 1980 Housing Act's Right to Buy policy meant they could purchase their homes – and not at high market rates, either: council tenants could command a huge discount, starting at 33 per cent and rising to 50 per cent for those with twenty years' residence.

This policy was extremely popular among ordinary council renters. Why wouldn't it be? For more than a decade there had been a broad political consensus that owner occupation was the ideal (in fact, the only respectable) housing outcome. Council estates were cemented in the popular imagination as ghettos for the most destitute, and therefore as undesirable places to end up. Municipal and NCB renters of all incomes had experienced varying degrees of housing quality and instability in their public housing up to that point.

Government subsidies had fallen, rent rates were rising as wages stagnated, and maintenance was a frequent battle. The private rental market clearly did not offer a safety net. Owner occupation may not have been so popular had there been tenant-centred, secure tenancies as a viable alternative in the first place. As Sarah Glynn states in her book on lower-income housing and the effects of neoliberalism, 'there is no intrinsic reason why public housing should not be a tenure of choice'.[1]

Nonetheless, Right to Buy was passed, and council-owned property stocks dwindled as local authorities sold what was on their books. Many words have rightly been spilled over Margaret Thatcher's privatisation bonanza, and I'll touch upon its impacts on the availability of municipal and Coal Board housing later in the chapter. First, I want to highlight a policy you might be less familiar with: the National Coal Board had its own fire sale of public housing first – with much worse outcomes for many sitting tenants.

Buyers wanted

In 1976, the NCB policy decision to 'get out of housing' and concentrate on moving coal meant selling all its remaining housing stock.[2] By this point the NCB property empire had halved, from the highs of around 166,000 Coal Board houses in the late 1950s, to around 85,000 by the mid-1970s. Sales were the result of surplus stock and the surrender of leaseholds, as well as the demolition of old houses. Yet even this reduced stock was still proving burdensome. Many of the houses – both brick and factory-made – were in desperate need of maintenance and modernisation, but the cost of building works had risen dramatically over the previous decade, partly because of the growth of the building sector and rising costs of materials. The NCB was neither able nor willing to keep up – and of course these houses were static assets that lost their relevance when mines closed and labour was needed elsewhere. So the NCB decided to sell off its properties at pace – with tenants and councils being first in line to purchase.

Even though the Labour Party pursued a slimmed-down policy of municipalisation (local authorities purchasing private residential properties) when it was in power during 1974–9, NCB properties were excluded from the subsidies that local authorities could access for this purpose. So the Coal Board had limited wiggle room with sales prices. This could have been a good thing for sitting tenants, as they were offered favourable low prices based on the NCB's 1976 policy (often a 50 per cent reduction on the market-value rate), preceding the similarly cut-price Right to Buy reductions.

If tenants were not able or willing to purchase their home, or took too long to decide, the NCB moved down the list to the next potential buyer: local authorities. In one case in Bolsover, Derbyshire, in 1978, the NCB attempted to sell an entire estate to the local authority, as the majority of sitting tenants did not want, or were not able, to purchase the houses themselves. The NCB was having to sell them dirt cheap because Bolsover Council were 'reluctant purchasers and are only interested in purchase from the moral and social point of view', according to contemporary records.[3] The houses were nearing the end of their life, and Bolsover Council's assessment of their condition was that, by 1980, they'd cost about £100,000 per year for maintenance and modernisation, so there was no choice but to sell them for pittance. Other options were to sell the Bolsover estate to a housing association or a private speculator, but the council worried that housing association ownership might lead to rent rate rises, and a private speculator purchase was ruled out (for the time being) because such a move would not be approved by the local authority.

Alan Dickie, national director of NCB Estates Management noted about this case that, although Bolsover Council had offered only half of the sale price, with the housing association and private company offering substantially more, it was better to sell to the local council to avoid stoking political difficulties with the National Union of Mineworkers. News of a potential private sale had already caused 'some minor NUM rumblings which it would be better to allow further time to quieten down'.[4]

While the NUM was never geared up to fight for housing rights in the same way as miner labour rights, it committed from the outset to intervene on behalf of all aspects of a member's life, including housing. This made housing a reactive, rather than coordinated, aspect of union work. John Grayson writes that where there were tenants' associations for Coal Board housing, they tended to deal with communicating minor housing complaints and the social side of housing. Where larger housing disputes emerged, the NUM would step up for the cause and represent a tenant worker at court or to the Coal Board.[5] Throughout NCB records, there are scattered mentions of NUM intervention in individual cases, or instances where influential figures such as Arthur Scargill lobbied for an entire estate (in the late 1970s Scargill was president of the Yorkshire NUM, then president of the whole union, and ultimately led the strikes against the Thatcher government in 1984).

Nevertheless, as in Bolsover, fights waged and won by the NUM were usually heavily localised and reactive. As miner housing conditions worsened over the 1970s and more concerted action was needed to secure tenant rights, coalfield housing had become completely enmeshed in local political dynamics, including venality and local corruption.[6]

Right to Buy

The idea of municipal tenants being able to buy their homes had been around for decades before the 1970s. The Housing Act 1936 permitted local authorities to sell their public housing stock to tenants with ministerial consent, though John Boughton notes that some Conservative councils had been doing it since the 1920s already.[7] Labour also floated right-to-buy opportunities for some local authority tenants in the 1950s. But by and large, ordinary people – even some owner occupiers – still liked renting: a 1960 housing survey revealed that a fifth of homeowners would have preferred to rent.[8]

The idea of a right to buy your council home then gained

policy momentum over the 1970s, where it was implemented with trial-and-error experimentation (one Tory council in Nottingham put its council homes on the open market, booting out sitting tenants).[9] Thatcher boosted the idea and made it one of her key election planks in the 1979 election. When she moved into Downing Street in June that year, before she even had time to rearrange the apartment's 'worn leather furniture', she set about putting it into policy. By 1980, the Housing Act was passed, and sitting council tenants could purchase their rented homes at substantial discounts. Thatcher turned municipal house divestment into a bargain-bin sale.

For someone who so strongly believed in markets and competitive pricing, this move should have been abhorrent. In fact, Thatcher had opposed heavily discounted public housing on market grounds in previous years.[10] And yet, as the 1979 election neared, she realised the move might provide momentum for bigger goals to reduce government spending on welfare, reducing what she viewed as dependency on the state and creating a 'property-owning democracy'.

Local authority house stocks plummeted by around 1.5 million between 1980 and 1990, and between 1976 and 1987, the Coal Board had sold off 74,000 more houses, too.[11] After the 1980 act came into force, councils were prevented from reinvesting sales income in new housing: money from the sales went straight to Treasury coffers and reduced national debt. And then, to make matters worse, the government reduced new construction subsidies by 43 per cent between 1981 and 1991.[12] So it was getting harder and harder for local authorities to fund the building of new rented housing, even though such homes were desperately needed.

Rent rates were also rising in the dwindling public housing stock. Where council tenants were not willing or able to buy their homes – primarily occupants of high-rise flats in deprived areas – many of the properties transferred to separate organisations, such as housing associations or tenant management organisations, and were therefore also removed from state books. These housing association transfers, coined 'Tenants' Choice' and formally enacted through the 1988 Housing Act, are what Daniel Renwick and Robbie Shilliam argue introduced the financialisation of public housing because of their reliance on private investment. It was certainly one among several factors.

Following the 1988 Housing Act, 'any large housing project had to be administered through a housing association. Associations were thus given access to private sector finance for public projects.' This included the ability to take loans for repairs and maintenance – something local authorities could not do. As Renwick and Shilliam continue, however: 'The interest on private loans incurred by housing associations was too high to afford the subsidisation of good housing necessary to meet the needs of the poorest.'[13] The result: higher costs for tenants; the managed decline of increasingly scant public housing; and the further impoverishment and stigmatisation of public housing tenants. So for those on low incomes wanting or needing to continue renting, options from the state were increasingly limited. What about those renting from industry?

Well, the other ideological commitments Thatcher made in her 1979 election pitch were to tackle inflation, take on trade union power, and improve law and order. Coal Boarders in Oulton were to feel the sharp end of several of those sticks. First, the 1980s Conservative government privatised key British industries, selling shares off for a pittance. It also oversaw massive spending cuts, and not just in housing. Linked to that, Thatcher reduced the power of the unions by responding harshly to strikers and then making it harder to strike. For coal specifically, Thatcher led the cruel confrontation with miners and their unions during the 1984–85 strikes, and closed down mines. The Conservatives then privatised the sector in 1994. In doing so, she removed yet another state-owned industry from the government's books (and with it, the industry's assets).

It was not just the mines and their surrounding land that needed to be sold off over that decade of asset disposals; there were tens of thousands of Coal Board houses still on the accounts. The NCB set itself a goal of getting rid of all its housing by 1988. In a so-called property-owning democracy, the fair step (in as much as neoliberal economics is ever fair) would have been for sitting tenants to continue to have the opportunity to purchase their Coal Board brick and prefab homes. Certainly, the NCB had been running that policy since 1976. Unfortunately for Coal Boarders in Oulton, and many other prefab municipal and NCB tenants across the country, they fell foul of poor building-sector workmanship and yet another Conservative law: the 1984 Housing Defects Act.

'Poor workmanship, poor quality materials or lack of maintenance'

Public housing tenants keen to buy their rented homes often didn't have the outright cash and therefore had to get a mortgage agreement from a lender. That was easier for brick properties than for non-traditional structures. As prefabs such as Aireys had primarily been built and managed by local authorities and the NCB up to the 1980s, many money lenders were unfamiliar with valuing this non-traditional type of building. Surveyors working on behalf of lenders had limited experience assessing the integrity of these structures, and therefore insufficient knowledge to value the financial risk and lending possibilities for mortgages.

Oulton Coal Boarder Mick Wagstaff recalled that his family moved off Cardboard City in 1969 due to his dad being told they'd never get a mortgage on the house. By the 1980s and the large-scale impetus to divest public housing, however, government policy propelled financial organisations to look a bit harder at the issue. That decade, the government commissioned the Building Research Establishment (BRE) to carry out a series of condition surveys and to produce referenceable reports for surveyors to carry out future lending assessments.[14]

Airey houses were some of the first to be investigated, and the pre-cast reinforced concrete (PRC) structures were found seriously wanting. As the BRE reported, carbonation or chlorides in the concrete resulted in the corrosion of some houses' steel frames, as well as 'cracking and spalling' of the concrete.[15] Some cracking had already been discovered in a couple of council-owned Airey houses undergoing renovation in Barnsley in 1981.[16] Where found, corrosion and cracking rendered the houses potentially dangerous. Such defects were not uniformly discovered in all Aireys, but were common enough to warrant the inspection of each unit. On top of that, the houses were made with concrete cladding slabs that were no longer in production and so difficult to replace. Construction companies just didn't have the commercial incentives to keep factories tooled for replacement parts.

The problem was not just limited to Airey houses. Unity, Cornish, Boswell, Reema Hollow Panel, and many other types of PRC non-traditional systems were soon to be designated as having defects. In other words, hundreds of thousands of houses, primarily those belonging to local authorities and the NCB, were suspected of being structurally unsound. Lenders were spooked and refused to offer mortgages on the properties without serious remedial work and guarantees, and government panic ensued. The BRE reported at the time of its initial inspections in the early 1980s, and again in the early 2000s, that the majority of the structural problems it identified in non-traditional house inspections were due to 'poor workmanship, poor quality materials or lack of maintenance'.[17] Suddenly the six-unskilled-men-build-house-in-two-weeks approach of the post-war industrialists seemed a little shaky.

The subtext within the BRE observations was that many well-built and well-maintained prefab houses could turn out to be fine if inspected. But of course, these houses were built by innumerable different private building contractors and unskilled labourers across the 1940s to the 1960s, so there was no easy rule of thumb when assessing build quality. Then there was the question of maintenance: when you're a tenant, structural maintenance is often out of your hands, and requesting it from a landlord can be difficult. As a result, by the 1970s, many of the tenanted prefabs and other council and NCB properties were in an appalling state of repair, even though some were little more than a few decades old. Crucially, in a financialised sector where the risk-averse lender dictates what's possible, the mud had already stuck: all Airey prefabs and others like it were judged ineligible for mortgages without substantial refurbishment.

These conclusions came in the 1980s, a nadir in public opinion about factory-made housing. In 1968, Ronan Point – a London-based systems-built tower block constructed by Taylor Woodrow Anglian – had partially collapsed following a gas explosion, killing four people and injuring many more. Subsequent investigations found that design flaws and poor workmanship in the construction process contributed to the incident.[18] The BRE looked into systems-built tower blocks in the 1980s, alongside their factory-made house research, and recommended safety inspections and changes to design codes for many of them. By this point, though, the reputation of tower blocks would have been difficult to salvage, even with repairs. This declining public and financial-services confidence in non-traditional housing created an urgent problem for the governing Tories, who had just offered millions of local authority renters the right to buy their homes. Who would buy the factory-made housing now?

A fair number of tenants had moved quickly and already bought their factory-made houses in good faith – including some 4,000 ex-NCB households.[19] These new owner occupiers were left with houses they were being told might be unsafe to live in, and that they might not be able to sell on. Such a situation draws parallels decades later with the tens of thousands of flat residents living in blocks covered in combustible Grenfell-style cladding. While many of the better-maintained prefab houses will have escaped structurally compromising defects in the 1980s, the BRE's findings created a significant publicity problem, making Right to Buy and the NCB's house sale look like duff deals for many thousands of citizens. The Conservatives turned out to be unwilling to fund the inspection of all houses so as to reassure tenants and prospective buyers. Instead, they sought rapid workarounds.

First came a discretionary scheme where private owners of an ex–local authority Airey house were able to apply for a maintenance grant to repair the defects in their homes (this is because even defective Airey houses could be refurbished – many still stand as happy homes today after timely interventions). Some councils were also willing to buy Airey houses back at almost-market rates, which the government encouraged local authorities to do. This was problematic in its discretionary character: not all local authorities across the country were willing or financially able to buy back the homes. It was also problematic in its focus on Airey homes, as many others were also being labelled as defective. So it was quickly followed by a statutory scheme for grants or repurchase of ex–local authority homes, and that was incorporated into the 1984 Housing Defect Act, which was later consolidated into the 1985 Housing Act.

This statutory scheme provided a government grant to the homeowner for 90 per cent of the repair costs (leaving the owner with a bill for the remaining 10 per cent), or the option of local authority repurchase at 95 per cent of the market value. Owner occupiers who sold their house to the local authority and re-entered the world as municipal tenants were allowed to maintain their duration-in-the-house record for the purpose of claiming another Right to Buy discount on their home once it had been repaired.

But it wasn't a universal policy. The scheme was for private owners only, not public landlords. That's not to argue for a race to the bottom in housing security; it is a good thing that some owner occupiers of Airey and other supposedly defective prefabs were not left with huge unanticipated costs as a result of poor design and shoddy building methods. But the policy further emphasised the Conservatives' disregard of council and NCB tenants' rights and securities: some 2,000 households were still living as tenants in NCB prefabs without a guarantee of repairs, or much opportunity to move elsewhere. Thousands more local authority prefab tenants were experiencing the same uncertainty up and down the country.

MPs with the highest number of defective prefab homes in their constituencies were quick to raise the various problems with the act in 1984. Unsurprisingly, these were primarily Labour MPs representing urban industrial constituencies in the middle and north of England, with higher proportions of local authority and NCB prefab tenants. Jeff Rooker, Labour MP for Birmingham Perry Barr, raised concerns about whether the financial provisions for ex–local authority owners were even workable. Rooker argued that this act placed a huge financial burden on local councils whose budgets were already tightened following wider Tory cuts:

> Extra responsibilities are being imposed on local authorities as a result of the discovery, after all these years, that several hundred thousand non-traditional dwellings may be subject to structural defects and they will all require individual inspection. That was never budgeted for by local authority housing departments … They should not have to take money from existing programmes for housing improvement grants, general repairs and so on.[20]

While the government made agreements with *some* local authorities to help fund the repairs or purchases by late 1985, this happened neither quickly nor uniformly across the country. Many local authorities had to fulfil the remit of the Act from their own housing allocations, which was to reduce resources for other public housing expenditure down the line. But it was not just a money issue. In a 1984 debate in Parliament, Robert Litherland, Labour MP for Manchester Central, pointed out the standards implications for local authority tenants that were not being addressed:

> The Government are dealing with a limited number of [owner-occupied] dwellings because they are interested only in the value of property. That is why there is discrimination. The Government are obsessed with money values. Where are their social values? Where is their consideration for council tenants who have to endure the misery of poorly-constructed, condensation-ridden properties which are expensive and difficult to heat?[21]

For the thousands of tenants sitting in NCB prefab properties (as opposed to council prefabs), the situation was even worse. There was no government money that the Coal Board could draw on to shore up the houses and make sure they were comfortably liveable and competitively saleable. This was another blow to the mining communities that had fiercely fought Thatcher's closure of the pits.

The Coal Board's policy upon discovering the defects was initially one of action. In 1981, shortly after cracking was found in some Airey houses in Barnsley, NCB estates director Alan Dickie ordered a pause on sales of NCB Airey houses to tenants and an inspection of a large portion of the Coal Board's Airey stock. In these houses, supporting columns classified as Cat A were not in any immediate need of attention but should be 'inspected in future intervals not exceeding ten years'. A Cat B column needed to be urgently replaced or strengthened, but only if three or more columns were adjacent to each other.

Otherwise, Cat B columns also did not pose any immediate structural problems.

Sixty-six houses in Cardboard City were inspected between 1981 and 1983 across Wordsworth Drive, Sugar Hill Close, Shelley Crescent, and Oulton Drive. More than two-thirds of these homes had columns classified as Cat A in the civil engineer's assessment. These figures roughly accorded with an earlier NCB sample of Airey homes, which found 60 per cent to have minor deterioration.[22] Of the nineteen homes that were listed as having three or more Cat B columns, it's difficult to see in the records whether these were adjacent and required attention. An earlier sample of Airey houses elsewhere showed that around 6 per cent of the total had significant deterioration. Presuming Cardboard City's houses followed this pattern, at least thirteen likely required some urgent remedial work.

Then – inaction. As far as I'm aware, no remedial work was undertaken on any of Cardboard City's homes. For owner occupiers elsewhere in the country, the Coal Board refused to buy back their houses, and would only refund homeowners' structural survey costs and the 10 per cent owner liability if defects were found. By 1984, in correspondence with Kevin Barron MP, the NCB indicated that it intended to plough ahead with its house disposal policy, selling whatever it could.[23] For houses that wouldn't sell, the NCB simply boarded them up when they became vacant. Tenants who couldn't afford to move elsewhere, or didn't want to, were soon surrounded by dilapidated unoccupied houses with plywood boards hammered over windows: 'Slum conditions', to quote Barron.

Gerald Howarth, MP for Cannock and Burntwood, a mining constituency in Staffordshire, reported in 1986 that he had received complaints that purchasers of defective Wates homes (another prefab builder) in his constituency were dividing their houses up and subletting, 'packing in as many tenants as possible'. Perhaps this was for greed, or because it was so expensive to repair their newly bought NCB homes that they wanted to recoup losses. Either way, Howarth reported that 'the standard of the area is declining' due to overcrowding.[24] In Cardboard City, nearly sixty Airey houses in the previously close-knit 210-house estate stood vacant by 1986. If NCB estates weren't already associated with poverty and neglect, they soon would be.

6

Going, going, gone

Everything about the NCB's 1976 house disposal policy was rushed. In just two years it had sold around 20,000 of its houses – more than three-quarters of them to sitting tenants.[1] While the sales discount given to sitting tenants was generous at 50 per cent, the time that tenants were given to decide on this life-changing financial commitment was not: three months to express an interest in buying their homes, and an additional three months after that to complete the purchase. Such was the rush that some NCB estates managers in Doncaster were unilaterally cancelling tenant house purchases if the contract exchange process went beyond the stipulated three-month period, even if completion was imminent.[2] There was to be no waiting around for dilly-dallying occupiers when stock needed to be disposed of as soon as possible. In that short space of time, lifelong renters had first to work out if they wanted to own at all, then whether they had the funds to repair the property, and whether they would be eligible for a mortgage considering their age and income.

Many NCB tenants, lifelong miners and their partners or widows, were in their fifties and sixties or older, and unsure about burdening themselves with mortgage payments for the remainder of their lives – so the sale option passed them by. For some, the idea of switching from a responsibility-light rented home to a troublesome and onerous house ownership seemed ridiculous. Others were eyeing up work options and considering whether pit closures meant they'd have to chase coal jobs elsewhere. Barry and Mavis Abbey from Cardboard City remember that they were briefly given the opportunity to purchase their Airey home on Oulton Drive in the mid-1980s, but they hesitated as they weren't sure if they were going to move to the new Selby Pit, which was slated to open in 1983.

Then, Barry explains: 'We went away on holiday and when we came back, we were going to sort out buying the house. But they'd already passed the houses, the [whole] estate over to a developer. We'd no neighbours. Nobody at each side of us, nobody over the road. All gone.' They were no longer able to purchase their home, even if they wanted to. It is unclear whether this was because the Abbeys missed the three-month window, or whether their holiday timed with the NCB's pause on Airey house sales to tenants due to defects. Either way, purchase was suddenly no longer on the table.

Other miners across the country who had managed to consider the offer during the short window of opportunity and were keen to press ahead were then met with additional wrangles around value and maintenance. One prospective purchaser, Mr Mills in South Nottinghamshire, was unable to get a mortgage on his home because of its state of disrepair, and wrote to *Coal News*. Addressing the concern, the NCB noted it would not take any 'special steps' to carry out repairs or improvements that might assist a tenant in getting a mortgage.[3] It asserted that it always did, however, keep up with everyday maintenance. This raises the question of how a property became unmortgageable from disrepair?

In another case, Mr C. Utley – a Barnsley-based miner of forty-eight years' service – wrote to the Board complaining that he had been offered the opportunity to purchase his home for £3,000 (minus the adjacent land and garden he had been using throughout his tenure), yet the house still had a 'horror story' list of outstanding repairs. These included attic roof subsidence, damp, rotting window frames, 'appalling' sewer smells, and more. Utley requested that the repairs be undertaken, and then he would purchase the house. The NCB's response? Sold as seen. Alternatively, any repairs it undertook would result in the house needing to be revalued, and therefore a higher sales price for Utley.[4]

While not making things easy for sitting-tenant purchasers, there was always the NCB's second option of selling to local authorities, right? Not for long. In July 1979, two months after a Conservative election victory, the NCB management caught wind that the Department of the Environment was further restricting local authority capital expenditure on municipalisation to cases of 'exceptional circumstances'. The Coal Board had to rethink its market. This anti-municipalisation policy, reflected NCB estates director Alan Dickie, would likely have reduced the number of local authorities and housing associations able (let alone willing) to buy remaining houses, so the NCB had to be pragmatic. While the first priority was to sell to sitting tenants, property companies and private investors 'remain a potential channel for the disposal of houses' – at least until sales to individual tenants hit the defects hurdle.[5] From there on, it was clear that tenants would be even less able and willing to buy their homes. Against this backdrop of apparent desperation, the last resort – private speculators – shot up to first place.

Although private sales had always been the fourth option on the table, the NCB was initially reluctant to consider it. As touched upon in the previous chapter, before the Miners' Strike in 1984–85, the background threat of a National Union of Mineworkers protest caused some Coal Board reluctance. In 1978, G. C. Shephard of the industrial relations department within the NCB expressed concerns about approaching the NUM for any kind of 'mute endorsement' for the sale of houses to private companies. Shephard pointed out: 'Communities everywhere are alive to the existence of the growing army of speculators enthusiastically studying the return to a period of rapidly rising property values.' He stated that approaching the unions on this particular subject could be a 'political "timebomb"' to be avoided.[6]

By 1979, NCB records indicate it had only made one or two sales to private companies (it is unclear whether that means one or two houses or one or two estates), and the line from the top was that these sales had to be undertaken with the utmost discretion.[7] This was the case until the NCB got desperate, until the political climate changed with the new Thatcher government, and until the NUM ceased to be such a threat. On top of that, the whole housing sector went through dramatic changes, to which the NCB was not immune.

SOLD!

By 1986, the Coal Board had decided that it would no longer offer its prefab housing stock to sitting tenants *at all*, as it was concerned that the apparently defective housing might prove a 'heavy liability'.[8] Yet the NCB had still set itself the target of disposing of all its housing stock by 1988. Few options remained and time was short, so the NCB ramped up its sale of estates in a swath of public auctions.

At these auctions, NCB houses and entire estates were sold off for a pittance, often without warning to sitting tenants or councils. It was a fire sale, and the main beneficiaries were private speculative companies hoping to turn a profit.[9] Shelter reported on this phenomenon in 1987, calling it out as a 'new form of Rachmanism'. Their *Pits and Mortar* report highlighted a pattern of landlord behaviour emerging: a company would buy NCB houses cheap, run them down without any maintenance or modernisation, and sell them on for vast profits.[10] It was not just majority-prefab estates, but any NCB estate where sitting tenants and local authorities were unwilling or unable to buy the dilapidated NCB stock. This Rachman approach was called out in Parliament, too, with MPs citing some egregious examples. In Creswell, Derbyshire, a speculator bought a bunch of NCB houses at an auction for £3,000 apiece, and sold them on to another speculator within six months for £6,000 each without doing a thing to them.[11] It was becoming hard for tenants to know who their landlord was, let alone to organise desperately needed repairs.

As with all housing injustices that came before, these speculator estate flips were met with objections and protest. Tenants formed federations, and some organised protests outside auction houses to try to put off sellers – including in Wakefield, not far from Cardboard City.[12] Such activism was heavily localised, however, and ultimately had little effect on the sales or on the subsequent behaviour of landlords.

Tenants in NCB houses bought by speculators were reportedly receiving a knock on the door as late as 10:30 at night, or a form posted through their letterbox with a one pound coin payment taped to it, asking the tenant how many lived there, the state of their health, what repairs needed to be done, and why they had turned down the offer of purchasing the freehold. 'Obviously,' Joseph Ashton, MP for Bassetlaw in Nottinghamshire pointed out, 'those questions are asked with the intention of [reselling the houses and] making a quick profit.' Fellow Labour MP Allen McKay told Joseph Ashton that in Elsecar a speculator had bought a bunch of NCB houses and their 'first action was to knock on the door and ask for £100 up front before starting on any improvements'.[13]

What is clear by this point is that coal industry tenants, particularly those in non-traditional prefab housing, had fallen through the deepest of cracks. In the space of just a few decades, they had gone from moving into the most modern and affordable of family homes and working in a thriving industry to renting dilapidated, even defective, houses next to closed (or soon-to-close) mines. These tenants were soon being charged market-rate rents for homes that *they* were not able to buy, but private speculators somehow could.

Cardboard City tenants were no exception. By the mid-1980s, the closest collieries at Water Haigh and Rothwell had closed down; all of the houses the miners had made into homes over three decades had been declared defective by government decree; NCB policy was to dispose of its housing stock entirely; and no sitting tenant on the estate had been able to buy their home up to that point.

Several tenant households in Oulton had enquired about the possibility of purchasing their homes when they first got wind of the sales policy. As mentioned, Mavis and Barry looked into buying their house but seemingly did not act on it quickly enough. Lynn and Diane's father, Mac Dickinson, had a survey done on the house for mortgage purposes, but because the tie bars were in a bad condition he did not pursue the purchase. Only two households progressed quite far in the process. Mavis and Barry recall that two separate neighbours, Dennis and Eric, got offers to buy their respective houses, and these miners managed to sign documents and put the first payment down. Then, suddenly, the offers were withdrawn by the NCB and the two miners were eventually compensated – possibly because of the pause on sales of defective Airey homes from 1981.

Yet by late 1986 the entire estate had been sold to private investors (and was possibly sold on again that same year). In 1990, the land and 210 houses were then split up; as many as 140 were sold, demolished, and redeveloped – all turned over to speculators, in the blink of an eye, and without a single structural repair being done in the meantime.

The details of the multiple sales are murky and cloaked in commercial jargon. On 31 October 1986, the Oulton estate popped up as 'for sale' in a *Financial Times* advertisement. An agency called Manchester Square Associates was selling this apparently 'HIGH YIELDING HOUSING ESTATE ... by direction of clients'. Of the 210 houses included in the sale, 155 were noted as still tenanted by miners. Who the landlord clients were, however, is unclear. According to the estate's title deed, it was still under NCB ownership at the time – it did not transfer to a named private company, Corrielek Ltd, until December

1987. I suspect there was a middle company turning around a fast buck between these two dates because of the advertised sale price for the estate and land: a cool £2.2 million.

Equating to nearly £10,500 per house, this was an unbelievable sum for the Coal Board to be pitching to prospective buyers. At this point in the NCB's ten-year house-sale journey, the Coal Board was desperate to sell the last of its stock. Houses were being valued on their (usually poor) state of repair at around the £3,000–£4,500 mark for sitting-tenant purchasers, or even less for local authorities – and the price for private buyers often fell somewhere in between. For example, in late 1986 in nearby Wakefield, 149 NCB houses were sold to private owners at auction, of which fifty-five were factory-made and categorised as having defects. The average price per house sold on that estate was £3,600.[14] In Staffordshire, another fifty-five houses went to private buyers for just over £4,000 apiece.

The higher end of the price scale tended to be for brick houses and not the supposedly defective prefab NCB homes that had by then been declared unmortgageable without costly repairs. But many brick properties were also going dirt cheap. In the case of Creswell in Derbyshire noted earlier, speculators also bought ex-NCB (brick) houses for £3,000 each, selling them on for double – still only amounting to £6,000 per house. In October 1986, the *Evening Sentinel* reported that Stoke-on-Trent miner tenants had mounted a protest following the sale at auction of their estate, Galley's Bank, to 'London-based' investors. Residents, a local councillor explained, were cheated of the opportunity to buy the houses themselves and he'd heard from a Coal Board 'mole' that the houses were sold at auction for as little as £1,000 each – a figure strenuously denied by an NCB spokesperson, who offered no alternative price.[15] Galley's Bank estate's new private landlord then failed to set up any mechanism for collecting rents, sending tenants into arrears despite their willingness to pay. These low prices were a far cry from the £10,500 per Cardboard City house advertised in the *Financial Times*.

It could be that Manchester Square Associates were flying a kite with a £2.2 million price tag – after all, they also described the estate as having 'all amenities close by', which was not true. Or it could be that £2.2 million was an astute valuation in a booming speculation market. Either way, it seems extremely unlikely that in the last throes of its life the Coal Board suddenly made a killing on defective Yorkshire Airey houses when they were selling everything else off for peanuts. There must have been a private owner in between.

To put that price into a wider sales context, by the mid-1980s council homes were being offered to tenants with the Right to Buy discount for around £9,000–10,000 – though this average includes huge nationwide variations. Council homes situated just 25 miles from Oulton, in Calderdale, West Yorkshire, were sold to sitting tenants for an average of £4,200 in 1981–82 – in other words, less than half of the asking price for Oulton's defective NCB Airey homes just a few years later.[16] In nearby Doncaster, 255 NCB tenants had bought their Airey homes for an average of £3,500 per house in 1983.[17] The same type of defective Airey house!

Could there have been a middle company owning and selling Cardboard City in between the NCB and Corrielek? There was certainly another company publicly associated with the estate between the date of the sale advert (in October 1986) and Corrielek's title deed registration in December 1987. Local newspaper the *Rothwell Advertiser* records in January 1987 that the estate had been bought by Manchester-based investment company Samuel Renshaw & Sons Ltd. The article states: 'It is thought that the property firm paid around £250,000 for the houses' – equating to a meagre £1,190 per house. A far cry from £2.2 million advertised (and a pretty big reduction on the £3,500 paid by Doncaster miners in 1983 for their identical Airey homes).

Goodness knows whether or how Samuel Renshaw & Sons Ltd was related to Manchester Square Associates or Corrielek, and goodness knows whether the houses were sold as a £2 million rip-off or a £250,000 steal. With the boom in property investment that followed Right to Buy, and investors' preferences for hiding behind complicated subsidiary set-ups, it was becoming harder and harder for tenants to have any idea of the name of their landlord (and it is still difficult for researchers to discover these details several decades later).

Following on from the NCB, British Coal (as it became in 1987) also refused to divulge who the purchasers were as a matter of 'commercial confidentiality'.[18] Not that knowing the name of a purchaser is always helpful: Corrielek Ltd was based on the Isle of Man and dissolved in 1993 – though not before either selling on the estate again or rebranding, as by 1990 the estate was suddenly owned by Oulton Drive Residential Estate Limited. If you think this one might at least be a local company – located on the estate itself perhaps? – you'd be mistaken. Oulton Drive Residential Estate Limited was associated with Johnson Fry Financial Services, a Belfast-registered financial services and property management group. The *Independent* noted that, by 1995, Johnson Fry owned 22,000 properties worth £900 million.[19]

Oulton Drive Residential Estate Limited (a.k.a. Johnson Fry) moved quickly to parcel up the estate. It sold more than half the houses to Beazer Homes in 1990, but kept a portion of the houses for land value and rental income. Then in 1997 Johnson Fry sold the remaining houses to Oulton Properties Ltd, a new subsidiary of Worcester-based investor Pemberstone – which remained the freeholder and landlord for two more decades. Corporate Watch reported that Pemberstone bought the estate in 1997 using a £1 million bank loan.[20]

Buy low, sell high

It's impossible to disentangle what was happening with NCB housing in this period from what was happening in council housing and local authorities more widely. The fact that local authorities across the country were in no position to purchase the majority of NCB homes by the 1980s was by design. The Conservative government's goal at this time was to transfer the long-term costs of building houses, owning houses, and maintaining them to the private sector and private individuals. In many ways, it wasn't much of an evolution from the post-war 'state-supported accommodation of private interests'.[21]

The Conservatives had already put council – and therefore Coal Board – rent rates on more of a market trajectory, passing the Housing Finance Act in 1972, which required a significant raising of rates. This Act saw widespread protests and opposition. Labour reversed the contentious parts of the policy on being elected in 1974, though never fully diverted tracks away from a mixed market; the new government's policies rejected radical financing reform, cut housing expenditure, and boosted housing associations rather than increasing new municipal stock. Labour then lost to Thatcher and the Conservatives in 1979.

For the 1980s' phase of municipal-housing privatisation, in addition to selling council houses to tenants, the Conservative government came up with 'innovative ways of starving local authorities of the financial means to invest in and repair their [remaining] housing stock'.[22] This included preventing councils from reinvesting money made from sales into repairing existing stock or building new homes. It also came in the form of starving councils of the ability to purchase available NCB homes.

Councils would have been the obvious purchasers of Coal Board housing once the NCB decided it could no longer be a landlord because councils had maintained, since 1945, the primary responsibility to provide and manage affordable and locally relevant public housing. Cardboard City would never have been NCB housing had the local council moved faster with building in the 1940s and 1950s, when coal mining was ramping up. The NCB's prefab stock was a top-up for council housing at a time of urgent need. Yet by the 1980s, the Conservatives had ensured there was no money left even to contemplate a wholesale transfer. Many prior Labour councils hadn't done public housing any favours either, as municipalisation had slowed even during the 1960s and 1970s Labour government years, with the party leaning into the owner-occupier ideology.

That said, most Labour local authorities weren't happy with the wholesale destruction of council housing stock through Right to Buy. Stuart Hodkinson writes that many Labour-run councils in Leeds across the 1980s and 1990s tried to resist the Conservative government's housing-privatisation initiatives, 'but were powerless to stop the Right to Buy programme ... or to do anything about the slashing of central housing budgets that left over 50% of council housing at an "indecent" standard by the late 1990s'.[23]

The NCB should not be let off the hook for its role in the financialisation of worker housing either. It never saw itself as a landlord, despite being one of the country's largest. It reluctantly responded to an urgent need – providing houses to enable workers to work. It inherited dilapidated brick accommodation and built many flawed new houses. As a consequence – or perhaps despite the condition of these houses – the NCB never meaningfully invested in the maintenance of its stock, racking up repair bills that were unaffordable by anyone's standards. When it was clear that the NCB wanted to rid itself of housing by the late 1970s, the NUM spent some of its advocacy time lobbying the Coal Board to give the entire housing stock over to local authorities for free. While perhaps a morally justifiable argument, the NCB was in no mind to listen. It was in economic crisis by this point: deep-mine outputs had fallen massively; lots of pits had closed; and the Coal Board had recently faced two damaging disputes, which resulted in electricity blackouts and factory closures.

Ideologically, the managers running the Coal Board had also bought into the notion of houses as investment assets. In response to a 1979 complaint from Arthur Scargill, then president of the Yorkshire NUM, about the fact that local authorities were getting lower purchase offers than sitting tenants, W. W. Burke, deputy director of NCB administration, argued:

> [Half] of the vacant possession value is a fair price to ask a sitting tenant ... He is buying the house for his own occupation and enjoyment and may sell it for the full market value at any time. The profit he makes whenever he chooses to sell his home is clearly a private, rather than a community profit.[24]

Ignoring the fact that some NCB homes would soon be unsellable because of maintenance issues and defects, Burke's logic here is that the tenant is being offered an *investment*, an opportunity to participate successfully in *the market* as an individual. Burke continued to explain that local authorities could buy the houses at a lower price because they 'do not expect any financial benefit from the purchase': rent is charged by councils simply to cover management and maintenance costs. In other words, local authorities were being offered prices that reflected living costs, while tenants were being offered prices that reflected market benefits. By the 1980s, the Coal Board had therefore clearly bought into the idea of houses as assets. Perhaps that's why it seemingly preferred bargain-bucket auctions to giving the unsellable houses to councils for free. So, what happened to tenants who suddenly found themselves with a private landlord after years of renting from the NCB? For that story, we travel back to Oulton.

Pay up or get out

Cardboard City was publicly declared as being in private hands in December 1986. This initially came as something of a relief to residents and local councillors, because by late 1985 the estate was in a dismal state of repair. Around sixty houses stood vacant after tenants had scarpered, but no purchasers could apparently be found – Leeds City Council and local housing authorities had turned down the opportunity to buy and the option had been withdrawn from tenants. The vacant houses were left to rot, as were the tenanted houses occupied by the remaining 150 households.

Locals hoped that new purchasers would revive the estate. A change of hands also ended the restriction of houses being rented only to miners, so there was the potential for Cardboard City to become a 'mixed community', some forty years after Bevan popularised the notion. Who might manage the estate was anyone's guess. In keeping with policy, the NCB did not initially name the new purchasers, with a representative explaining: 'That is a confidential matter. The estate was sold through a tendering process.'[25]

Unfortunately, the hope for better-managed homes was misplaced, as Cardboard City residents soon realised. Less than two weeks after news broke of new purchasers, a front-page headline in the local newspaper followed: 'Massive rent increases for coal estate': the new landlords – Samuel Renshaw & Sons Ltd – had started the process of 'reassessing' the rent rates and, if their application for a rise was accepted by the fair rent officer, it could lead to increases of 200 per cent or more.[26] While Cardboard City's housing conditions were poor, the picturesque rural setting of the estate and its proximity to Rothwell (where house prices had shot up by almost 10 per cent that year) would have fed into a hefty hike for former Coal Board tenants.[27]

While the rent rises were being disputed by sitting tenants, the new landlords were already advertising the vacant properties to prospective tenants unconnected to the mines. One local couple were reportedly horrified to have a two-bedroomed Airey house on the estate offered to them in January 1987 for over £2,000 per year in rent and rates – around £38 per week.[28] In response to the publicised complaint, Cardboard City's new estate manager, let's call him 'Mr M' for reasons that will become clear later, clarified that two-beds were being rented for £30 per week and three-beds for £35 per week, which was perfectly reasonable in his eyes. Some of the additional costs being quoted to the couple could have been additional utility rates charges, but it is unclear why there was such a discrepancy.

Regardless, to put those numbers into perspective, that same year local authority houses were being rented out across the country at an average of £17.40 per week. In Rothwell specifically, rents for council homes averaged £14 per week.[29] For the private sector across England as a whole, rents typically fell between £18 and £33 per week.[30] So Samuel Renshaw & Sons Ltd was continuing the newly established tradition of flying a kite when it came to valuing houses on this neglected estate.

Through manager Mr M, the new private landlord argued back against local complaints of ridiculous rent charges by stating that it was undertaking essential repairs and decorations to turn this estate into a 'high class residential area'. Though nothing was done about the structural issues that many of the houses faced: simply a lick of paint here and there and a bit of rewiring and plumbing where necessary, but nothing to extend the life of these neglected homes. Bear in mind that two-thirds had cracked columns.

Residents started to mobilise in outrage about the situation and received support from their Labour MP Bill O'Brien as well as by local councillors. They attended a meeting at a local pub in late January 1987, where senior representatives from

Samuel Renshaw & Sons were meant to answer residents' questions. But the landlord didn't show, sending manager Mr M again to act as a spokesperson. Residents were infuriated and the meeting got very heated.[31] They felt ignored and there was a growing anxiety that the liveability of their homes was increasingly out of their control. Just as with the middlemen of the nineteenth century and the letting agents of today, distance was being deployed as a tactic in maximising rental profit and minimising landlord accountability.

Following a second fruitless public meeting in late January 1987 (where the landlord and the Coal Board again failed to show in person, despite requests that they attend), the residents formed an action group. This was headed by Frank Allatt (recorded elsewhere as Allott) as the secretary, and twelve others who joined to form a committee. Their plan was to make a representation to the fair rents officer about the rising rent rates, and then to liaise with both the council and the NUM for support.

Frank Allatt had previously been a union man for the pits. He wasn't a resident at that moment, though he had lived on the estate for nine years before moving to nearby Stanley in Wakefield. It is notable that the residents didn't choose a secretary from within their own neighbourhood ranks to represent them, as they did three decades later with Cindy Readman and Save Our Homes LS26. I asked Mavis and Barry whether they recalled the formation of any organised tenant action against the NCB prior to Frank Allatt and the Oulton Estate Tenants Committee (as it became known). Mavis explained that the residents didn't really organise together for housing issues while it was managed by the NCB – not formally anyway: 'We didn't know what power we had and didn't know our rights.' Certainly not in relation to housing.

This aligns with housing researcher John Grayson's observation that in coal areas tenants tended to see the NUM as their 'tenants association', dealing with ad hoc housing complaints alongside workplace issues.[32] Even after the 1984–85 strikes, when the NUM was defeated and demoralised, the union still led housing fights in many areas across the country. In the North East, the NUM set up the Durham Mineworkers Housing Association, which took over hundreds of Coal Board houses in 1987. Other union-backed tenants' associations demanded repairs from new (and increasingly absentee) landlords. In nearby Wakefield, activists from the housing charity Shelter teamed up with the locally constituted British Coal Tenants Federation to pressure the council to survey the condition of a local estate. The Federation produced its own report that revealed 'general environmental neglect and deterioration … [and a] desperate need of modernisation'.[33] This modernisation would cost the council £3.75m, by their own figures.

Perhaps Frank Allatt had been involved in, or at least knew about, these similar fights on his Wakefield doorstep and applied that learning to the Oulton tenants action group. At the very least, as an NUM man, he would have known about wider union fights going on up and down the country – and by the late 1980s, there was growing national attention focused on fighting the privatisation of housing. It would have been hard for him, and the 1980s' residents action group committee, to have missed nationwide housing activism: the homelessness charity Shelter was active throughout the country; also, organisations such as SCAT – Services to Community Action and Trade Unions – were publishing and distributing action plans to help tenants fight the sale of estates, and explain the implications of changes in housing laws. Left-wing news publications such as *Public Service Action* and *Militant* were documenting estate sales and the actions of 'greedy landlords' (including Cardboard City's sale in 1986).[34] Local newspapers were filled with stories of rent swindles and resistance.

Cardboard City residents managed to make some initial headway with their complaints and advocacy about the condition of their homes. By June 1987, Labour-led Leeds City

Council had agreed to step in and supervise consultations between the residents, their representatives in the action group, and Mr M, the landlord's agent. Labour councillor Brian Walker reported that the council would consider what action it could take under the Environmental Health Act in relation to the long-documented disrepair.[35] By November 1987, the council had reportedly agreed to organise a structural survey of two of the homes in relation to the 1984 Defects Act.[36] Then, nothing.

The Oulton Estate Tenants Committee complained in a letter to the local newspaper in December 1987 that they'd heard nothing directly from the landlord about what it intended to do with the estate, nor about the ever-growing list of outstanding repairs.[37] The silence and delays were preventing tenants from undertaking the most basic of maintenance because they had no idea whether the investment would be worth it. In February 1988, Wetherby Magistrates Court had to order Samuel Renshaw & Sons, via Mr M, to carry out urgent repairs on the dilapidated back door of elderly resident Mrs Cott's home. The repair had been outstanding for more than eight months and was already the subject of an abatement notice by Leeds City Council requiring the landlord to undertake the work.[38]

As for the two-house structural survey, I haven't found mention of its results in any local news reports. Given that sixty-six of the houses had been surveyed by the Coal Board in 1983 and the majority were found to have at least minor defects, I presume any structural survey a few years later would have come to similar conclusions. Whatever the case, remedial work on the houses had ground to a halt. Unsurprisingly, tenants were leaving the estate in their droves.

By January 1989, only ninety-six of the 210 houses remained occupied – primarily by pensioners, widows, and older couples. This meant a loss of more than fifty households in less than two years and should be viewed as eviction through neglect. Remaining tenants were freezing in their homes, surrounded by broken fittings and fixtures, rotting window frames, and vacant houses next door. Frank Allatt told the *Rothwell Advertiser*: 'By not doing the repairs, the new owners are just waiting for everyone to get fed up and leave so they can knock the whole lot down and rebuild.'[39]

It was a classic case of Rachmanism. By 1988 local house prices in the Rothwell area were soaring, in some cases by as much as 20 per cent. With more than half of the Oulton estate now empty, Samuel Renshaw & Sons could smell a huge profit. Without notice or detail, the landlord announced plans in June 1989 to redevelop the estate and build new houses to sell off. Such a plan would require the rehousing of remaining tenants in similar properties because they had regulated tenancy agreements. Then, by September 1989, the landlord had sold it on to someone else to do that dirty work.

Cardboard City residents and other Coal Boarders across the country were not alone in finding their homes to be a bizarre mix of dilapidated yet valuable. The Conservative government was in the process of creating a private rental market which required an increase in demand and supply – changes that would take time to bed in. In 1985 the private rent accounted for around 9 per cent of total housing types. Tenants in private lets were predominantly on low incomes and often needed to move to a specific location in a hurry for their work and had limited other options. There wasn't much scope for charging them more than a basic rate.

For another few years, rents were still regulated – apparently discouraging landlord investment in maintenance or expanding stock. Moreover, ordinary people were only just beginning to buy their own houses on any significant scale, and so there weren't a lot of second homes to be rented out by individual landlords. Some speculators got a shot in the arm with the sudden availability of lots of NCB housing. But their poor state of repair resulted in new private owners banking on demand increases to offset product quality and quantity. Thus, as with the slum landlords of the nineteenth century, the main way to make money from housing was to raise rents without spending any money on improvements – or to evict, demolish, and redevelop. Luckily for aspiring property investors in this period, tenant rights were being demolished, too, so these two options would become much easier.

Prior to the Conservatives' 1988 Housing Act, most private renters had quite solid tenure protections. The regulated tenancies that accompanied the 1965 Rent Act meant that tenants could not easily be evicted, and tenancies could be passed through two generations. In 1988, the Conservative government suspended these terms and deregulated renting, so from early 1989 it was only possible for renters to get assured or assured shorthold tenancy agreements. The former had some protections, as a landlord couldn't evict without meeting a particular set of conditions, such as the tenant being in significant rent arrears. An assured shorthold tenancy (which became the *default* tenancy, from 1997 onwards) gave landlords the power to end a tenancy with a reasonable notice period, without finding fault or arrears. With the 1988 Housing Act, the policy of fair-rent determination was also abolished for new private tenants, so landlords could charge whatever the market could bear.

After 1989, then, shorthold agreements were the only tenancies available to incoming Cardboard City residents; this cemented a precarity that culminated in the eviction of my parents and many others some three decades later. Yet the remaining miner tenants who had occupied their Oulton Airey homes for any length of time before 1989 still maintained their regulated protections from the Coal Board. Council tenants across the country benefited from similar protections – as did any tenant still in possession of this pre-1989 agreement. Theoretically, a regulated tenancy meant that a landlord could not evict a tenant without good reason – such as health and safety problems with the homes – and would have had to take the tenant to court for possession. In the event of a legitimately enforceable eviction, households had to be offered like-for-like accommodation. Sounds like a decent compromise, right? Better than today, of course, but not without its own swindles.

Sheffield-based campaign organisation SCAT reported in 1989 that tens of thousands of council homes had been sold off to developers under this type of circumstance across the late 1980s. Councils had supposedly suddenly discovered asbestos or similar dangerous substances (often years after tenants had already highlighted these hazards), moved tenants elsewhere for the duration of repairs, then sold the valuably located blocks or houses on to developers so the tenants could never move back.[40] These council tenants were not dispossessed of the physical benefit of a council house (guaranteed shelter), as they had the right to similar local authority accommodation and therefore would retain a roof over their heads. But in the transfer, tenants were dispossessed of the personal and emotional connections that made up their home and community. With a creaking, depleted and oversubscribed stock, local authorities would match relocated tenants in accommodation that was as similar as possible in terms of number of bedrooms required and other features. But this rarely extended to similarities in layout, condition, access to amenities, or proximity to long-standing neighbours, friends, and carers.

In many ways, this renovation as relocation also fits into the nineteenth- and early-twentieth-century pattern of slum clearances. While better houses are ostensibly built by the state to replace dilapidated stock, there is no consideration for the lives, homes, and relationships made by those who have lived in the original building – connections that are broken by forced relocation and dispersal. Local authority tenants in these cases were treated as occupiers of someone else's property (the state's) rather than interconnected people who had made homes and essential relationships with neighbours.

Back in Cardboard City, tenants – now exposed to landlord market forces – saw a further and more rapid decline in the condition of their homes, in the affordability of rents, and in the protection of new tenancies. Some residents were forced to relocate, experiencing the same social dispossession as council tenants moved out of dilapidated blocks. Yet Cardboard City residents also resisted some of these impositions – sometimes individually, and sometimes collectively. They leaned on networks of support that had been built on the estate and in the wider area over decades.

7

Subcontracting accountability

Local news reports make clear that after a private landlord took over Cardboard City from late 1986, repairs and maintenance stopped entirely. Residents began regular battles over rent, rates and basic facilities. While some of those battles were waged by Frank Allatt and the Oulton Estate Tenants Committee through letters, public meetings, and newspaper coverage, other battles were reactive and fought separately by individual households.

'When it became a private landlord, we got nowt done,' Barry Abbey recalled. The only way to sort anything was to badger the salaried housing manager, Mr M: 'You'd have to have a real go at him. And then you'd get bits and bobs done.' The landlords changed, but Mr M was kept on to manage the estate – well, apparently until he was caught stealing. Barry continued: '[Mr M] got kicked off because he'd [managed] four estates and what he'd done as new people were moving in, he'd put the rent up. Only a fiver a week or something like that. He'd say, "It isn't me, it's these [landlords] what have done it. I can't do owt about it." He was putting it in his pocket.'

The Abbeys recall that Mr M used to sit in the reception area of one of the privately owned blocks, and people used to go to him to pay their rent in cash or by cheque. Under the NCB, each household had a rent book where all rent transactions were recorded for the benefit of the tenant and the landlord. When the first private landlords took over, they sent a paper form through the post. Barry made sure that whenever he paid rent, Mr M had to sign for a receipt. On one of the last collections before Mr M stopped working on the estate, Barry remembers the manager's son was there to collect in Mr M's stead. The son questioned the spreadsheet form, and Barry replied, 'You have to sign that, or you're not getting this cheque.'

Shortly after, Mr M was apparently let go and the management of Cardboard City was passed to a company based in Newcastle, some hundred miles away. Out of the blue, Barry and Mavis received a £500 bill for unpaid rent. Barry called the company to challenge it, explaining he was fully paid up and if they had any issues, they should take it up with the previous manager. The new company refused to accept that and pushed him again for the money, so Barry dared them to take him to court and hung up the phone. Later, Mavis called them with the same result. 'We never paid anything,' Barry said. But many other residents did, because they'd previously paid cash and Mr M did not sign anything – 'no receipt, no proof'.

It's difficult to establish today whether Mr M was stealing rents in the late 1980s or whether there was negligent landlord record-keeping around rent payments in the switch between one managing agent to another. Skimming from the top could account for some of the £8 discrepancy between what prospective tenants were reportedly told were the new rent rates (approximately £38 per week), and what Mr M publicly confirmed the new rents were (£30 per week) to the *Rothwell Advertiser* in January 1987. Equally, it could be that the new managing agents in Newcastle were trying their luck in asking for additional payments where none were owed.

Whatever the case, additional rent charges were demanded from Mavis and Barry where none were due. This pattern of landlord pressure echoes Barnsley MP Allen McKay's experiences of his constituents being asked to cough up £100 for repairs by private landlords in 1987 as soon as the new companies had taken over. It was only Mavis and Barry's diligent record-keeping and robust rebuttal to the Newcastle agency that prevented them from having to pay twice. The Abbeys had retained the power of the rent book in their own hands, using an unofficial spreadsheet to hold the landlord to account on payments. Their neighbours were forced to cough up, as they were too trusting or had no evidence of previous payments.

After winning this small personal battle over their rent rate, Mavis and Barry were forced out of their Oulton Drive home anyway. As mentioned in the previous chapter, in 1990 the estate was parcelled up and sold to Johnson Fry with plans for redevelopment that, as far as I can tell, were to be undertaken by Beazer Homes. So many houses on the estate were vacant by this point that there was no need to fight regulated tenants in the court for possession. Instead, the new landlord clustered remaining tenants in one corner of the estate and redeveloped the rest. Such a move was technically permitted under regulated tenancies, as the Airey houses required repairs and the new landlord was rehousing tenants in like-for-like properties – well, on paper anyway. In practice, Barry and Mavis experienced something quite different.

First, there was a battle to get a driveway of comparable size so that Barry could have space to keep his small boat. The house the private landlords had allotted for the Abbeys had a completely unsuitable twisted driveway, 'and you couldn't even get anything in the back garden'. Barry continues: 'I said I wanted the one next door. They said, "Someone's taken that." Oh right, I said [sarcastically], "You've sorted everything out" ... I said, "If you can't do any better than what you've offered, then I'm staying where I am." So he said, "You can't." I said, "I can – and you can't start the building work while I'm still there."'

The Abbeys were then offered another option – the house that is their current home. Barry asked for a few modifications such as a concrete resurfacing of the driveway for his car and boat (as per the previous house), adding a coal bunker round the back, and the installation of radiators downstairs (by then commonplace in houses across the country). These were basic requests to make the house liveable up to a modern standard and to meet the terms of the regulated tenancy. Like for like shouldn't be used as a punishment because the starting position is poor. The landlord agreed, but asked the Abbeys for a contribution towards the radiator installation and the driveway, which they eventually made. Yet the landlord didn't stick to the bargain. For the driveway, 'They put loose hardcore down which kept spilling out onto the street. So, it cost me £1,000 in concrete' (at least £2,500 in today's money).

Decoration of the new property was also the responsibility of the landlord that was moving them across. The local newspaper reported in mid-1990 that Johnson Fry Properties – a subsidiary of landlord Johnson Fry Financial – had begun decorating the remaining seventy-eight Airey homes.[1] But again, the promise of like for like was not kept. Mavis and Barry had to choose from a small pre-selected set of carpet, curtain, and paint options offered – another cost-cutting exercise on the landlord's part. A neighbour, Dora, was one of the few residents who managed to have her interior decor entirely recreated in the new property – but only after taking the landlords through the courts.

The rent rip-offs continued. Mavis recalls having to call the estate manager (whoever it was at the time) every three to five years and argue against rent rates, as they crept up and up. She was always armed with a calculation formula, arguing that rent-rise proposals were unfair in relation to previous rates, the condition of the property, outstanding repairs, and so on. While she often won in terms of securing a lower rent rise than originally proposed, it was always within the boundaries of an already marketised increase. Other neighbours didn't or couldn't fight, and so absorbed the differences – accelerating the unevenness of rents across the neighbourhood.

Situations like these were occurring throughout the country, as the private-landlord sector grew, and more and more private tenants found themselves paying higher rents to ensure landlord returns on investment. A 1998 government housing report on renting highlighted that average private sector rents almost doubled in real terms between 1988 and 1997 – far outstripping increases in tenant income, particularly for the poorest in the country.[2] Where increased rents were not feasible, for example in some of the poorest housing estates, residents saw the return of slum-like conditions.

A 1998 Coalfield Taskforce report highlighted 'dreadful conditions' of ex-NCB estates now owned by absentee private landlords who neglected maintenance. The number of vacant properties in these ex-coal estates was on the rise, encouraging vandalism and antisocial behaviour. The Taskforce pointed out that tenants trying to make absent landlords undertake essential repairs faced a 'complicated, lengthy, easily abused' set of procedures, and landlords were subject to a maximum fine of only £2,500 – insufficient to cover much-needed maintenance works, which were often significant.[3]

With landlord neglect and occasional trouble from antisocial tenants or opportunistic vandals, ex-NCB estates increasingly became associated with poverty – like their council estate counterparts. Proposed solutions to those social problems often came at the expense of apparently troublesome tenants – either through their evictions, or court proceedings. As John Boughton writes, impoverished estates were increasingly labelled as the problem but this 'conveniently shifted responsibility for the structural causes of poverty and inequality – which it had been thought in the past the duty of the state or government to address – to supposedly failing neighbourhoods'.[4]

The structural causes of housing inequality faced by Cardboard City residents were clearly the result of the flawed prefab design, followed by years of maintenance neglect by the NCB, then a fire sale of its dilapidated homes to private speculators who cared little for resident living conditions. While impoverished council housing estates across the country increasingly became labelled as 'sink' estates, Cardboard City escaped this designation to some extent. It did gain a reputation locally as being run down, which wasn't entirely unwarranted – and was certainly not the fault of residents. Perhaps it escaped the scorn reserved for much council housing because half of this isolated mini-village suddenly became a desirable owner-occupier estate.

Daily battles

Beazer Homes completed its redevelopment of half of 'Oulton Park' – the new name it had given the ex–Coal Board estate – between 1991 and 1997. The construction company built mainly three-bed and four-bed detached houses as well as a smattering of two-beds and flats on Oulton Drive, Shelley Crescent, and surrounds. After demolishing around 140 Airey houses, 110 new houses were built in their place, plus nearly 30 flats.

Land registry sold prices only date back to January 1995, but as far as those records show, prices on Shelley Crescent ranged from nearly £80,000 for a three-bed to a whopping £130,000 for some of the four-bed detached homes on the estate (sold during 1996).[5] The national average for a detached house that year was a little under £60,000, with houses in the Yorkshire and Humber selling for £56,000 on average.[6] So new owners in Oulton Park were paying well over typical prices. Not that it stopped the flow of buyers. By the late 1990s, more than half of Cardboard City – a long-time tenanted miners' estate – was now owner-occupied.

While many ex-miner families stayed on in their Airey home rentals in the Wordsworth Drive and Sugar Hill Close part of the estate – either finding new jobs beyond the mines or enjoying a quiet retirement – many more fled during the 1990s. With empty houses, an influx of non-miner tenants came into the community.

The new tenants, from the 1990s right up to the 2010s, tended to be lower-income workers. Rents were increasing in relation to wider market rates, but because of the estate's remoteness, draughty prefab housing, and low turnover of tenants, Cardboard City remained one of the last bastions of affordable family-sized homes in the LS26 postcode.

Cindy and John Readman moved to the estate with their family around 2006. John was an ex-miner, and his personal connections to the estate stretched back decades. As well as familiar friendly faces, the Readmans were looking for an affordable and comfortable home for their family. After experiencing a period of housing instability in the early 2000s, including one point when the family of five was homeless and camped out at Cindy's sister's house, the Readmans spotted an opportunity to get onto what was left of the Cardboard City tenanted estate. Their first home was a two-bed Airey, which was too small for their family (two boys and a girl) in the longer term, but it still felt 'massive, with big bedrooms' that could more easily be partitioned and accommodate living. Plus, Cindy and John figured they could keep a closer eye on upcoming three-bed houses from within the estate. And they were right: not long after moving there, a three-bed became available and they moved across to their most recent home – 46 Wordsworth Drive.

Cindy recalls that back then the tenanted part of the estate 'had a bit of a reputation', mainly for being run-down. The Readmans didn't anticipate staying permanently – just long enough for the family to get back onto their feet – but the house and the community quickly grew on them; they made fast friends, and they stayed. Their garden was huge in comparison to those available elsewhere in the area (something you hear time and again from sitting and former residents of the estate). In addition, the rent was affordable, it was a quiet area, everyone was friendly, and there was a real sense of community. Cindy's children attended local schools and loved playing in the safe green spaces surrounding the two streets – on bike and on foot.

Both John and Cindy continued to work locally, with Cindy taking on a role as a teaching assistant at a local primary school and John doing a range of jobs after the mines closed, including in administration and acting as vice chair of the Oulton and Woodlesford Sports and Social Club. While family and community life thrived, like others they soon found themselves battling the vagaries of tenant estate management.

Both the Readmans and the Abbeys recount that during the early 2000s, the quality and speed of maintenance and repairs to their Airey homes depended almost entirely on who was the estate's contact person – sometimes an office manager, sometimes a handyman, all organised through a property agent (such as Grainger or Watson Property Management) rather than directly with the landlord. Andy, Mick, Mike, and Shaun were a few faces among many and offered varying degrees of workmanship quality.

Andy was apparently a good egg – he was a self-employed handyman that the Readmans remember Grainger using from some point before they moved in until around 2012. Andy would tell residents straightforwardly that they would not get certain modernisations – such as new plug sockets – because Pemberstone would be unwilling to pay for an electrician to come round for such a small job. This honesty was appreciated by the tenants as it saved them precious time requesting and chasing the agent over things that would probably never happen anyway. But it highlights a resignation to poorer service and living standards that so many private and council tenants suffer: the idea that there is a ceiling of good will from a landlord when it comes to basic repairs and upgrades.

Such buffering practices also prevent landlords being held accountable for refusals of maintenance, even if well intended as in Andy's case. No formal request for basic repairs or upgrades means no paper chain to record landlord unresponsiveness or neglect over a longer period (which can be vital should the repair issue prove dangerous). An atmosphere of resignation can also mean that tenants across different households unwittingly end up with the same maintenance issues but miss chances to coordinate and communicate as a group to get something done. Of course, subcontracting management to an agent, and then repairs to a worker, has long been a strategy of landlords to avoid accountability (as in the case of the nineteenth-century middleman). So too is the frequent turnover of contracted managing agents and maintenance workers. Paper trails are broken and key contacts changed, so tenant–landlord relationships and requests are forced into a reset.

The estate management company changed from Grainger to Watson Property Management sometime around 2012; Andy stuck at the job for a while but is said to have become increasingly frustrated by long delays in getting paid for his work – a consistent problem across both agents. 'Nice Mick' was up next and became another familiar face on the estate for a while. John recalled that, as well as fixing reported problems like windows and gutters, Mick spotted and act on problems whenever driving around the estate – at least until he too became fed up. John recalls that it took Mick ages to get paid for his proactive maintenance work, and the managing agent was constantly querying why he did these 'costly' repairs if they were not absolutely necessary (according to the agent, at least). Mike was told only to work on repairs that had been called in, had a job number, and had been sanctioned by the agent. The attitude running consistently across all managing agents over the last couple of decades seems to have been, in Cindy's words, 'We're not gonna spend money unless we have to.'

There were also instances of shoddy workmanship resulting in outright damage to these ageing Airey properties, which still hadn't been refurbished some three decades on from inspections that had revealed defects. Cindy and John's windows needed replacing at some point in the 2010s. They recalled a contractor who wanted to cut out some of their house's supporting pillars to get the job done. That day, the contractor brought the wrong-sized window frame and planned to come back another time to complete it; luckily for the Readmans he never returned, and Nice Mick finished the job instead – with the right-sized windows, no destruction, and little fuss.

The Abbeys didn't fare so well. At a similar time to the Readmans' experience, Mavis and Barry also called the managing agent to get someone in to fix their back window, as the frame was old and rotting. As Mavis explains, that same first workman and his colleague 'put a brown one in when we asked for a white one ... and it didn't fit. So, they chopped out the concrete on the sides and you could see the [supporting] pole, and they chopped out the middle [of the pole], which I was never happy about. But they wouldn't listen to me.'

Mavis kept protesting at their shoddy work while they were doing the job and highlighted the damage it was doing to the house. In response: 'The man said, "Do you think I don't know what I'm doing? I said, "Yeah. I know you don't know what you're doing. It's part of the support of the house is that."' Barry suspects that it was all in the name of penny-pinching. The contractor had 'come three times to measure it then turned up with one that didn't fit. He'd nicked it off a building site, that's what I reckon.'

These were not isolated incidents at the hands of a few incompetent contractors; they were symptoms of a wider disease impacting council and private rental housing across the country well into the twenty-first century: 'organised negligence'.[7] Renwick and Shilliam point out that council estates over the 1990s and 2000s – under both Conservative and Labour governments – saw the state neglect its responsibilities to provide for the safety and security of its citizen-inhabitants.

In Peter Apps's powerful account of state failings and commercial greed that led to the deaths of seventy-two people in the Grenfell Tower block in 2017, he explains how concerned residents were labelled as serial complainers and disruptors, how essential repairs were put off wherever possible, how materials were swapped out time and again for cheaper – in this case, dangerous – alternatives, and repair works were undertaken without regard for the needs and convenience of the occupants. In one example, workmen moved boilers to speed up the refurbishment work, placing the bulky sharp-edged units outside the flats and forcing residents to squeeze past them to get in and out of their homes.[8]

In another tragic case, in 2020, two-year-old Awaab Ishak died as a direct result of mould exposure in his Rochdale social-rent home. Awaab's parents had repeatedly raised concerns to the landlord about the mould and living conditions in the property. The housing association, Rochdale Boroughwide Housing (RBH), failed to act and blamed the parents for the dangerous conditions – blame that was based on racist assumptions about the family's cooking and bathing practices. A subsequent investigation found that RBH had been dismissive and discriminatory to other residents and routinely ignored complaints about damp, mould, and other repairs.

These accountability gaps are not mistakes; they are baked into the housing ecosystem. Scholar Stuart Hodkinson writes about the 2000s trend for private finance initiatives – public housing regeneration outsourced to private companies – across London. He highlights that in three cases in Islington, Camden, and Lambeth, public bodies relied on contractors to self-report their progress and any problems on a job – a system that is obviously flawed given the millions of pounds at stake.[9] Where contractor failings were evident, authorities typically issued the most minimal of penalties. The priorities in these schemes were always the partnerships and contracts with private companies, rather than the empowerment or involvement of tenants affected by the redevelopment works. Huge profits were made by corner-cutting with impunity.

Renwick and Shilliam argue that disregard for residents must be understood as organised negligence rather than abandonment, because 'a neglected community remains trapped in rules that do not serve their interests or even provide for their basic safety'.[10] Organised negligence takes on a more complicated hue in the private-rental sector, with the proliferation of individual and small-scale landlords. (Buy-to-let mortgages were only introduced in 1996, yet in just over ten years they accounted for 12 per cent of all mortgages, accommodating around 2.5 million households).[11]

While individual landlords are unlikely to outsource maintenance and renovation to big corporate and industrial contractors, they still subcontract – using letting agents, casual building contractors, and other service providers. These outsourced companies (or sometimes just mates of the landlord) are paid by the landlord, in whose interests they operate. For ad hoc tasks such as plumbing maintenance, damp removal, general repairs, and so on, these are often one-off jobs where the invoice-payer is not there to see the quality of work. In such instances, the tenant can be ignored and the job rushed.

As another example from the Abbey household, some time ago Mavis and Barry needed a new fence in the garden because their chain-link fence had been pulled down by the plants growing through it over the years. Mavis recalled it had been up over twenty years by that point, so the Abbeys asked the agents for a replacement. 'We didn't ask for any particular fencing,' she explained, and the workman came with something adequate but, for some reason known only to him and the agent, he wouldn't run it all the way to the top of the garden where the previous fence ran. He took it part-way to the edge of Barry's shed in the middle of the garden, stating, 'That's the boundary and I'll go no further.' That was that.

Daily battles to get work done and retain some sort of agency over one's home have been common across tenanted properties for more than a century and a half. Landlords began to distance themselves from accountability through the cash-in-hand middleman in the nineteenth century. But by the end of the twentieth century, subcontracting and outsourcing had made this accountability vacuum standard.

A shock in the post

Fast-forwarding through the late 2000s and early 2010s, tenant–landlord relations in Cardboard City bumbled along. Rent was marginally increased every year, pretty much in line with both inflation and average private rent costs for the region. Mum, Dad, and my brother moved to the estate in 2006. At that time, their three-bedroomed home cost about £380 per month, comparable with a regional average for Yorkshire and the Humber of £390 for private rent.[12] Tenants of housing associations and local authorities however, were paying an average of £247 and £222 per month, respectively. That made private sector tenants around £143–68 worse off per month than fellow tenants in housing association and council houses.

Ten years later, Mum and Dad were paying £490 for the same property, compared with a £590 private rent average elsewhere in the region, or £312 for local authority housing elsewhere in the country – slightly better off than other private renters in Yorkshire, but significantly short-changed when compared to public sector tenant compatriots across the country.[13] Landlords were clearly no longer worried that tenants might have cheaper public housing choices – the supply just wasn't there.

For many years, Mum and Dad were also charged an annual £60 administration fee by the letting agent, just to roll the same contracts on for another year. Despite being a charge for nothing, this amount was on the lower end of the national spectrum. By the late 2000s, households up and down the country were being charged anything from £12 to £220 annually to renew a tenancy – sometimes per household, sometimes per tenant – using exactly the same contract.[14] Other spurious charges were front-loaded: rent in advance (by as much as six months); high deposits; and reference checks – the latter costing anywhere between £10 and £275. Up until 2019, when these charges were made illegal (2012 in Scotland), low-income tenants often had to borrow or get into debt just to pay these charges and get a foot in the door. Many more couldn't pull the cash together and ended up on friends' sofas.

Yet, to repeat the pattern of decades, little of this extra money went into maintenance. By 2006, at least one in four rented houses – both private and social – failed to meet decent living standards.[15] And while there was a moral and legal obligation for landlords to provide safe homes, they were not averse to punishing tenants who requested that maintenance work be done.

A 2005 Shelter report highlighted that the third most common cause of homelessness was a landlord ending a tenant's shorthold tenancy agreement (with causes one and two being relationship breakdown, and family or friends unable to put someone up any longer).[16] This eviction was not just about rent arrears. Citizens Advice Bureau reported the following year that it was becoming increasingly common for tenants to be served eviction notices when asking for basic repairs to be done. Echoing Chapter Two's 1948 *Yorkshire Evening Post* report about 'Mrs X' (who lived in a rat-infested, unlit, cracked-window cellar room with her husband and baby), Citizens Advice Bureau shared the experience sixty years later of a couple in Yorkshire with an eighteen-month-old baby who lived in a privately rented three-bed:

> The house was in serious disrepair: windows were cracked, one bedroom and the bathroom windows were boarded up and a shower had been installed in the main bedroom with no associated ventilation. The immersion heater had wiring hanging off the wall, secured insufficiently with black tape and the gas fire

> in the living room had been condemned by a gas engineer. The landlord replaced the gas fire with a two bar electric heater but their home was still cold. As the bathroom was unusable the baby was bathed in kitchen sink, which was increasingly unsuitable as the child grew. The family were living in conditions which were a health risk, especially for the baby. However, they were concerned that if they sought the help of the Environmental Health Department they ran the risk of eviction.[17]

That was 2008.

By 2011, some 40 per cent of private rentals failed to meet basic decent living standards.[18] Yet tenants were stuck: reports from environmental housing officers and tenancy relations officers showed that in *the majority of cases*, landlords were threatening eviction when tenants sought external intervention for essential maintenance.

In Cardboard City, no one to my knowledge called in external officers about the state of the houses. That was, in part, because they were able to undertake basic repairs and decorating themselves. It may also have been because extensive local press coverage over the 1990s seemed to make little difference. Eventually though, without structural maintenance, the prefab stock was always going to reach the end of its life. Work needed to be done and, like landlords before them, Pemberstone apparently wasn't prepared to fund it.

In late September 2017, Wordsworth Drive and Sugar Hill Close neighbours were waking up or returning home from work to find the usual pile of bills and junk mail in their hallways: take-away leaflets, discount leaflets, utility bills, bank statements and the like. Nestled in the pile was another nondescript glossy one-page leaflet – one that contained a familiar map. This leaflet was blank on the back, addressed to no one, and the only hint it might be relevant to the residents was that their street names were at the top. For those who took a few minutes to read the dense, tiny text, they saw that it was an invitation for a public consultation event to be held a few days later at the nearby sports centre. The organising agency – JRP Architecture Planning Landscape – was advertising the consultation on behalf of 'the landowner who is looking to submit a planning application for replacement housing on this site'.

Reading the leaflet, you'd never think anyone actually lived on the estate. The text refers only to 'land', houses, and dwellings – not homes and people. It boldly invites ideas for how the development scheme could 'meet the needs of the local community'. The obvious answer, of course, would be not to demolish their homes. But in this case 'the local community' clearly referred to the neighbouring owner occupiers of Oulton Drive and Shelley Crescent, rather than the soon-to-be-displaced residents of Wordsworth Drive and Sugar Hill Close. This depersonalisation of the estate and its tenant community served to obscure the truth that up to seventy low-income tenant families would be turfed out to make way for a wealthier class of owner occupiers.

Until this moment, the shorthold tenants had no idea that their landlord had any plans to change anything on the estate, bar the predictable annual rent rises. Hazell, my mum, remembers finding the leaflet on the floor in the hallway and not really understanding its implications at first – hoping in fact that the new houses might be for them. At this point in 2017, Mum, Dad, and my brother had lived in their Airey home for eleven years. I didn't grow up in this Wordsworth Drive house because, like many tenant families across the world, we'd had to move around a lot due to other people's choices. In 2005 I'd left our previous home in nearby Rothwell to go to university. But that Rothwell house, also a private let, was nothing more than a temporary stop-gap for my family after an unexpected no-fault eviction in 2004 forced us out of the previous house – a cottage in Oulton that had been our home for seven years … until it suddenly wasn't.

Our chaotic 2004 eviction was caused by the company that owned the house going bust. It was a tied cottage, so our home depended on the patronage of the company. Mum and Dad both worked there: Dad as a caretaker (it was his job that was tied to the house); and Mum as an administrator. So not only did we lose our home, but Dad lost his job. To prevent the loss of our entire household income, Mum transferred to a sister company in Tingley, which was an hour away by two buses that each came only once an hour at best. As a non-driver, Mum relied on lifts from kind colleagues, while she frantically searched for a more commutable job. My brother and I were aged fifteen and seventeen, both in crucial exam years at the time.

Mum put us straight on the council house waiting list, and after several weeks a property was offered in East Leeds. Unknown to me and my brother, Mum and Dad took a reconnaissance trip to the street that weekend. Mum said they slowed down past the house, noted the boarded-up property on one side (with a panel removed that looked like it might be an entryway for squatters) and an apparently burnt-out house on the other. The property they'd been offered had thick yellow grime on the outside of the windows. Another council estate plagued by organised neglect. They turned it down when they got home. It's one thing to change your kids' school in exam years; it's another to change their home to somewhere demonstrably less safe, as Mum later told me.

With limited options, we had to move into a much smaller semi-detached, two-bed private rental on a steep street in Rothwell, paying a hefty deposit, agency fees and six months up front in rent (pretty much all of Dad's redundancy pay) in order to convince the landlord that we – a family of four adult-sized people with one income – were worth the renting risk. It's all Mum and Dad could afford at the time. As well as being uprooted from our cottage home, that unsettling 2004 eviction saw us parted from our beloved two dogs and three cats, as the landlord refused pets. It also cost us a significant chunk of personal space. It was just a two-bed, so my parents slept in the living room on a sofa-bed, folding it away every morning and putting their duvet and pillows at the back of the room so we could watch TV and eat dinner as a family. Eventually, Mum found a job as an administrator for the NHS in a Wakefield hospital, far more commutable from Rothwell – though with a significant pay decrease from an already low starting point. My dad struggled to find work for some time. My brother's schooling suffered, and he sought escape in ways that at times got him in serious trouble.

Our private renting experiences were not unique – not then, in 2004; not 150 years ago; not now. Nor were they particularly terrible when compared to that of many other evicted families over the past century and a half. But frequency shouldn't mean acceptance, because it was difficult: it was confusing, embarrassing, and disruptive – in more ways than I'm prepared to spill onto these pages. I got out in late 2005 to go to university, falling into my own whirlwind of student-tenancy rip-offs. The rest of my family moved out to Cardboard City in late 2006. They put in their notice to the two-bed Rothwell landlord, but the opportunity to leave was timely, as the landlord said he was already thinking of evicting us, to give the house to his son and new wife.

It was against this backdrop of eviction that 8 Wordsworth Drive and Cardboard City became a secure home for my family. An added relief was that rents were affordable on NHS salaries – and my parents and brother have been able to make it their own over many years. Mum and Dad took back the surviving one of our two dogs – our Burmese Bramwell died in the interim – as well as our three cats. My parents also rapidly formed strong connections with neighbours, some of whom – like Mavis and Barry – had lived there for decades. It was this band of neighbours who started exchanging calls and text messages the moment they understood the meaning behind the

2017 glossy leaflet – first to close family, and then to each other and anyone else that might help. Cindy and John Readman emailed local Labour Councillor Karen Bruce that very day (residents contacted councillors from other parties, too). Push-backs against outstanding repairs and landlord neglect were about to become coordinated efforts to save their homes.

PART III

FIGHTING BACK

8

#SaveOurHomesLS26

Save Our Homes LS26 was started by those most affected: the tenants of Sugar Hill Close and Wordsworth Drive. Residents came together immediately after receiving the leaflet, not least because external events seemed to be moving at lightning speed: the landlord set up the public 'consultation' to take place on 2 October 2017, a week after dropping the news of the demolition. The site of the event, Rothwell Sports Centre, was a ten-minute walk from the estate, located on the erstwhile land and fields of the Coal Boarders' youth club and Miners' Welfare Club. Where miners used to walk for social gatherings, Cardboard City tenants now trudged to find out when they might be booted out of their homes.

That evening of the consultation, Mum walked down to the sports centre with long-time friends and neighbours 'Auntie' Linda and Susan. Susan had lived on Sugar Hill Close for a decade, Linda nearly four years. Both Linda and Susan worked with Mum at the water utilities company that went bust in 2004 and forced my family out of our home. Susan went on to work at the NHS hospital Mum was based at, though she and Linda had since retired. Other residents also walked down to the sports centre with their neighbour friends that cloudy October evening. Everyone wanted to know what would happen to them, their families, and their homes.

Mum described the whole event as a farce. 'Council man was there,' she wrote in WhatsApp messages to me on the day. He 'only found out the day before us. Rabbit in headlights.' Mum and Dad were advised to get straight onto the council house list (again), passively accepting the landlord's agenda rather than informing tenants about various options to oppose the redevelopment. It was already approved in their minds.

Pemberstone was conspicuously absent, sending its architect firm to collect 'feedback' on a blank form rather than answer any questions directly. Managing agency Watson Property Management was represented too, reassuring residents that it'd be at least eighteen months before they'd be forced out. It seemed that – with assured shorthold tenancy agreements allowing for just a two-month notice period – a warning of any longer than that was considered generous. In the end, the Rothwell Sports Centre meeting was a public consultation without any actual discussion at all.

The next day, Mum said she felt 'very alone' at the meeting, as the council and the landlord's representatives were already separating their attention and advice for residents depending on the strength of the household's tenancy agreement, creating a hierarchy of tenants. For the ex-miners with regulated tenancy agreements, some care was taken to offer reassurance and direct support. Watson had given them a courtesy phone call a week before the pamphlet dropped, warning them of the impending planning-application submission before shorthold tenants knew anything about it. At the consultation, regulated tenants were then separated from assured shorthold tenants, with the council explaining directly to the former how the redevelopment and rehousing would work, leaving the latter to their own devices. This dedicated attention to regulated tenants did not give the ex-miners much power and wouldn't prevent their eventual upheaval. But these limited gestures – a courtesy call and extra guidance at the meeting – show that stronger protections translate directly to an improved and more humanised treatment of tenants.

Scholars Vickie Cooper and Kirsteen Paton explain that the division of tenant communities has become particularly heightened in the past three decades, as market forces have reshaped tenancy agreements and diversified rent charges. This marketisation is fragmenting housing tenure and dividing class struggle.[1] In other words, renters are being pitted against other renters. The division is visible at the everyday level through the intense competition private renters face to secure a property viewing, let alone sign a tenancy. The BBC reported in 2023 that there was an average of twenty requests to view each available rental property, reaching as high as thirty in the North West.[2] In Yorkshire and the Humber, viewing requests went up fourfold, from five to nineteen per property, between 2019 and 2023.

Private renters have to offer higher rent or more cash up front to secure a place over other hopefuls, pushing up market rates. Prospective, often desperate, social-rent applicants who approach cash-strapped councils are being told to accept whatever properties are available, even when they are unfit for habitation, inappropriate for health needs, or miles away from family networks. This postcode lottery means some very vulnerable people are being told to take what's offered, wherever it's offered, or render themselves homeless.

Private landlords can, of course, be far more selective about who they take on as tenants. Landlords frequently discourage pets, forcing people into agonising decisions about what to do with dogs, cats and other furry companions, many of whom are not only family members but have also been vital emotional support during difficult times. While a blanket ban of pets isn't legal, landlords can currently make 'reasonable' refusals based on size of pet, number of pets, and other factors. Desperate renters don't tend to challenge.

Other landlords won't consider tenants in receipt of housing benefits, even though discrimination against housing-benefit claimants can break equality law. Judges ruled in two landmark cases in 2020 that refusal to rent to someone because they receive housing benefit can be 'indirectly discriminatory on the grounds of sex and disability contrary to sections 19 and 29 of the Equality Act 2010'.[3] Yet it's still happening, because landlords can cloak prejudice in general concerns about affordability, credit checks, or simply because there's no need for transparency in explaining why they've chosen one applicant over another. Few tenants have the time or knowledge about their rights to challenge individual landlords and estate agents about viewing or application refusals.

This fragmentation and renter competition is a result of the hamster wheel of poverty: low-paid and insecure jobs triggering frequent moves; spiralling costs of rent triggering evictions or relocation; a high turnover of tenants and increasing demand for private rent pushing rent costs up. The constant effort of running to stand still depletes energy, and people can barely keep pay in their pocket. If a Section 21 no-fault eviction notice gives you just two months to find a new home, there's little chance you'll find the reserves to fight given the challenge of getting a new roof over your family's head. And who's there to support you? Chances are, you'll be in a minority of one, as the multiplication of small-scale landlords through buy to let and accidental landlordism has meant that tens of thousands of tenants have faced eviction every year, one household at a time.

At the time of writing, renting reform is on the horizon. The new Labour government, elected in July 2024, has put forward a Renters' Rights Bill that updates the previous government's stalled Renters (Reform) Bill. If passed, it promises to end Section 21 no-fault evictions, increase landlord notice periods from two to four months, prohibit eviction in the first year of tenancy, and ban discrimination against people with disabilities and parents, among other things.

The Bill also commits to the extension of both Awaab's Law and the Decent Homes Standard to the private-rented sector. Awaab's Law, introduced under the Social Housing Regulation Act 2023, requires social landlords to act on hazards such as mould and damp within a set timeframe. The Decent Home Standard, established in the early 2000s, set statutory minimums in fitness, state of repair, amenities, and thermal comfort for council and housing association houses, and later private properties housing vulnerable people.

While reform is long overdue, these changes are ultimately piecemeal. Four months' notice is an improvement on two, but still inadequate for the task of finding somewhere new in a market of dwindling private-rental options, and with the challenges of funding the move, packing, and uprooting a family. Four months is also well below other European countries: Italy and France require the landlord to give six months' notice. In Germany, the notice period increases with the length of time a tenant lives in a property – notice can be as high as nine months. Moreover, the Renters' Rights Bill says nothing about affordability.

The Bill also doesn't change the requirement for landlords to act as de facto immigration officials. The 2014 UK Immigration Act contained a 'right to rent' provision requiring landlords to check the immigration status of all individuals set to live in a property. Since then, academics and housing advocacy organisations have documented numerous examples of racial, ethnic, and linguistic discrimination preventing applicants from being considered for a tenancy. However, the high number and disparate nature of individual landlords make it challenging to enforce discrimination legislation – not least because it's very difficult to investigate and prove individual bias by a single landlord.[4]

The power of numbers is one of the areas where Cardboard City parts ways from conventional eviction stories. With a slightly longer warning time of eighteen months and a whole community facing the streets, residents had a little more time to think and more boots on the ground for action. And it was soon after the farce of the October consultation that tenants began rallying. Within a few weeks, neighbours had banded together to form a Save Our Homes LS26 Residents Action Group.

Activists by necessity

As with so many social-change movements, the Save Our Homes LS26 campaigners were ordinary people thrust into action because it was their lives affected and their homes on the line. And everything happened so quickly. Two weeks after the late-September leaflet drop and early-October sports centre consultation, Leeds City Council organised a residents' meeting to talk through the implications of eviction. In this meeting the focus was again on encouraging Cardboard City's shorthold tenants to put their names on the council house waiting list rather than outlining ways to oppose the redevelopment.

For those not familiar with council housing provision, allocation works through a bidding system. You must be registered with the council, meet certain criteria to be considered eligible for a house, and show your interest in a property by bidding on it. Those who pass the criteria are then assessed on the basis of urgency and other factors, and the council will then allocate the house to one family.

The trouble is, increasing numbers of renting families have found themselves in urgent situations and supply has not met demand for a very long time. Leeds City Council has overseen a loss of at least 35,000 council houses in the past thirty years due to Right to Buy – homes that were never replaced. In the more sought-after Leeds postcode areas (those with lower crime rates and better transport links), waiting lists for council properties range anywhere between 70 and 200 weeks – and that's for families in Priority Band A, with the most urgent need to move.[5] In fact, Leeds is one of the councils with the highest demand for council homes, alongside nearby Wakefield, Sheffield, and Liverpool in the North, Birmingham in the Midlands, and London's Brent, Newham, Greenwich, Tower Hamlets, and Lambeth.[6]

At one point during the campaign, Cindy and John bid on a council house within reasonable distance of Rothwell centre so that they could be near their daughter, their jobs, and the community they'd spent most of their lives contributing to. Yet they were the 693rd family on the list. Only 1 of those (at least) 693 families could get the house, and in the end it wasn't John and Cindy, even though they were on the cusp of homelessness. At the time of writing, there were 27,000 households on Leeds City Council's social-housing waiting list, and more than 5,000 are in Band A, with an urgent need to move because they're already homeless, in temporary accommodation, threatened with homelessness, or living in squalid conditions.[7]

The Labour-led council is actively considering just deleting 18,000 people off the social-housing waiting list – pretty much all of Bands C and D, those with 'low or no housing need' according to ungenerous criteria – because the council does not have the resources to meet unprecedented increases in demand. A council spokesperson said that this action would be to help 'manage expectations' of lower-band applicants who 'have little or no realistic prospect of being offered a home'.[8] This removal is not because people don't need housing, but because there's simply nothing available.

Yet data massaging does not improve the overall housing situation. Band C families are often on the list because they're in insecure or inappropriate accommodation, and removing them from social-housing waiting lists neither improves their private-rent situation nor does it create more social housing. Leeds City Council recently recorded the ending of private tenancies, usually through a Section 21 eviction notice, as one of the main causes of homelessness in the region, accounting for 16.48 per cent of all cases.[9] They expect this figure to rise steeply with the uncertain legal environment around renting as well as the cost-of-living crisis and a ramping up of house repossessions. All those soon-to-be booted out Band Cs might soon return as Band As in urgent need of accommodation. And then what? Even if there were other houses elsewhere for my parents, brother, and their neighbours to go to, Cardboard City was a social community as well as a collection of households – and residents wanted to stay together. So in the early days of the campaign, they leaned on whoever they could for help.

First they reached out to their elected Labour and Lib Dem ward councillors, who supported the organisation of another residents' meeting on 4 November 2017 and encouraged the community to formalise themselves into a structured campaign so that, in John's words, 'everyone knew everything was above board'. It sought to be an issue-based movement without political affiliation, characteristic of many tenant movements across the preceding century. Within four days, members of our new Residents Action Group stood in front of Leeds City Council, giving a deputation to ninety-nine councillors asking them to save the homes of Wordsworth Drive and Sugar Hill Close. My

Residents, from left to right: Susan Gould, Mark Field (Dad), Cindy Readman, Mavis Abbey, and Sadie Somers, standing outside Leeds City Council offices after the deputation. Credit: Save Our Homes LS26.

dad was one of those resident representatives, resurrecting the only suit and smart pair of shoes he owned for the occasion. Councillors listened intently and even gave them a standing ovation. For a time, there was camaraderie and optimism in the air.

To share information and garner publicity, we picked up the usual tools at the disposal of a grassroots group: we set up a private Facebook group for community updates; a Twitter account @SaveOurHomeLS26 for public advocacy, hashtag #SaveOurHomesLS26; and a website – saveourhomesLS26.org.

From the outside, the campaign must have seemed relatively slick. We garnered thousands of petition signatures and gave deputations to the council. We received financial and vocal support from the National Union of Mineworkers. We also received generous financial support and people power in key moments of protest from activist and union organisations such as Hands off Our Homes, Sisters Uncut, ACORN, Unite, and many others. Cindy, John, Mavis, Barry, Hazell, Mark, Linda, and Susan became regular figures in local and national press; they've told their story in national newspapers, on *ITV News*, BBC *Newsnight* (2018), and in several housing-focused prime-time television programmes including *Losing Your Home: The True Cost* (ITV) and *We are England* (BBC), both broadcast in spring 2022.

Residents were interviewed by countless journalists, regularly featuring in online news stories on the *i Paper*, *LeedsLive*, the *Yorkshire Post*, and others. In 2020, an award-winning short documentary film was made about the eviction, called *Hanging On* by Cosmosquare Films.[10] Its director, Leeds local Alfie Barker, and creative producer Hollie Bryan organised for residents to be hoisted up by cranes and filmed clinging onto the sides of their homes. My dad was the poster boy for the docu-short.

BBC Newsnight *crew filming in Susan Gould's home in 2018. Residents on the sofa, from left to right: Susan Gould, Hazell Field (Mum), and Linda Elsworth. Credit: Save Our Homes LS26.*

Hanging On *film poster, featuring Mark Field (Dad). Copyright Cosmosquare Films, designed by Scott Woolston. Printed with kind permission.*

Cosmosquare Films shooting Hanging On *in 2021. Mark Field (Dad) is being hoisted up by a crane. Credit: Save Our Homes LS26.*

Cosmosquare films shooting Hanging On *in 2021. John Readman, centre, is being attached to the hoist. Credit: Save Our Homes LS26.*

Alfie's goal was to tell the story of a tight-knit community visually and convey what it means to have, and lose, a home. This theme resonated personally as he was having troubles with his own landlord at the time, back in 2021 in the thick of COVID-19 lockdowns. As repeated requests for essential repairs and the cleaning of mould went unanswered, Alfie felt he had no choice but to stop paying rent to force the landlord's hand. 'I just kept thinking, how can this government ask us to stay at home during the pandemic, when where I'm living is uninhabitable?'[11] He wasn't alone. Around this time, the Health Foundation reported that 25 per cent of privately rented homes had at least one major problem relating to urgent maintenance concerns, overcrowding, or affordability.[12]

Hanging On went on to be selected for big-name film festivals (the Toronto International Film Festival, the British Film Institute London Film Festival, Sheffield DocFest) and shortlisted for many prizes; it won multiple awards (at the Encounters and Aesthetica festivals) and was well received across the global short film circuit. The message was cutting through.

There was a working-class architectural-heritage element to our campaign, too. From the get-go, we spotlighted the local nature of the Airey design, the post-war context of the construction, and the strong links between housing design, location, and coal-mining community heritage. The Twentieth Century Society, which campaigns for the conservation of significant twentieth-century architecture, submitted an objection to Pemberstone's redevelopment proposal, emphasising the social and historical value of our prefab estate, the size of which, they pointed out, is relatively rare. Two years running, ordinary people visited our estate on coaches as part of the National Trust's national Heritage Open Days, exploring residents' homes and gardens and – guided by Cindy and other neighbours – learning about the history of our streets.

So in just a few years, Save Our Homes LS26 had become a focal point for local and national discussion around the plight of renters in the national housing crisis, as well as for the critical issues of housing supply, refurbishment versus demolition, working-class heritage preservation, and tenant communities. Our Twitter following swelled, and fellow campaigners from across the country were offering solidarity and tips or seeking advice in turn. As chair, Cindy was increasingly spending most evenings on the phone or emailing journalists and supporters. But in many ways our momentum was a product of luck as well as hard work.

We were fortunate that there were enough of us with diverse networks, skills, and interests to undertake specific roles and bring in invaluable resources. The ex-miners – especially Mavis and Barry – brought the connection, interest, and resources of both the NUM and wider mining community. Cindy and John, long-time members of the Labour Party, brought local councillor support and the experience of volunteering in organisations that have to account for actions and funds. Their networks and outreach in turn brought in other unions. The Lib Dems had members in the community too, and councillors took an early and active interest in preventing demolition. The territorial rivalry between both parties also served a purpose, accelerating coverage of competition between the two, which ultimately heightened our profile and shaped their commitments to preserving our homes. (The Conservative MP at the time, Alec Shelbrooke, responded to correspondence but visited the estate just once at the beginning.)

My mum Hazell took a dogged approach to posting on Twitter, with the result that the @SaveOurHomeLS26 handle and tweets were mentioned frequently in council meetings. I set up and ran our website. I uploaded historical context and resident profiles and kept churning out regular blog updates, which were utilised by journalists. Exposure brought different housing-interest groups and individuals on board – including ACORN, Sisters Uncut Leeds, and Judicial Domicide – as well as expert individuals. For example, John Lynch, director of the Department of Planning and Environment at Leeds City Council in the early 2000s, attended the first planning meeting where our case was presented and felt sufficiently incensed to support us the rest of the way with vital planning expertise and in funding legal representation when things got that far.

We weren't a particularly special community; neighbourhoods up and down the country have their own valuable combinations of skills that come to the fore in a time of crisis. But for every community with the ability to fight and such strong combinations of skills and networks, there are dozens more communities and individual households who just don't have the time or social resources to draw on in their moment of eviction. Most evictions are isolated, fought household by household.

That said, the Save our Homes LS26 campaign wasn't all plain sailing; the five-plus years of intense activism took a great toll on individuals and households. From the day the leaflet dropped, residents shared feelings of constant unease and stress. Anxiety hit children, older residents, and those with dependents the hardest. Parents shared across garden fences and in community meetings that their children were struggling to sleep, feeling powerless. It wasn't just about seeing their worried mum or dad that made them upset – it was the potential of homelessness, of changing schools, losing friends, and further disruption during an already difficult period.

Simply the *threat* of disruption and unplanned moves are detrimental to a child's education and well-being, especially if there's nowhere to go but temporary accommodation. Anxiety affects concentration levels in schools, interpersonal relations with family and friends, mood, eating habits, and confidence. When finally evicted, these challenges compound. A recent Shelter report documented that almost half of homeless children have had to change schools since moving into temporary accommodation, making it much harder for them to keep up educationally and socially with their peers. One in five of these children travels more than an hour to get to school. On top of that, their temporary homes are often small and cramped, with 35 per cent of children reported to be sharing a bed with their parent. This leaves little space for homework or play.[13] Children who avoid homelessness but have to move frequently or unexpectedly between rentals also perform worse in school assessments than their peers. Parents self-report worse mental health the more frequently they have to move, too.[14]

'The years of fighting have really taken a toll on our family's mental health and stress levels,' Cindy told me in the midst of the campaign. 'Our youngest son has suffered with anxiety in the past when at high school, and there's the fear that all this upheaval will be detrimental to his mental health. All this after eighteen months of pandemic hell, too.'[15] Another resident, Robert, has lived on the estate his whole life and spent much of the campaign caring for his elderly ex-miner parents, who have since passed away. He shared that he has previously experienced poor mental health, and the eviction threat kept pushing him to the edge all over again; he was more angry, more upset, and drinking more, because he didn't know how else to cope with this relentless anxiety.

Mum's back condition was worsened by sleepless nights, both complaints rendering her vulnerable to tears at work and in other situations. Sleeplessness plagued Dad on and off for years after the redevelopment leaflet dropped through the door. My brother kept his redundancy secret for a while, not wanting to add his impending loss of income to family stress. Then there was the constant guilt all of us felt about not doing enough for the campaign in case that one tweet, blog, or news interview might have made all the difference. 'You were always thinking, "Right, I need to get in touch with this person, that person,"' Cindy explained. 'We were spending weekends doing stalls,' every spare minute scheduled. The relentlessness of the campaign and the anxiety around eviction ate away at family time, downtime, and any sense of inner peace – for more than five years.

These tactics and responsibilities were learned on the hoof while juggling low-income jobs and family care responsibilities. None of us knew how to do any of this before it started. Balancing advocacy alongside care and domestic responsibilities in addition to holding down a job is a gendered barrier to campaigning, as women undertake most of a household's care responsibilities. Cindy felt that she went from teaching work in the daytime, to social media messaging in the evenings, to – at the campaign's peak – petition collection, marches, and fundraising on weekends. All this was on top of doing most of her household's cooking, cleaning, laundry, and budgeting. And supporting three children, two of whom lived at home.

Like all the campaigners, Mum used her limited annual leave to attend meetings, and spent sick days online. One day in mid-December 2017, 'bunged up' with a cold, she messaged me just after a local BBC *Look North* presenter had left the estate following another round of interviews. 'I have run out of ideas who to tweet now. I think the only people I have not done is the Royal family hahaha.' She recalls that she and Cindy were lucky to have sympathetic bosses who approved last-minute leave requests against protocols.

While campaigning seems, and often is, exciting and solidaristic when groups are taking to the streets in marches and running fundraising stalls at fairs, protracted campaigning to prevent eviction is always punctuated with feelings of anxiety about the future, guilt about not doing enough, and frustration and anger about things or people that appear as obstacles, buffers, or additional challenges – inadvertently or otherwise.

For example, Save Our Homes LS26 existed through local and national election cycles. With fierce local competition between Labour and the Lib Dems for council seats, the campaign increasingly became a flashpoint for local party-political grievances. We saw, at various times via comments on private-community Facebook groups, one side accusing the other (or the absent Tories) of disingenuous activities: 'playing politics', not being there when it counted, and lacking credibility. Passive-aggressive remarks about inaction and hypocrisy abounded. Some residents and supporters were dragged in, and others felt the need to tighten their political football scarves and call out the other side for apparent foul play. There was occasional public mudslinging on Twitter, not to mention random trolling. Mum and Cindy didn't come through their active social media presence unscathed.

Losing wars, winning battles

On 3 October 2019, two years after the community first received that redevelopment leaflet through the door, Leeds City Council were to decide on Pemberstone's planning application. It was a council-plans panel meeting that followed a fairly standard template: an overview of updated proposals; an opportunity for Cindy (as Residents Action Group chairperson) and Pemberstone to speak, and to ask and answer questions; a discussion among the councillors; and a vote on whether the proposal should be approved. Pemberstone was represented by the man who'd previously appeared at the 2017 community consultation for the company Blue Marble. Like most investors, the landlord preferred to linger in the background and employ other companies or subsidiaries to manage their assets.

By this point Pemberstone was over thirty years old and majority-owned or controlled more than 100 companies. Its interests included travel agents, tech design, and manufacturing companies, a water-quality monitoring system – as well as Blue Marble Asset Management, which managed most of its property dealings. Pemberstone's portfolio was a successful one. Corporate Watch reported in 2020 that its founder Andrew Barker is a millionaire, and the company had made nearly £2 million in profit from Cardboard City's rents between 2007 and 2016. The estate's land value had more than trebled to £3.8 million between 2000 and 2018.[16] It was clearly a prime time to sell.

At the Leeds City Council planning meeting that day, Pemberstone's representative offered the usual explanations. First: that the development would have a low social impact because there was no community. Specifically, Pemberstone argued that the majority of the estate's tenants were 'transitory'. This is a common assumption about privately rented communities – that somehow any turnover of residents (typically caused by weak rights and frequent evictions) means that tenants are unable or willing to make the social links that constitute a community.

While landlords may wish this to be true as it can make evictions feel less cruel, it's not borne out by how people live within neighbourhoods. Neighbours, renting or otherwise, undertake the everyday community responsibilities of watching out for each other's homes, babysitting children, feeding pets, taking in parcels, and putting out bins. They chat over garden fences, compare notes about landlords, host street parties, and come together when maintenance work needs to be done. They also rally in times of hardship and ill health. Mum often accompanied Linda on doctor and hospital visits. Then, during the COVID-19 pandemic, neighbours provided essential care, check-ins, and food parcels while the country was on lockdown.

Moreover, some turnover of tenants doesn't mean that all households are equally flighty or lack social roots in the neighbourhood. Pemberstone based its conclusions on statistics that measured how many households had been on the estate for fewer than five years, but these figures were flawed. First, they excluded the dozen households on protected tenancies who had been living there for decades and had made deep friendships with subsequent arrivals. Second, the stats didn't account for the fact that a sizeable proportion of residents had moved into this estate from neighbouring areas. These families were rooted in the LS26 postcode, with kids at local schools and friends and family living nearby.

Next up at the plans panel meeting, Pemberstone offered that the new homes would have Airey-inspired features, attempting to address concerns that the demolition would destroy significant architectural and cultural heritage. These features included a timber-appearance cladding, dark-grey window frames and a vertical window in the front door. Setting aside the fact that timber-like cladding looks nothing like pebble-dashed concrete slabs (the Airey houses' most characteristic feature), this offering failed to appreciate the intangible elements of what makes Airey houses non-designated heritage stock: their prefab manufacture method, post-war context, and working-class community history. It was heritage-washing.

Pemberstone and the like can get away with tokenistic nods to working-class heritage preservation because of the wider crisis facing the heritage sector. Working-class built history, as journalist Jennifer Sizeland recently wrote, has long suffered from 'institutional neglect'.[17] Government, councils, museums, historic, and heritage organisations have never meaningfully championed this type of heritage – preferring to invest culturally and financially in their upper-class counterparts – so it has been left to demolition and disrepair.

Most heritage grants are small and wouldn't cover the preservation of single buildings, let alone entire estates, and they are usually one-off and time-restricted. Moreover, as Sizeland points out, to apply for this money you have to be fluent in grantspeak – the funding jargon of the heritage sector. Alongside work and care responsibilities, people on low incomes have limited time and resources to dedicate to institutionalised heritage preservation, let alone for navigating the sector's complicated funding bureaucracy and jargon. All this means landlords and developers proposing to demolish a heritage asset can get away with perfunctory nods to history without having to do any meaningful preservation. For renters the problem is especially acute, as what heritage organisation would grant funds to preserve an aspect of a building that doesn't belong to the applicant, no matter how significant the structure or long the place has been their home?

Pemberstone gave some perfunctory nods to council-mandated environmental adaptations, too, in efforts to sail the application through. At some point in proceedings the council questioned how many trees would be lost with the demolition, and Pemberstone's rep admitted (not for the first time) that he didn't have figures to hand. But if we could 'wait a moment', he could count the trees in the pictures on Pemberstone's application. Awkward silence ensued while he rustled through pages and counted out loudly to seven.

When asked what exactly Pemberstone will do to ensure the properties meet minimum climate standards, the representative then replied (I paraphrase, but only slightly): What typically happens is that you give us the approval and we sort out these things later down the line. To which a councillor enquired, 'Does that then mean the council have the capacity to test the houses and then tear them down again if they don't comply?' The answer, unsurprisingly, was no. Next, the rep admitted that Pemberstone had failed to do a requested climate-cost estimate for refurbishment versus rebuilding. This, he explained, was because the company apparently couldn't find any consultants to do the job. Had they done any research, they might have discovered that demolition and rebuilding have, typically, a far greater climate impact than refurbishment due to the excessive environmental costs of resource extraction, manufacturing, and disposal.

Disregarding – or selectively prioritising – environmental-impact considerations is not unusual in the housebuilding sector. While large house developers and builders in the UK pay lip service to climate and biodiversity concerns, they often lobby in the other direction. One of the UK's largest house-builders, Persimmon, revealed in a 2019 select committee hearing that it had lobbied the 2015 Conservative government to scrap the zero-carbon homes policy brought in by Labour – which the Tories did, thanks to their newfound majority in Parliament. Another megabuilder, Taylor Wimpey, lobbied the Conservative government in 2020, arguing that targets for better insulation standards were 'too demanding', and targets to cut carbon emissions 'too ambitious'.[18]

The costs of such inaction ultimately filter down to homeowners, and those who pay the highest prices are tenants. Where houses are not insulated to the highest standard, their efficiency levels go down and energy bills go up. In owner-occupied properties, residents have money-saving incentives to insulate the property themselves; in tenanted properties, the opposite is true. Landlords gain little from updating the insulation of a property they do not live in. A BBC investigation in 2023 revealed that six out of ten rental homes in the UK failed to meet energy-efficiency standards because landlords just weren't doing the work.[19] And a common thread throughout the past 150 years is landlords punishing tenants with eviction by hook or by crook should they request even the most basic of repairs, let alone upgrades.

The consequences of a profits-first deregulation attitude have proven to be horrific. Refurbishment cost-cutting contributed to the deaths of seventy-two people in the Grenfell Tower fire in London, 2017. Substandard insulation was one of the factors contributing to the ferocity of the fire, as combustible cladding and insulation were wrapped around the building. Both the cladding and insulation were known to be combustible and to have failed key fire-safety tests by the companies flogging them, but they were chosen by the developers to keep costs down.[20]

As a side note, Pemberstone has launched battles on the cladding front too. Running parallel with our battle over Cardboard City in the late 2010s, the investor was fighting a dispute in Manchester, where its property portfolio included the clad

Cypress Place and Vallea Court towers. When, post-Grenfell, the government ruled that all dangerous ACM (aluminium composite material) cladding had to be removed from tower blocks, Pemberstone took Cypress Place and Vallea Court leaseholders to a tribunal to force them to pay for the removal costs, equating to around £10,000 per flat. The tribunal not only awarded in Pemberstone's favour but required leaseholders to pay Pemberstone's legal fees on top. Residents faced ruin – that is, until a successful leaseholder-led social media campaign and negotiations supported by Manchester City Council prompted Pemberstone to establish a fund to cover the £5 million cost. It was another rare battle won.

Legislation around insulation remains weak as developers continue to lobby the government to keep sector costs low, and recent successive Conservative governments have failed to engage meaningfully with concerns over the sector's environmental and safety standards in favour of leaning into the culture war about net zero. Such inaction is creating damper, colder, less safe properties – and is causing thousands of excess deaths among tenants and leaseholders every year. Let alone untold damage to the planet.

Back in Leeds, after discussing environmental concerns, Leeds City Council turned to the issue of community and housing availability. Here the tide seemed to be turning. Councillors variously remarked: 'Planning should be about people … houses should be designed around people'; 'I think it is right to take the impact on the community as a material planning matter'; 'I'm concerned about the loss of affordable rental housing – we are obviously in deficit. We support affordable housing for public sector workers.'

In planning panels up and down the country, so many decisions around development are made purely on the basis of physical concerns: are the driveways large enough for a car; does the building overshadow any other building; how will the proposals impact local amenities? But, as councillors rightly pointed out in this Leeds meeting, what sits behind development considerations are people – tenants and their communities.

At the end of deliberations, the panel chair took a vote, and it was unanimous: application refused. Councillors from all major parties and independents voted in sync. Two reasons were noted for this decision. First, community protection: the council was keen to prevent 'the potential and disproportionate harm that would result to the existing local community, particularly to those with protected characteristics relating to age and disability, through the loss of their existing homes and the dissipation of the community'. This harm to the community would, in planning terms, outweigh the benefits associated with local and national planning frameworks. Councillors also refused the application on the basis that some of the gardens *still* remained smaller than the required minimum, and therefore Pemberstone 'fail[ed] to provide adequate private external space for families to use'. Needless to say, the community felt euphoric at the verdict; it came as a complete shock. We all bundled out of the council offices and posed for jubilant photos by the local press on the grass just outside, banners held high.

Whether protecting the right of the privately renting community to stay in their homes would have been sufficient on its own for councillors to reject the planning application remains to be seen. English planning law technically does allow for planning applications to be refused on grounds of community preservation, but this rarely happens in practice – especially for private-tenant communities. Planning decisions are primarily influenced by built-environment concerns regarding a proposal's alignment with national and local development plans, internal or external space calculations, amenity access, character and appearance, and so on. Within those areas, arguments can be made about impacts on a community – for example, that developments might be out of scale or character for the current built environment, thereby undermining community cohesion. But a straightforward argument about the need to prevent community dispersal rarely holds water.

It didn't in our case in the end, either.

In late March 2020, less than a week after the country was first locked down to try to curb the spread of COVID-19, Pemberstone notified Leeds City Council that it planned to appeal the decision. The case then went to an independent inspector, as per due process. Cindy, Mum, and the others wearily regathered the troops and restarted campaigning – but the national terrain had totally changed with the onset of the pandemic. At the national level, there was some respite for tenants – the government banned evictions between March 2020 and June 2021. At the same time, holding landlords to account for maintenance became much more difficult as all but urgent repairs were stalled (and even then, were not always acted upon – as Alfie Barker described earlier in the chapter).

For the Save Our Homes LS26 campaign, petitions, rallies, fundraising stalls, and other actions to gather support were much more difficult as the country dipped in and out of disordered lockdowns. Many residents were elderly with health vulnerabilities, or they were families trying to survive through chaotic daily changes to schooling. Mum and Dad worked for the NHS, and my brother for Royal Mail, so they all had to keep going into work. Any remaining energy went into caring for family and neighbours, and lifting community spirits through socially distanced garden gatherings. Campaign momentum was much harder to sustain.

Eventually, across two weeks in October 2020, the appeal came to a head. The community attended two weeks of deliberations online over Microsoft Teams. We had to raise substantial funds to cover basic legal representation, as Pemberstone lawyered up with Sasha White KC, 'one of the top Planning Silks currently practicing in England and Wales' as noted in

Legal 500, Chambers and Partners, and *Planning* magazine.[21] They also came suited and booted with a range of other legal experts and consultants from planning, engineering, heritage, and chartered surveying – which just shows how much money there was to gain from these redevelopment proposals. The inspector then took his time to deliberate.

Finally, in January 2021, the war to save my parents' estate was lost. In the report outlining his decision, the inspector didn't dispute the core thesis of Leeds City Council's position that 'the proposed development would have a damaging impact on the community of existing residents'. He also recognised the heritage value of the estate. But the final decision ultimately rested on the condition of the houses:

> If no scheme [of refurbishment] for the existing houses is put in place, I anticipate that the dwellings would become unsafe to occupy. In this situation, it is reasonable to expect the Appellant [Pemberstone] would give [an eviction] notice to the existing occupiers ... That would dissipate the community on the appeal site.[22]

In short: the planned obsolescence and managed decline of the houses would give Pemberstone the right to evict eventually anyway. And evict, they did. By April 2022, almost all shorthold tenancy households had left Cardboard City and gone elsewhere, to whatever accommodation they could find.

Despite the community's dispersal, Cindy has remained active in representing former residents at Leeds City Council level. Mum continued tweeting. Towards the latter stages of the campaign, there were whispers that Pemberstone might sell the land to a housing association with planning approval. Public pressure and sustained publicity pushed this option all the way, giving us perhaps our biggest victory yet.

In September 2022, Leeds Federated Housing – a local housing association with 4,300 properties in Leeds, Wakefield, and North Yorkshire – confirmed it had bought the estate from Pemberstone and would redevelop it as a mixed rental and ownership estate. With a £2.8 million boost from Leeds City Council money, Leeds Fed committed to upping the affordable-rent portion of the houses from fourteen to thirty. Another thirty will be sold under shared ownership. The remaining ten are earmarked for the surviving miner households living on the estate under regulated tenancies. In all, that's forty rental homes.

This new scheme is partly funded through Homes England's Strategic Partnership with Accent Housing as part of the government's national Affordable Homes Programme (AHP) 2021–26. Initially, the AHP was set to deliver 180,000 new homes, 50 per cent of which were slated for 'discounted rent'. While it might seem lucky that Cardboard City's new houses will count towards the scheme, the reality is that the government is desperate to make up numbers. A review of the AHP in September 2023 revealed a status way below target, delivering fewer than 35,000 completions, mainly shared ownership and affordable rent – only 4 per cent were social rent.[23]

Moreover, while the ex-miners are guaranteed a house on the new estate due to their legacy tenancy agreement, it was less certain how ex-shorthold renters might return ahead of the tens of thousands also jostling for council or housing association homes in Leeds. At the time of writing, no roadmap around the bidding system has been laid out, though Leeds Fed say they are 'working closely with the council to enable former residents who did not have assured or regulated tenancies to be given, where possible, an opportunity to move into the newly built affordable rented homes'.[24]

If these plans come to pass, it means residents will be able to leave the private-rental sector and move back into their old estate, but in shiny new housing association homes. A limited win. Yet, with only forty earmarked for affordable rent, not all of Cardboard City's seventy households will be able to secure a place.

Even then, 'affordable' is a thorny concept. As a word, it's synonymous with inexpensive: a cost that is well within a person's ability to pay. Yet in the social housing sector, 'affordable rent' has a very specific meaning: a rent chargeable at 80 per cent of market value. Policy discussions around this calculation stretch at least back to the late 1980s, when David Edmonds, then head of the non-departmental Housing Corporation, hit headlines stating that affordable rent equated to one-third of disposable income. More recently, the term has been tacked to market rates.

In 2011, the Conservative–Lib Dem coalition government introduced the Affordable Rent tenure. Social rents were significantly below market rates, and the Treasury wanted to reduce house-provider reliance on government grants for developments. Prior to 2011, housing associations received 50–75 per cent of the cost of building a home as a grant. For Affordable Rent properties after 2011, only 25–30 per cent of the development cost could be covered and housing associations were told to pay for the rest themselves – so they have pushed the cost onto tenants through higher rent charges. The stated intention behind the policy was to enable local authorities to raise the cash to build more Affordable Rent housing than the previous social-rent model would allow, but this framing was effectively smoke and mirrors. More Affordable Rent housing (capital A, capital R) doesn't mean more genuinely affordable housing (synonymous with reasonable, or within a person's means). In fact, the policy has resulted in an upward trend in housing costs for everyone.

This is because, as the building of Affordable Rent properties has increased, social-housing construction has fallen off a cliff. Nearly 40,000 social-rent homes were completed in 2010, but they numbered only 6,000 ten years later. In contrast, 24,000 Affordable Rent homes were built. This shift in government-funded housing tenure has contributed to driving up the cost of the private rental market as a whole, because the competition for private-rent rates at the lower-income end of the market is no longer social housing, charging 50 per cent of market value (paltry though that supply was). Competition is now Affordable Rent, set at 80 per cent of the private-market value, feeding into a general market-rate rent inflation.

Those at the sharpest end of poverty in England simply cannot afford 80 per cent of market-rate costs, yet they are also less and less likely to get a social-rent home with the ever-dwindling supply. One housing association told *Inside Housing* in 2021 that it has a higher volume of applicants who fail the affordability assessments for Affordable Rent than it had under social tenure.[25] Those poorer tenants have to go somewhere – likely to the private-rent sector and into overcrowded, less safe properties on precarious (sometimes exploitative) rent deals to try and keep costs down. Another housing association told the magazine that its Affordable Rent tenants struggle more in everyday money management due to the high level of rent they must pay – in other words, they are cutting back on other essentials like food and heating to keep up with rents.

The virtual removal of a cheaper rental option through the lack of social-housing building can only inflate overall rent costs as people have no choice but to fall back on the private-rental sector. They will pay more per property through overcrowding, or they will pay more per person through cutting back on essentials. Such private-rent inflation leads in turn to a gradual creeping up of so-called Affordable Rent rates, tacked to market rates – a virtuous circle for housebuilders and property investors, a vicious one for renters.

Look at the future trajectory of Wordsworth Drive as a concrete example. Before the 2022 mass eviction, Linda was living in a two-bed Airey house paying £485 per month to Pemberstone. This was a fairly low private-market rent based on the micro-economy of the isolated and poorly maintained Cardboard City. Rents went up for each household every year roughly with inflation, and certainly weren't discounted to account for the income levels of residents. It just so happened that many residents had lived there long term, so incremental increases were more common than the sharp rate hikes that come with higher tenant turnover.

When Mum, Dad, and my brother were finally evicted in April 2022, they simply could not afford a market-rate three-bed house elsewhere, so they moved into a two-bed mid-terrace in Rothwell on a main road and without a garden. Rent for that terraced property started off at £700 per month and rose to £750 in year two. Other two-beds in Rothwell currently being advertised start at £825. Based on those figures, let's put the LS26 market rate at roughly £775 at the time of writing (summer 2024). That means, should my family move back to the new Leeds Federated 'affordable housing' homes in the upgraded Cardboard City, they will likely be paying around £620 per month for a two-bed home (80 per cent of £775). This is £135 per month more than a similar-sized property on the same streets just a few years ago. It's also around £200 per month more expensive than two-bed council properties in neighbouring areas (though the cost of council properties is on the rise, too). Far from a 20 per cent affordability reduction for the new housing association houses, my family will be shouldered with a 25 per cent price hike compared with 2022, for one fewer bedroom than their previous three-bed Cardboard City home.

These high costs are mirrored up and down the country, which is why rent payments take up such a huge proportion of household income, and why so many tenants are falling into arrears. In 2023, 35 per cent of private landlords reported tenants in rent arrears, a number growing year on year. Two months of arrears is reason enough for a landlord to issue a Section 8 eviction notice, which gives a tenant just fourteen days to leave their home if a possession order is granted. The current Renters Rights Bill retains Section 8 (though increases the arrears threshold to three months). Over 5 per cent of housing association tenants are also in arrears.[26] While housing association and council tenants have stronger tenancy protections, non-payment of rent or service charges are also some of the most common legal reasons these social landlords can evict tenants. English housing courts are stuffed full of cases of landlords trying to get their non-paying tenants out, with just as many other tenants fighting to get their landlord to do some basic maintenance to make their homes liveable.

For the ten surviving ex-miner households of Cardboard City, Leeds Federated Housing's redevelopment promises must feel like déjà vu: shiny new houses with a promise of security, affordable rents, and a social landlord that isn't the council, but isn't a private landlord either. It'll likely be their last move – *hopefully* their last move – as these pensioner miners are in their seventies and eighties, and packing up a home at this age isn't a task to take lightly. When they eventually pass on, their regulated tenancies will end – a historic artefact of a sliver of time when renters had multigenerational housing security.

For the remaining private-renter households booted out of Cardboard City, the new Affordable Rent houses feel like crumbs flicked off a very high table. Pemberstone made millions of pounds out of renting poor-quality houses, then sold them on for millions more, evicting everyone in the process. A housing association pays market rates for the estate's land, and can afford it because the government and local authorities slosh money around for much-vaunted affordable-rent schemes, yet (like private developers) fail to meet targets and commitments by dramatic margins. And affordable doesn't mean affordable anyway, given the 80 per cent market price tag.

Mum calls the Leeds Fed takeover of Cardboard City 'a bitter-sweet deal': the best outcome that they could have hoped for given the wider private-rental terrain. But, she says, the 'housing association rents will still be too high for a lot of working people. I haven't found out the exact cost yet, despite asking several times.' No news either on when the houses might be completed or what the process is for applying for them. This makes it hard to budget, and hard to plan. Cardboard City's now dissipated residents are stuck in a kind of limbo – moveable masses waiting to accept whatever's on offer because that's all that's left.

9

Taking up space

In recent years, just a handful of tenant campaigns have caused enough of a stir to prevent the worst excesses of mass eviction. One of them came from the New Era estate in Hoxton, East London – a mixed-tenancy community. This ninety-six-flat block was built by Middlesex property developer Arthur Barsht in the 1930s – a decade when slum clearances in the inner cities had picked up apace. The design of the four-storey New Era building with integrated shops on part of the ground floor was architecturally typical of the period – aesthetically nondescript, rectangular in layout, with an inner block as well as the four outer sides, and no real green space. The building was divided into twelve houses with ground-level access through mostly street-facing doors.

While high rise was the flavour of the 1930s, the rise couldn't be *too* high: five storeys were judged as the maximum number of floors that a housewife should lug shopping upstairs, or their husbands drag coal.[1] Also typical of the interwar period, these weren't flats for owner occupiers; they were to rent to private tenants – working Londoners who could afford slightly better than slums. And so it stayed for decades; as in Cardboard City, New Era rents stayed much lower than the ever-escalating London rental market. But it wouldn't last.

In 2014, American private equity firm Westbrook made an offer to buy New Era from Robert Lever, grandson of Barsht. Covering the purchase with a cluster of articles, the *Guardian* revealed Westbrook's reputation preceded it. In the US, part of its investment model was to purchase tenanted blocks populated by low-income renters who couldn't afford market-rate rents in cities such as New York. It then either hiked rents or scrimped on maintenance to try to make money for its investors. Tenants were left festering in 'sub-human', pest-ridden conditions.[2] After some time Westbrook would sell on the blocks for a huge profit.

It's a well-trodden model, writes Brett Christophers in his recent book *Our Lives in their Portfolios*.[3] Asset-management companies specialising in housing acquire cheap assets (people's homes), then cut operating costs to the bone with skeleton management and rolling back repairs. They maximise income through raising rents. Eviction is, of course, a key weapon in their armoury – those who can't pay are out on their ear to make way for those who can. Finally, these corporations sell their housing assets on for huge profits – in fact, selling is the end game: it's where the real profits are.

Westbrook brought its modus operandi to the UK. In 2005, it spent £190 million buying the lease of a 1,234-flat block in Pimlico, London – Dolphin Square, favoured accommodation of MPs, spies, and other notable people. The block had begun life as a mixed community with affordable-rent levels that meant MPs and other establishment figures rubbed shoulders with junior clerks, drivers, and shift workers. Rates remained low in comparison to the local private market and the flats were well maintained and serviced by porters.

Until Westbrook bought the lease, anyway – that very year, the private porter service was axed. Then the firm paid off some of the subsidised tenants for £24 million and forcibly bought the freehold for another £176 million, all so it could undertake an expansionist and rate-rising redevelopment that the tenants didn't want (plans for which were eventually rejected by Westminster City Council).[4] Westbrook didn't shy away from aggressive asset-management methods. In 2014, a Dolphin Square tenant took Westbrook to court claiming it had tried to evict her using harassment. While Westbrook was cleared of any criminal activity, the judge still found the company's behaviour 'unreasonable and oppressive'.[5] This was the same year it swooped in to buy New Era in Hoxton.

After Westbrook's New Era bid was successful, London property firm the Benyon Estate bought a 10 per cent share and took over management of the estate. The Benyon Estate is owned by the family of Richard Benyon, who was at that point MP for Newbury, Britain's wealthiest politician, and one of the largest landowners in the country. He had previously held a ministerial position in David Cameron's government. While some of the press hinted at political enabling in Westbrook's purchase and management, Richard Benyon stated he did not have a direct role in the Benyon Estate, which was run by his brother Edward Benyon (though the Newbury MP did have a controlling part in Englefield Estates – the Benyon Estate's parent company).

In a meeting with tenants, New Era's new manager Edward told the community that the firm intended to build the block upwards, adding new flats to the top floor, and would raise rents initially by 10 per cent and then to market levels – which for some households would have been a 300 per cent increase. Such a hike would have destroyed a community made up of generations of extended-family households.

Up to that point, vacant flats in New Era had rarely been advertised on the wider private market; they were let via word of mouth. Many children who grew up on the estate would take up a vacant flat when they became adults, keeping families together. It wasn't social housing, but rents were kept low at around 50 per cent of market rates or less. Some still paid rent in cash to the caretaker.[6] Residents were responsible for their own repairs and refurbishments, and many took out loans for new kitchens and bathrooms, which they were just about able to afford because their rents were so reasonable. Even a 10 per cent rent hike (the initial increase the households were set to face) would have rendered the estate unaffordable for so many – it was essentially eviction by the back door.

When residents received the news of Westbrook's rent rises, they mobilised to form the New Era Tenants Association. This predominantly women-led group – spearheaded by residents Lindsey Garrett (Tenants Association chair), Lynsay Spiteri, and Danielle Molinari – contacted news organisations, gathered petition signatures, and sought to draw national attention to the unaffordable rent rise and inevitable evictions that non-payment would entail. Molinari, a single mother of a two-year-old boy, told the *Socialist Worker* at the time that any eviction would have a devastating ripple effect on her small family.[7] Her mum lived in the block and, since her dad died, Molinari cared for her with the help of neighbours. Eviction would mean her mum moving into a sheltered home elsewhere, ending the possibility of family care and isolating her mum from wider neighbour support networks.

Eviction would also have meant statutory homelessness and Molinari moving into temporary accommodation with her son, altering his life chances significantly. Homeless children in temporary accommodation find it harder to keep up with schoolwork, harder to make and keep friends, and are more likely to lose sleep and suffer negative mental health consequences than their non-homeless peers.[8] Molinari knew this was what she and her son Frankie were facing. Other tenants shared similar fears and their 'New Era 4 All, Social Housing Not Social Cleansing' campaign quickly gathered huge media attention.

Comedian Russell Brand, now charged by police of rape and sexual assault, became one of their more famous supporters after meeting the group during a petition signature collection. He joined protests and publicly clashed with a news reporter at a Downing Street demonstration. The filmed confrontation went viral, bringing the nation's attention to Westbrook's treatment of the community. Other supporters included then London Mayor Boris Johnson as well as a swath of media outlets from across the political spectrum. By the end of 2014, just a few months after purchasing the estate and threatening rent hikes, public pressure led the Benyon Estate to sell its shares and then Westbrook to sell the estate on to affordable-housing provider Dolphin Living.

Dolphin Living is the brand name of the Dolphin Square Charitable Foundation, which was set up in 2005 by the Dolphin Square Trust after it and Westminster Council sold leasehold interests in Dolphin Square (the luxury Pimlico block of flats) to Westbrook. Westbrook then ran the Pimlico block under the company named Dolphin Square Limited.[9] Proceeds of the 2005 Pimlico lease sale went towards creating the new charitable foundation.

While there's no suggestion of dodgy dealings in Westbrook's sale of the New Era estate to Dolphin Living, and the companies are separate, the revolving door of firms underlines the symbiotic relationship between developers, investors, and landlords of all types when there's lucrative property or land value and below-market rents. On the rare occasions that landlords are forced to sell their properties for social reasons – as during slum clearances across the nineteenth and twentieth centuries or because of public pressure in the twenty-first – owners still make their money. Rinse and repeat.

What did Westbrook leave in its wake? Back in Pimlico's luxury block, Dolphin Square, low rents are now mostly market-rate rents but, as Westbrook was not able to redevelop the building as planned, it sold the block to AXA Investment Managers for a reported £850 million in 2020. AXA are now accused by tenants and their MP of forcing through 40 per cent rent hikes under cover of a new refurbishment plan.[10]

In Hoxton's New Era block, Dolphin Living promised tenants they could remain in their homes under a new model of 'personalised rents' that would be tailored to a household's income. This personalised-rent model has since been rolled out to other accommodation in limited ways, though Dolphin Living admitted it was facing 'challenges'. The 1930s New Era building that many in the community were so keen to save will now be demolished, as Dolphin Living has said it can no longer afford to resolve the building's maintenance issues on the personalised-rent levels that tenants are paying.[11] So the new plan is to demolish and rebuild, rehousing the existing ninety-six households. The planned development will add over a hundred additional homes to the block, more than doubling its residential capacity. But the new homes will apparently be a mix of social, affordable, and living-rent tenures – essentially higher-rate rented flats.

Such redevelopment will involve evicting existing New Era tenants while refurbishment is ongoing, which could take years, and then moving them back into the block, mixing up erstwhile neighbours. While most tenants are apparently happy enough at this compromise, the effects of dispersal, temporary rehousing, and a reshuffling of neighbours won't go unfelt. Critics of the personalised-rent model also suggest that it ultimately causes more polarisation in rents and tenants don't have the tenancy protection that social renters enjoy.[12]

The rates are well above social-rent levels, as well. Where previously New Era tenants were broadly paying 50 per cent below market rates, Dolphin Living's own reporting in 2023 stated that 73 per cent of their 819 homes were available for 'intermediate rent at an average discount of 34% to the local market rent'.[13] As in Cardboard City, New Era tenants will be evicted, have their current homes demolished, and will end up paying more. The new homes being added to the rebuild will also serve to push up market rates and Affordable Rent levels in the area.

Looking at the positives for the community, New Era protestors and tenants across the estate have at least been able to remain housed in their local area, on rents they can afford, and they've been consulted on all Dolphin Living's development proposals – for now. These are small victories, hard won, and not to be taken for granted.

Another high-profile group, the Focus E15 Mothers, campaigned against eviction from their hostel in Stratford, London in 2013, which was closing its mother-and-baby support programmes due to swingeing funding cuts imposed by the Tories' austerity agenda. The programme housed these otherwise-homeless single (often teenage) mum-headed families in one-bedroom apartments for below market rents while they worked to get themselves on their feet. The rooms were grotty, but they were better than the streets, and they enabled the women to live near friends and family.

After the cuts, the council advised newly evicted mothers that they'd have to accept subsidised privately rented accommodation in far-flung areas of the country if they wanted housing support – severing the women and their children from family safety nets, schools, and local support networks. In other words, the plan would cut them off from their communities.[14] Refusal of relocation would, the council warned, result in these women being classed as making themselves intentionally homeless and therefore ineligible for further assistance.

Without any political or campaign experience, the group of twenty-nine single mothers garnered a petition and set up a stall alongside that of the Revolutionary Communist Group, who happened to be there the day the women marched with their petition, but became long-term allies in the fight. The Focus E15 stall became a weekly fixture, and the group loudly campaigned under the banner 'Social Homes, Not Social Cleansing'. Within six months, all twenty-nine women were rehoused in the borough – though this time in private rentals, which were expensive, insecure, and run-down. In an interview with the *Guardian* in 2024, one Focus E15 mum recalled finding a mouse skeleton in her new house; another found a sewage leak.

Little seems to have changed since for other women in similar situations. The hostel continues to operate as temporary accommodation and new mothers finding themselves suddenly homeless are still being pushed to accept private-rent housing miles away, or they have to live in cramped dismal conditions with their children in the hostel – sometimes for years.[15] So yes, another battle has been won; but a wider war for secure housing has been lost to the rental market.

Eviction as care work, eviction as violence

It's no coincidence that the New Era, Focus E15, and Save Our Homes LS26 anti-eviction campaigns were mainly spearheaded by women; housing insecurity disproportionately impacts women. They shoulder most of the domestic labour, emotional labour, and care work in the home – cooking, cleaning, laundry, household management, childcare, and the associated tasks of nursery and school runs, doctor visits, clubs and social groups, and communication with and among these venues.

There's economic inequality within households, too, which sharpens with housing insecurity. Women living in couples with a male partner are twice as likely to manage household budgeting (37 per cent versus 22 per cent, according to the Fawcett Society).[16] Women also pay a larger proportion of their individual income as rent because they tend to earn less. In fact, there is nowhere in England that a single woman on average wages can afford to rent privately.[17]

Against this backdrop, eviction can only be seen as additional care work that lands upon women in the household. It requires, in just a two-month timespan with a Section 21 notice: searching for a new home that meets all family requirements; reworking household budgets; endless estate agent form-filling; managing school and job impacts; switching healthcare; and meeting the various social needs of different family members. That generalisation does not even account for additional, contextual challenges that families might face, such as working around specific care or disability needs, or owning pets.

Though data is sparse on how individuals share responsibilities within households, particularly in times of housing crisis, I'd wager that women do most of the sorting and packing that comes with a move, too – their own belongings, plus shared household items, and sometimes the menfolk's personal belongings, too. After all, with women still managing the lion's share of the household chores, it's not a stretch to assume the domestic grunt work of packing falls on them. This is certainly true in my family and friend network.

The violence of housing precarity and eviction also falls disproportionately on women. While most rough sleepers are men, and so are the most visibly homeless (there were nearly 4,000 rough sleepers in 2023, including around 550 women), women make up two-thirds of people living in temporary accommodation (279,390 in 2023) – the statutorily homeless.[18] That makes about 190,000 homeless women, and the figure is rising year on year.

As journalist Vicky Spratt highlighted in her recent book *Tenants*, these statistics intersect with domestic violence.[19] Many statutorily homeless women have fled violent households and are living in temporary accommodation with their children. Leeds City Council has noted that the second-biggest local cause of homelessness is domestic violence (at least 16.5 per cent of all cases).[20] Deep cuts to funding for domestic violence centres and dedicated women-and-children housing programmes have reduced the number of safe places that vulnerable women can turn to when they're made homeless – as the Focus E15 campaign showed.

Women are also more likely to be victims of predatory landlords who abuse and exploit tenants, often through offering accommodation in exchange for sexual favours. Research undertaken by YouGov in 2022 on behalf of Shelter revealed that nearly one in fifty women had been propositioned for 'sex for rent' in England over the previous five years. Refusals can result in harassment and eviction. This phenomenon is increasing as the cost-of-living crisis and an acute lack of housing worsen.[21] Cycles of displacement and eviction through domestic and landlord violence push vulnerable tenants repeatedly back into the exploitative private-rental sector or into inappropriate temporary accommodation. With these stark facts, eviction should be understood not just as a form of structural violence, but as *gendered* violence.

In response to these experiences, women at the margins 'have been pushing back', to quote late housing writer and activist Dawn Foster: 'Grassroots women's groups have begun to fight – not by voting for parties that have shown little interest in them – but by taking up space, and refusing to budge.'[22] Focus E15, New Era, Save Our Homes LS26 – they've all done exactly that. Such tenant activism is a form of direct political action that can be traced back to the 1915 Glasgow rent strikes and further. It's about more than just defending a single home in the private sphere. These protests demand radical social change, recognising that gender and class intersect – and the reality that housing crisis is the norm for poorer communities.[23]

The 1915 rent strikes offered political visibility, highlighting the pressures of poor wages, appalling living conditions, and profiteering landlords.[24] The protests involved direct confrontation with a private power (rather than the state) who, through rent or debt collectors, was violently intruding into everyday life.[25] As Pam Currie writes, these experiences of confrontation and protest then gave the women 'a voice and an impetus for further campaigns, extending beyond the "politics of the kitchen" to wider demands around suffrage and peace'.[26] For example, strike leader Mary Barbour founded the Women's Peace Brigade in 1916, went on to become one of Glasgow's first female Labour Party councillors in 1920, and took on a range of other political positions subsequently. She remained an ardent and prominent activist for working-class communities, healthcare, and women's welfare.

Other women-led housing movements over the last century have seen similar radical political mobilisation rippling outwards. The 1972–73 Kirkby rent strike, for example, saw thousands of tenants in Kirkby, Merseyside, withhold rent and take to the streets in protest at the Conservative government's 1972 Housing Finance Act, which reduced council subsidies and raised rents for local authority houses. These protests were led by women from the Tower Hill estate in Kirkby, which was a new town near Liverpool built over the 1950s to house 50,000 tenants cleared from nearby city slums.

This strike was loosely linked to the 1968–69 Abercromby rent strike led by Ethel Singleton (featured in Chapter 4). In fact, Merseyside saw several major rent protests and strikes develop between 1968 and 1973, each in reaction to localised, abysmal living conditions and often coupled with charges of negligent management and spiralling rents.[27] Ethel Singleton declined to take an overtly political role after the conclusion of the Abercromby strikes, though she and fellow Abercromby tenant activists Lilian Kerruish and Marjorie Gallimore continued fighting – including campaigning against the Housing Finance Act.[28] In Kirkby's Tower Hill, the protests went militant and national.

By the 1970s, the Tower Hill estate was still unfinished – crudely built with pokey, poorly insulated flats and no real outdoor play space for children. Scholar Kerrie McGiveron writes that local authority officials were viewed as slum landlords because of the way they ran things. Several years before the rate hikes tenants had already written to the (Labour) prime minister to complain about paying high rents for shoddy housing.[29]

In response to the 1972 Act, strikes erupted around the country. Kirkby was the only area to undertake a total strike, with mass action also directed against redundancies occurring at the same time. Kirkby's labour market was unusually dominated by women, who made up 55 per cent of the local factory workforce.[30] Housing and labour issues publicly collided in real time.

Rent-strike momentum grew organically from the tenant community, and then was propelled by the revolutionary mixed-sex feminist group Big Flame and other militant organisations. Several Tower Hill women were members of Big Flame and established its base there to help organise protestors alongside the Tower Hill Unfair Rents Action Group. These women-led protestors planned action and discussed principles in the domestic spaces of the block, they followed and obstructed rent collectors from accessing the tower, and debated the rights and limits faced by waged women. Big Flame leaflets kept tenants up to date with news; activists organised a strike system across the block; and they stormed council offices alongside other activist groups. The strikes saw two men jailed, court orders, and financial hardship for fourteen months, and were eventually called off. While it did not achieve a reversal of rent hikes, this feminist group successfully politicised working-class housewives and their living conditions alongside industrial labour concerns. For the participating women, it provided a blueprint for future community activism.[31]

Also in the 1970s, a community of women squatted in empty local authority properties throughout Hackney's Broadway Market and London Fields. These women-only squats were formed in part to ease the acute housing shortage for single women with children, but they were also a refuge for victims of domestic violence, gay women, evicted single-woman families, and other marginalised groups from across the country.[32] Some private landlords wouldn't rent to single women or female-headed households; others kept properties in an appalling state of repair. Many women had been on council house waiting lists for years with no progress. Squatting ended up being the only safety net – a case of women housing and protecting themselves when the state failed them.

Yet the state didn't take ceding authority lightly. Squatters were routinely issued with repossession orders and evictions were violent; police and bailiffs were not afraid of using battering rams to gain entry to properties, and physical force to shove women and children out of the houses and into the back of police vans.[33] Nonetheless, the solidaristic and affordable nature of this women-only housing enabled an extension of politics beyond the domestic sphere: residents provided support and safe spaces for discriminated-against lesbians; some trained in traditionally male skills such as construction and became active in relevant unions; others formed political book groups and debated all manner of social change.[34] Confrontations with a violent and intrusive state tightened resolve that something was fundamentally wrong with housing and gender justice in this country.

While the housing activism of the Focus E15, New Era, and Save Our Homes LS26 campaigns are perhaps too recent for us to chart the wider political ripples resulting (watch this space!), we can already see that skills and experiences the women gained in the fire of eviction are being aimed at other housing crises and political issues.

Focus E15 have, very publicly, taken on other housing causes beyond their hostel and their own lives. For the past decade, they've been campaigning to prevent the demolition of the Carpenters Estate in Newham and raising their voices against the violence of homelessness, insecure tenancies, and unsafe properties more generally. They joined forces with the Carpenters Against Regeneration Plans group, formed in 2011 by residents who have now been fighting for well over a decade to prevent displacement. Carpenters Estate residents are mainly from Black and other ethnic minority backgrounds. These marginalised groups are disproportionately affected by estate demolition and renewal programmes, particularly around London.[35]

Focus E15 members also extended solidarity to the Palestinian people in the wake of the recent genocidal atrocities committed by Israel against Palestinian civilians in Gaza, holding campaign events and supporting national marches. 'The struggle for housing in Newham,' they wrote in November 2023, 'is part of the international struggle for justice for the poor and oppressed all over the world. A struggle against capitalism, against racism and imperialism.'[36]

The New Era protests gave those involved a feeling of political empowerment. The campaign was relatively short – 'efficient', as scholar Lisa McKenzie put it, because celebrity pressure and media coverage expedited a resolution to the stand-off. As a result, the movement 'lacked building class-consciousness and solidarity that often comes out of grassroots campaigning'.[37] Nonetheless, it still gave the participating women a sense of power, with one woman remarking to McKenzie in an interview, 'I want to do this for the rest of my life'. For a time, chair of the New Era Resident's Association Lindsey Garrett planned to run as a London mayoral candidate for the Something New political party in the 2016 election, but withdrew for personal reasons. Housing was the key plank of her campaign, as she explained in the *Guardian* in May 2015:

> We are lucky. Because of the publicity our campaign raised ... we were able to embarrass our landlord into selling up to a trust with a different attitude. But so many Londoners don't have that luck. People are facing rent hikes or keeping quiet about maintenance problems in case it leads to a rent increase. And every time a renter moves, they are forced into more cramped and degrading conditions.[38]

She could have been speaking for renters across the UK with that description.

The New Era protests also contributed to expanding the experiment in personalised rents, where rates are based on income rather than what the market can bear. While I mentioned earlier that the experimental funding model hasn't prevented the demolition of this historic estate and is not without flaws, it is still a departure from the dominant market-based model. Radical experiments are what's needed if we're to find new ways of making rent work for tenants.

The Save Our Homes LS26 campaigners have been active on the wider advocacy circuit too, engaging in discussions beyond their own housing estate while they continue to wait for the campaign to be resolved. Cindy and Hazell attended the Justice for Grenfell protest in Leeds a year after the tragedy, with Cindy addressing the crowd to talk about housing injustice. They and others in the campaign have represented Save Our Homes LS26 at online meetings hosted by ACORN and Axe the Housing Act. Discussions included job losses, evictions, and homelessness across the country. Cindy, Hazell, John, and Mark also travelled to London to address the Parliamentary Campaign for Council Housing meeting, invited by Hands Off Our Homes and Defend Council Housing. Other residents

Residents outside Cindy and John Readman's house on Wordsworth Drive in 2018. Credit: Save Our Homes LS26.

Residents on a march through Leeds in 2018. From left to right: Susan Gould, John Readman, John Davis from Hands Off Our Homes, and Cindy Readman. Credit: Save Our Homes LS26.

Sisters Uncut Leeds holding a protest in solidarity with Save Our Homes LS26 in Leeds city centre. Credit: Save Our Homes LS26.

have joined countless protests about housing, inequality, and injustices outside Leeds Town Hall over the years – standing shoulder to shoulder with ACORN, Sisters Uncut Leeds, Hands Off Our Homes, Unite, and other unions. 'It was always about the community,' says John of those times. 'We bounced off each other. You could talk to people. There were horrible times when everyone was feeling low, you did just have to try and pick each other up.'

Silencing resistance

As Lisa McKenzie writes, these types of grassroots protests are far from rare. Every day, tenants up and down the country are finding ways to fight David-and-Goliath battles against their (or others') eviction. Yet these stories of protests and resistance rarely make headlines in a way that might sow the seeds of a transformative movement – a silence that helps to maintain the status quo.

When the media covers social protests of any kind, the frame tends to be negative – portraying protestors as deviant, if not criminal. Recent coverage of Just Stop Oil protests, for example, have overwhelmingly focused on disruptions to road traffic, damage to heritage, and hostile responses from the public, rather than the climate crisis that is behind the movement (or the members of the public who join their ranks). More typically, social protests just aren't covered.

A range of factors feed into this negative or absent coverage – including the cause itself. News organisations often struggle to portray protests challenging the political and societal status quo, and anti-eviction or rental-reform housing protests seek to do exactly that.[39] A reworking of the private and social-rent sector would upend the financialised housing market, upon which so much of our national economy is reliant. It is not necessarily an editorial conspiracy to silence dissenting voices (depending on the outlet!) – rather, the Overton window has shifted. Housing financialisation has been completely normalised. As a result, many mainstream and even left-leaning news organisations seem to lack either the vocabulary or the bravery to take a different angle in their coverage about anti-capital social movements and housing protests.

The identity of protestors also shapes the volume and character of coverage. Women with housing insecurity, especially working-class women, are only ever meant to be passive victims – individuals having something horrible done to them, rather than citizens pushing back against marginalisation and poor treatment. As carers and household managers in the out-of-sight domestic space, what could they possibly have to say about wider systemic inequality that those in power want to hear? McKenzie describes how working-class women protestors are delegitimised in the public space because they are presented as not knowing or doing the right things, in contrast to their middle-class counterparts who are more typically presented as 'concerned' about whatever issues they are raising.[40]

Linked to this, journalist and writer Owen Jones describes a broader media and political erasure of conventional class fault lines as a distraction from widening inequalities.[41] Where once there was a popular recognition of unjust class structures that diverse communities could rally to fight, Jones explains, there are now narratives about individual merit and hard work. Those who are successful (with steady, well-paid jobs) are celebrated for their intelligence and diligence; those who struggle (on a low income or receiving benefits, for example) are supposedly intellectually lacking and workshy at best – or criminal at worst. Systemic inequalities have been reduced to individual character flaws.

This framing is most famously demonstrated by the 2014 Channel 4 documentary *Benefits Street*, which followed benefit-claimant subjects through their everyday lives in Birmingham. The show was floated to its participants as being a programme about community. But it soon became a voyeuristic and judgemental gawp at the lives of those at the sharp end of Britain's economic inequality, showing residents committing crimes and enjoying life on welfare. It encapsulated and fuelled a growing sentiment that there is a moral underclass who want something for nothing, including housing.

While most mainstream media outlets may have moved beyond the nakedly exploitational format of *Benefits Street*, the media, politicians, and wider discourse have not diverted far from narratives of hard work and deservingness, especially around housing. The MailOnline, for example, recently ran a spectacle story about a woman living in a small council house with her children and husband 'despite' apparently earning a decent income from making TikTok videos. The piece is full of misogynistic objectification, belittling, and parent-shaming, all packaged as concern about entitlements to social housing.

These ideas and frames aren't new: the Victorians perfected the idea of the deserving and undeserving poor, the hardworking and the scroungers. But add housing and gender dynamics to the class mix, and you get a recipe for weak or mean-spirited coverage of evictions, let alone of working-class, women-led protests against them. Working-class women are more likely to be on lower incomes, precariously housed, and responsible for children, and therefore in receipt of some kind of benefit such as universal credit (even while in work).

Media outlets have been fed and watered on the moral-underclass narrative that has long demonised people for receiving benefits or living in low-income housing, so they often do not know how to tell counternarratives without falling back on reductive tropes. So if a working-class family's housing plight is to be covered at all, focus is often on the sob story rather than the fight – coverage homes in on residents' specific vulnerabilities or tragic backstories, or on shocking anecdotes of dilapidation and vignettes of – particularly children's – lives being upended. These may all be essential parts of a person's lived experience of eviction, of course, but so are moments of resistance – organised protests, confrontations with landlords or local authorities, and community solidarity. Despite the ubiquity of sob stories about housing poverty in Britain today, the media struggles to follow the narrative arc through to protest, resistance, and agency.

As well as the nature of the cause and the identity of the protestors, the level of media coverage is also affected by other circumstances: the type of protest and the tactics used, and the politics of the news organisation and its proximity to the demonstration. New Era was backed by Russell Brand and his spectacle tactics, which helped fuel coverage and a quick resolution.

Moreover, it's no coincidence that London-based New Era and Focus E15 are two of the most covered and most academically studied tenant-protest stories in recent times. The national news media establishment is overwhelmingly based in London. The capital also sustains an unusually large number of active local newspapers. Local news publications have long been the first to break housing scandals and cover stories of protest, but they've been on the decline for decades; since 2005, nearly 300 local newspaper titles have closed, with a small rise in local digital news outlets not making up for the overall loss.[42]

Up in Yorkshire, Save Our Homes LS26 had the benefit of scale (seventy households as opposed to one or two), the local iconography of the prefab Airey houses, and the living heritage of a former coal-mining community. It also helped that Cardboard City was an eminently filmable goldfish-bowl estate. Regional and local news outlets, including the *Yorkshire Evening Post*, *Yorkshire Post*, *LeedsLive*, and BBC Radio Leeds, covered the campaign extensively, building a foundational narrative that could be picked up nationally. Yet decent coverage of these three protests continues to be an exception. This shouldn't be the case because they have a significance far beyond their specific circumstances.

First, in terms of tactics. Tenant activism researchers John Grayson and Kim Singleton point out key commonalities in tenant struggles across the twentieth century: common strategies (such as formalisation through associations); links to outside parties – often grassroots Labour, but not exclusively; cultivation of the media; the mobilisation of women; and direct action.[43] The pressure tenant campaigners put on established housing interests extended beyond the authorities' abilities to endure. Focus E15, New Era, and Save Our Home LS26 show these tactics still work effectively today.

Second, in exposing the antagonists. Binding the New Era and Save Our Homes LS26 campaigns together is the light these women-led protests have shone on the murky world of financialised housing. Westbrook is a global real-estate investment and management company, while Pemberstone is a UK-based, director-owned investment company. Though they operate at different scales, both increase the value of their portfolios and profits by, among other things, the acquisition and sale of assets, including homes. Tenanted properties are lucrative as they have large growth prospects in addition to the accumulating value of land. Rent yields, as Nick Bano points out, drive property value.[44] It's a safe bet for investors. Local authorities have little power or resources to build their own developments, so to meet development targets (or sometimes to line pockets) they enable private investors and developers to swoop in, often incentivising purchases with public-money subsidies or flexible planning.

One of the latest developments in financialised rented housing is the build-to-rent (BTR) sector: properties, typically flat blocks, built for the sole purpose of renting. While the Resolution Foundation points out that build-to-rents typically offer more secure tenures, more transparent rent increases, more accessible management through on-site managers, and purpose-built facilities such as gyms – they come with hefty rent costs.[45] In 2022, the average rent for a two-bedroom BTR flat in Leeds was £1,250 per month – around half the average post-tax income for the inner-city area.[46] Poorer renters are priced out and, as these build-to-rent developments expand through inner cities, they contribute to gentrification, pushing poorer renters further into the outskirts.

Whether at the deprived end of the market or through luxury build-to-rents, investors are making huge profits from rent hikes, evictions, and redevelopments that are breaking up neighbourhood communities across Britain. Yet, as Brett Christophers points out, the asset-manager class achieve this almost invisibly in the housing sector: buying and selling occurs in private, often through subsidiaries or spin-off management companies, and without obligations to disclose property transfers or sold prices.[47] It can make the detail and scale of tenant rip-offs and evictions almost impossible to report. The untraceable trail of speculators that bought and sold Cardboard City across the late 1980s and early 1990s (before Pemberstone swooped in with Oulton Properties Ltd in 1997) are a case in point. To the same end, the multiplication of small-scale landlords means there's no single or obvious bogeyman for news organisations to expose, making tenant rip-offs and evictions from these homes difficult to build media interest around.

The political power of the New Era and Save Our Homes LS26 campaigns was ultimately the ability of these women and their families to sustain public attention on their communities and their landlords, and to put a spotlight on the intersection of global capital, local development, and the domestic space. Perhaps Pemberstone and Westbrook bailed quickly from their developments, not just because they could turn a profit regardless, but also because these protesting women threatened to shine an uncomfortable spotlight on an inequitable and unjust operating model that hits low-income communities the hardest.

Uncertain future

For Save Our Homes LS26, the campaign isn't quite over. There have been many mini-battles to fight since January 2021, when residents found out they'd definitely lose their homes – each fought household by household, which served to weaken their collective bargaining power.

Some of the older residents on shorthold tenancies were able to secure relatively local sheltered council accommodation. For tenants there to the last, Leeds City Council stumped up a deposit and one month's rent for new private lets – poor consolation for the fact that they had no alternative council properties in which to house the evicted tenants. Not all residents got this. Those who fled before the final ruling or did not fill in the application form missed out.

Pemberstone also offered the dwindling number of remaining residents a 'goodwill' payment of a couple of thousand pounds to help with house-move costs – subject to the tenants being in the green on rent, leaving the properties in a fit state, and complying with the eviction notice. The latter element was out of resident control and depended entirely on availability of private-let properties. Demanding that properties be left in a 'fit state' was ironic, bordering on hypocritical, given the history of poor maintenance and defects in the buildings. At least one tenant apparently managed to wrangle additional financial compensation on the basis that she'd installed her own double glazing. While other residents had also funded their own refits, they didn't follow suit in fighting, because it was just one too many fires.

The surviving ex-miners on pre-1989 regulated tenancy agreements, including Mavis and Barry, are promised equivalent houses on the new estate and can remain in their homes until these new properties are built – a better deal than most got, but not without its hardships. It will still mean an ejection from their home of decades, packing, moving, and dislocation – much harder to go through in your seventies and with bouts of ill health. They've lost dozens of close neighbour-friends in the shorthold houses, who've all had to disperse across nearby towns and further afield. Moreover, while construction gets under way, Pemberstone have boarded up neighbouring vacant properties.

The empty houses are regularly broken into and anything of value removed, including metal fittings. At one point, as many as six scrap-metal vans a day were spotted trawling the estate for detritus. Some drivers became unpleasant when challenged by residents about what they were up to. 'The scrap men have eyes everywhere,' Mavis said. 'You daren't leave anything out.'

Ordinary people, too, have made their way to the estate, hoping to find something that evicted Wordsworth and Sugar Hill residents have been forced to leave behind. Flowers have been dug up from the gardens of vacant homes, and remaining ex-miners receive regular enquiries about the availability of this

Two vacated and boarded-up houses on Wordsworth Drive in 2022. Credit: Hazell Field/Save Our Homes LS26.

or that on their driveways. Of course, some don't ask. At one point, a minivan was stolen from a lay-by in the previously quiet cul-de-sac estate. Cardboard City's two streets became a target for fly-tippers, too, dumping old washing machines, fridges, garden waste, and other rubbish in the front gardens of boarded houses.

While the ex-miners wait on the now dilapidated estate for their new homes to be built around them, the evicted have had to pick up the pieces from their dispersal. Close friends and campaigners Cindy and Hazell now find themselves six miles apart, living in smaller houses yet paying higher rent. Cindy, John, and one of their sons are in a small three-bed mid-terraced house outside of the LS26 postcode; my family are in a two-up, two-down terraced house in Rothwell centre – each household paying nearly double their previous rent, despite losing rooms, space, and gardens. Another of Mum's close friends, Susan, felt she had little choice but to move 100 miles away up to Newcastle where she has family. Private lets are cheaper up there.

'Auntie' Linda moved into sheltered council housing in Rothwell's John O'Gaunts estate – part council, part private, and plagued with a reputation for anti-social behaviour. Her one-bed bungalow was, to put it politely, filthy, when she was given keys and invited to move in: thick grime coating doors; damp, cracked flooring and a large exposed drain in the wet-room bathroom; messy plastering around room vents; an unauthorised extension with a single layer of corrugated plastic for the ceiling; and no carpets – leaving dirty, exposed floorboards, concrete, and uneven ledges between doorways. It looked as though the previous tenant had used one corner of the living room as a toilet. I even found his medical and care visit records strewn all over the floor – no one had bothered to clear up before handing keys to Linda. It wasn't fit to move into.

Despite a council's general obligation to provide houses (especially sheltered accommodation for elder tenants) that are clean, safe, and in a good state of repair, Leeds City Council initially told Linda that it was the tenant's responsibility to get the property up to standard. The council soon caved and paid for basic refurbishment when threatened with publicity and solicitors – a threat that only held power because we had developed a strong social media following and news contacts through the campaign. Linda's bungalow now has carpets and fresh paint, at least. Her new home is just over a mile from Mum's new house, but these longtime best friends hardly see each other nowadays.

All await news about whether and when they'll be able to return to the new Leeds Federated Housing development. Well, not all. Susan won't return from Newcastle; she's settled now, and with various health complications it's just too much to contemplate moving everything down again. Linda is in her mid-seventies and feels she doesn't have another move in her. Liz and Paul, Sadie and Steve – all are long-term tenants and friends who for one reason or another have had to make the best of what they have elsewhere, unlikely ever to return to Cardboard City. That's the thing with redevelopment. Even in the rare cases where former tenants are offered something of a comparable size in the same neighbourhood, it always results in eviction from a home and the destruction of a community.

Conclusion

A place to call home

When Mum, Dad, and my brother finally got their Section 21 eviction notice in January 2022, it gave them the standard two months to leave Cardboard City, their home of sixteen years. They'd had a five-year heads-up that this might happen; yet despite such a long run-up they had packed very little. Up to that point, packing felt like giving in – admitting the landlord had won. After the government inspector found in Pemberstone's favour, that was it. There were no more cards to play.

Mum was fifty-eight and Dad sixty-six when that long-fought notice arrived in the post – a time when they should have been making retirement plans. Instead, they began desperately searching for somewhere new to live that would take three low-income adults and a cat. Competition for private rentals in the local area was fierce, and my parents found it hard even to book viewings; houses were gone by the afternoon they went online. It's a landlord's market, leaving older renters – half of whom have pets, who tend to be poorer than their homeowner counterparts, and who might require household adjustments for mobility and access – at a distinct disadvantage in the rat race.[1]

In my parents' search, they ruled out dozens for being too expensive, then fell at the application hurdle of many more. 'Too many adults.' 'We'd prefer a young family.' 'The property has already gone,' they heard repeatedly. Two landlords rejected their application on the assumption that three adults would mean three cars parked outside, yet there was only one driver in the household. Neither landlord bothered to ask. The two-up, two-down mid-terrace they ended up taking was one of only two they were invited to view, and Mum almost rejected it outright as the stairs are steep and narrow: she's unsteady on her feet, and there was no banister.

Their cat Pumpkin was also a sticking point – 'no pets'. But Mum agreed to pay an extra deposit as security, on top of the higher rent, 40 per cent more than they were paying in Cardboard City. In the end, there were no other options. On the plus side, it was on decent bus routes for work and Dad was hopeful it wouldn't be too long before they'd be offered a housing association house on the redeveloped Cardboard City estate.

With the move, Mum and Dad lost so many precious things they had to throw away, give away, or just leave, because there wasn't space in the new house. A Yamaha motorbike in bits (one of Dad's many future 'retirement projects'), furniture inherited from Grandad, large plant pots inherited from Nanny, gardening tools, my bed. But they made do, as they always do. It wasn't our family's first eviction rodeo and at least this one seemed secure. 'We don't want anyone temporary,' the new landlord insisted. 'We want long-term tenants who'll treat this place like a home.' And of course, they did.

Then, in May 2023, just one year after moving in, Dad died. Suddenly and unexpectedly, while at work. He was just sixty-seven years old, and it threw us all into a tailspin of grief and death bureaucracy. We later found out it was a heart attack and could not have been predicted; though I strongly suspect chronic stress from years of housing insecurity was a contributing factor. The British Heart Foundation recently reported that deaths of under-seventy-fives from cardiovascular disease has risen year-on-year in England since 2019, impacting the poorest the hardest.[2] These rises have been driven by austerity and the cost-of-living crisis: income erosion, housing insecurity, and reduced access to health and other public services. People in more deprived areas develop cardiovascular conditions ten to fifteen years earlier than people in richer ones.[3] It is disease of the poor in their sixties. Housing isn't the only part of this health-deprivation story, but it's a key one.

Dad should have retired years earlier after a lifetime spent working manual jobs, but he wanted to keep earning to cover rent and pay off debts; he was sixty-two when they first got wind of Pemberstone's redevelopment plans and still felt retirement was an impossible dream while they were housing insecure. His and Mum's lifelong low wages (most recently on stagnating, bottom-rung NHS salaries) meant that neither had savings or pensions to shout about. So when Mum, my brother, and I should have been thinking about Dad's funeral, memorials, and taking time as a small family to grieve, we were instead frantically working out how they could keep paying rent on what were now only two low incomes. I was seven months pregnant at the time and had to work midwife appointments around visits to Leeds to filter through Dad's payslips, credit card statements, and previous employers' pension information. After trawling through paperwork and navigating NHS death-in-service bureaucracy, it seemed OK, though. Mum and my brother could manage.

Time ticked on, as it does, despite grief. Mum deepened friendships with her new neighbours: chatting on the doorstep, watering their gardens, sharing bin duties, and even receiving reiki treatment from a neighbour who needed volunteers for her student assignment. These neighbours offered care and support after Dad's death, attending the funeral, dropping round to check in on Mum, offering to run her about as there was now no driver in the household. They may not have been Cindy, Linda, Mavis, Liz, and Susan, but they were starting to become her new safety net.

Then, in January 2024, Mum got news of a 7 per cent rent rise; the landlord said she needed to offset her mortgage-rate increases after the Conservative government's disastrous 2022 mini-budget had sent interest rates skyrocketing. As always, the tenant bears the brunt of cost rises on something they don't own. This instigated new calculations on an already squeezed household. It also created anxieties about whether Mum would be able to drop her hours for health reasons, as she'd recently been planning. Mum is now classed as disabled due to a chronic back condition, which is daily exacerbated by severe delays in her employer's implementation of recommended adjustments. The irony that she works for the NHS has not been lost on us. But the resources aren't there. Mum now joins millions of other workers in cutting hours or leaving unemployment entirely due to ill health. My brother's Royal Mail contract is also part-time and has not been upgraded for years. Overtime is often available, but part-time contracts serve to reduce the company's bill for leave, sick pay, and pension contributions.

Underemployment, unemployment, and part-time working have huge impacts on whether a prospective tenant passes affordability checks, as letting agents and landlords impose thresholds that can be difficult to meet on anything but a decent full-time salary. Such checks risk disproportionately impacting older people who are increasingly likely to reduce hours for a variety of reasons; today a quarter of workers over the age of fifty work part-time hours.[4]

The national charity Independent Age, which focuses on improving the lives of older people, highlights that, without higher retirement income and increased protections such as indefinite tenancies, *half* of older renters will be living in poverty by 2040.[5] They'll be shelling out proportionally more for their rent while dealing with compounding – typically later-life – challenges that are often distinct from their younger renter counterparts: spouse bereavement, complex care responsibilities, and changing health and mobility needs. Moreover, health conditions raise welfare red flags to landlords whether a prospective tenant works part- or full-time. Implicit considerations include: *Are they on benefits? What adjustments will I be forced to make? How easy will they be to evict down the line?* Discrimination on grounds of age or disability may be illegal, but it is still rife.

Back in January 2024, our reworked rent budget seemed OK. Mum and my brother could stay, we thought – no house hunting yet. Mum could go part-time to manage her health as hoped, and she and my brother could still pay the rent, just about. Fast-forward six months to June – twenty-six months after moving in, thirteen months after Dad died, and just one week after signing her new part-time working hours agreement – and Mum gets a text message: the landlord needs to sell the house. So, Mum and my brother are going to be evicted again. Not immediately, but they can only stay as long as it takes the landlord to sell the property – Mum and my brother's home. 'I can't touch your dad's stuff,' she said in tears the day she got the text. His slippers are still by their bed.

While one landlord can't be singlehandedly accountable for plugging the country's glaring social-house and private-rent crisis, here we are. Again. Two part-time, low-income earners, one of them now sixty with disabilities, facing another eviction. Looking around at the four – just four – private rent options currently available in their area, the cheapest costing 10 per cent more than their already increased rent, it is hard not to despair.

This time, though, there is no campaigning community to rally around Mum. Just one tenant household versus an accidental landlord who rents out a property she used to live in, but now needs to sell. I didn't intend this anecdote to be the story at the end of the book; I didn't know this is where my parents would end up when I started writing. One dead, one facing eviction twice within two years. But evictions have a way of shunting families around to other equally insecure properties, and of shortening lives. Landlords have a habit of taking back their properties, and governments seem unwilling to protect tenants against the vagaries of the market.

In their book *In Defense of Housing*, David Madden and Peter Marcuse write that the idea of a housing crisis implies that there is some kind of well-functioning norm from which the country is temporarily departing. But as they point out, 'for working-class and poor communities, housing crisis is the norm'.[6] The term habitually reappears in the headlines when middle-class homeowners and investors face residential instability or sharply rising costs, making it seem that there are peaks and troughs in the business of shelter. In the present moment, it's the young professional, 'generation rent' dominating housing precarity stories. Yet, as this book has shown, governments, builders, and landlords have baked poor-quality housing, unaffordable rent rises, and evictions into the social contract for centuries. Low-income tenants from across the age brackets have always been treated as moveable masses occupying someone else's investment.

Nineteenth-century private landlords ran slum properties where eviction notices were as easy to issue as moralising sermons. The state started to intervene at the turn of the century, packaging eviction as progress: demolishing slums, dispersing communities, and building supposedly better houses for a slightly higher class of deserving poor, who were no more guaranteed well-built, secure homes than the previous inhabitants.

Cyclical government drives to build more or better rented housing in the mid-twentieth century resulted in rushed and shoddy constructions whose only long-term beneficiaries were private developers. Post-war prefabricated houses were built with a lifespan that would see families evicted within two generations. This is planned obsolescence of tenant lives.

Brick-built public housing did not stay secure, comfortable, and affordable either. Managed decline has resulted in rising complaints about damp, mould, and broken fittings. Since the

1980 Right to Buy scheme, more than 2 million council homes have been sold to their sitting tenants.[7] This stock was never fully replaced, let alone increased to account for a growing population. More than 40 per cent of the 2 million sold have since been converted to private-sector rentals, which come with all the trappings of housing insecurity: assured shorthold tenancies, market-rate rents, and no-fault evictions.

Eviction has long been enacted in different ways, through various means. While sharp rent hikes, maintenance neglect, and harassment might push tenants to leave their home 'voluntarily', these are essentially evictions by the back door – tactics landlords have been using for centuries to force tenants out when formal evictions aren't possible. No ruling party – the Conservatives and Liberals at the turn of the twentieth century, nor Labour, nor the post-war Conservatives – have developed meaningful, long-lasting policies to give tenants security in their rented homes, whoever the landlord. There's no better example of these failings than National Coal Board housing.

As this book has revealed, the state-owned Coal Board was one of the country's biggest landlords during an apparent golden era of public housing. Yet it watched its properties fall deeper into ruin while prioritising the pits. Maintenance of dilapidated brick-built stock was kept to a minimum. To fill housing gaps the NCB decision-makers, like their local authority counterparts, were swayed by quick-fix solutions, building between them more than half a million temporary and permanent prefabs destined for demolition. Private building companies reaped the rewards, and taxpayers were destined to pick up the tab at least twice.

For those living on Coal Board estates, tenant protections were weak; what were envisioned to be secure mixed-community developments ended up being miner-only estates and tied houses, with rental agreements that could see a family turfed out should the breadwinning miner die, sustain disabling injuries, or retire. The NCB never saw itself as a landlord, and managed housing only to service production needs. When the coal industry struggled, from the mid-century to its end, there was no state safety net to secure these tenant-miners' homes. Council housing was already on the decline. Instead, just thirty or so years after the country was buoyed by the promises of affordable, quality rented homes, Coal Board estates were being chopped up and auctioned to private speculators – heralding a rapid financialisation of rented housing. Rather than Thatcher's Right to Buy being the death knell of public housing, the National Coal Board auctions are what brought global capital rolling into housing estates. Tenants never stood a chance to make forever homes for *themselves*, let alone across generations.

These eviction trends, visible across all tenure types, are heavily classed and gendered. For low-income, job-insecure people across Britain, home ownership – the apparently only 'valid' housing aspiration these days – is out of reach. Council and social housing are scant, with the latter still proving unaffordable for many. Nowadays, working-class people have little choice but to fall back on the private-rental sector, where they are more vulnerable to eviction, dispersal, and community destruction – holes punched through their lives at frequent but unpredictable intervals. These holes can't be refilled with new, improved, or simply *more* housing – at least not in the same way. Safety nets are broken as neighbour-friends disperse. New ones might be made in the latest house, but meaningful social connections are violently severed all along the way. Income and savings take a huge hit with every eviction; individual health declines, children's education and life chances suffer, and the insecurely housed die younger than they should. Council and social-housing tenants aren't immune to these oppressive patterns, either.

The everyday repercussions of tenant insecurity and eviction are felt disproportionately by women, especially poorer women. They typically bear the larger mental and manual load of displacement within couple or family households. After all, moving house (famously one of life's most stressful events) is a cascade of chores and rebudgeting. Single women have fewer housing options due to comparably lower incomes, and they are more at risk of sexual violence and harassment by landlords.

Yet this book has also shown working-class women have long been at the forefront of tenant activism – fighting back against slum landlords, against unaffordable or unavailable state housing, against private speculators, and everything in between. Mary Barbour and the Glasgow rent strikers of 1915 mobilised mass solidarity through domestic networks, successfully leveraging the local Labour movement and cowing the at-war government into addressing the dire state of privately rented housing with a national rent freeze.

In the late 1960s, Ethel Singleton and her tenant neighbours forced Liverpool Council to rehouse them, after bringing a princess's – and then the world's – attention to the condemned University of Liverpool–owned slums they were forced to live in. The Abercromby Tenants Association, led by Singleton and others, made the most of university student allies and the press's appetite for a spectacle to secure relocation from uninhabitable conditions.

In this century, Lindsey Garrett and fellow New Era Tenants in London raised placards, gathered signatures, and garnered high-profile support from celebrities and political figures to force their private landlord's hand. Under intense scrutiny, global investment company Westbrook sold the property to a charitable foundation, which now rents the block to tenants on more affordable rents linked to income.

Then there's our campaign: Save Our Homes LS26. Cindy Readman; my mum, Hazell Field; Mavis Abbey; and the whole estate led marches, gave speeches, gathered signatures, and took up space in the national media, seeking to prevent the demolition of their tenant estate and a mass eviction. The community's relentless activism over nearly five years pressured

Pemberstone to sell the entirety of Cardboard City to a housing association, which is promising to rehouse many of the original tenants in new Affordable Rent housing.

None of these outcomes have been perfect. And the small wins have come with huge social and emotional costs. Yet, taken together as a long history of pushbacks against renting insecurity, they show what's possible with grassroots housing action – and who is doing the acting.

The bigger picture

Where to go from here? I wouldn't dare offer pat solutions to the insecure rent problem plaguing this country; regulation and policies are dense and complex, changing all the time – and that's part of the problem. Moreover, as this book has shown, landlords are a diverse bunch and find ways to resist or undermine improved conditions for tenants – whether through legal loopholes, such as the 1960s shift from unfurnished to furnished lets to enable easier evictions; or through raising rents, as councils did after the 1972 Housing Finance Act; or through simply selling property and removing another housing option from a decreasing supply, as the NCB did from the 1970s and accidental landlords are doing today. Tackling tenant insecurity purely as a policy problem misses the political and economic norms that shunt tenants to the bottom of the pile when it comes to housing rights.

Sitting behind the question of regulation is a bigger one: What is housing for? Peter King philosophically describes housing as a private good for the individual(s) living in the house. The essence of housing, he writes, is as a place 'that allows us the freedom to be', free from the intervention of others (criminal activity notwithstanding). A place where we can exercise rights to other things and where we can do what we need to 'live and flourish'.[8] In that sense, housing underpins all other rights, because it allows needs to be met, life to be lived, and social relations to prosper.

Regulations and policy around renting over the past 150 years have failed to get that balance right. Tenants have always been treated as economic and interchangeable – transient rent payers rather than social beings making a home and community. Speculator-investor landlords are driven by profits – a residential property investment is often just one of many interests. They do not care about the needs and social lives of tenants. The gradual distancing between tenant and landlord through the rise of middlemen, letting agents, managing agents, subsidiary companies, and so on has made this indifference easier – part of the operating model, even. Speculators are not in the business of providing homes, just managing assets. Industry landlords, similarly, have other priorities – namely, the success of their trade, which requires a steady supply of reliable workers, not a settled community.

For their part, small private landlords – the accidental ones and the buy-to-letters – undoubtedly feel hard done by. Popular culture has enjoyed bashing them at opportune moments. As we've seen since the First World War, the press can be quick to jump on an evil or enemy landlord running slum conditions, hiking rents, or, like Rachman in the 1960s, running criminal harassment campaigns. Most individual private landlords, I imagine, feel they run *their* properties very differently. But, like speculator investors, an individual landlord's priority is also their bottom line – whether as income top-up, a retirement investment, or a value-accumulating asset. They, too, exercise distancing through letting and managing agents and other subcontractors. As a result, they, too, lean into market-level rents, intrusive inspections, easy evictions, and a cultural mistrust of tenants more than they might want to admit. Just ask any private tenant.

If the purpose of housing, then, is to allow the occupier to live and flourish, stronger tenancy protections are essential.

In the history of Cardboard City, the tenants who saw better housing outcomes were those with pre-1989 regulated tenancies, which came with stronger protections against eviction, the possibility for family to inherit the tenancy, and the promise of like-for-like rehousing. Those regulated tenants, including Mavis and Barry Abbey, were not ultimately spared from upheaval. They will still have to move house, they have still lost close neighbour-friends. Yet in this book's spirit of acknowledging small victories, Mavis and Barry's regulated tenancy meant that they were guaranteed a replacement, that they did not have to move multiple times, and that their rent will remain stable (and low compared to shorthold private-sector alternatives). This enhanced tenancy also meant that Mavis and Barry received more humanised treatment throughout the campaign saga – again, it was not enough, but better than their assured-shorthold-tenancy neighbours. The landlord and council were forced to give them advance warning of the development by a personal phone call, forced to work with them to arrange their next home, and forced to keep them updated on the newbuilds.

In the absence of stronger tenancy agreements and without a cultural shift that recognises tenants' rights to flourish in their homes, collective action to fight mistreatment and eviction is essential. As this book has shown, activism and self-advocacy – 'taking up space' – is often the only weapon in a tenant's armoury, but its power lies in networks. Save Our Homes LS26's tenant activism was boosted massively by linking into existing campaign networks: unions, housing organisations, wider social-justice groups. Underfunded though they are, these volunteer and activist-led groups are extremely helpful and generous with advice, solidaristic in times of protest, and empathetic.

The Focus E15 campaign in Newham leant on a Revolutionary Communist Group stall to get their protest tactics rolling. Save Our Homes LS26 benefited from connecting with local councillors, local housing-support groups, and workers' unions. It is not possible to put politics aside in these fights: individuals and organisations come with political affiliations and ideas, which will be front and centre during protests. But it is also neither desirable nor realistic to rinse politics from the processes of eviction: everything about housing security is political; policy choices are shaped by elected and unelected establishment figures who make assumptions about who deserves housing security and what that security looks like. Navigating a course between unconventional allies can really help to boost the cause.

The closure of local newspapers and the parallel decline in national news outlets' focus on housing have a lot to answer for when it comes to connecting the dots of eviction and housing activism across the country. Anna Minton points out in *Big Capital* that, as recently as thirty years ago, newspapers had housing-and-planning correspondents and local papers were leading exposés of local scandals with national significance.[9] Vicky Spratt, housing correspondent of the *i Paper*, is currently one of the few frontline national journalists left standing in this field. Major publications that have played a role in exposing monumental housing failures – such as *Inside Housing*'s forensic coverage of Grenfell – sit behind costly subscriptions because investigative journalism is expensive. Yet dedicated and accessible coverage is essential.

Many of the stories in this book are drawn from local *Rothwell Advertiser* coverage, a now defunct publication, or other local newspapers that have since closed, but whose back catalogue has been digitised and made available online through the British Newspaper Archive (behind a paywall, I might add). Housing and landlord accountability requires transparency; transparency requires reporting; and self-reporting, where it exists, is not good enough on its own. With private rent rates and evictions once again on the rise there's a greater need than ever for dedicated and consistent coverage of policy changes, lived experiences of renting, and activism for better, more secure, conditions.[10]

Save Our Homes LS26 tried to maintain coverage through direct and regular contact with local news journalists – online, print, radio, and TV news – updating them with every development, step, and fear throughout the campaign. We kept up a regular online presence and via social media, too, which kept supporters informed and sustained attention – even though some of it was unwanted and fraught with tension. As the social media lead of the Save Our Homes LS26 campaign, Mum would receive messages from 'rent-a-mobs' offering to bus troublemakers up to any protest, as well as messages from trolls demanding to know why any of them deserved a 'free' house. This was before Twitter became the cesspit of nastiness that characterises a lot of discussion on the rebranded X.

A huge challenge in fighting evictions is that campaigners often only get their voices heard or a seat at the table when activists stick their head above the media parapet. Yet online spaces are increasingly dangerous places for everyone – especially women. More than one in three women have experienced abuse or harassment on social media or elsewhere online.[11] For women from minority ethnic backgrounds, the violence is even more pronounced. A 2018 study of Twitter by Amnesty International found that Black women were 84 per cent more likely than white women to be mentioned in abusive or problematic tweets; women from other minority ethnic groups were 34 per cent more likely.[12] Visible activism is not easy and isn't always safe, which is why networks can be a lifeline.

Inviting local and national news organisations onto the estate to tell the eviction story, and explaining it themselves on social media were just two of the ways the Save Our Homes LS26 campaigners made use of the physical and online spaces they already occupied in order to stake claims on their rented homes. Cindy, John, and other residents invited strangers into their homes through the Heritage Open Days visitor project.

Residents shared previously unheard stories of life in Coal Board housing. The whole community welcomed Alfie Barker and his crew onto the estate to film *Hanging On*. Residents organised and joined protests, marching down Rothwell High Street and in Leeds City centre. We ran stalls at local fairs. For the longest time, we refused to budge.

As with the 1915 Glasgow rent strikers, the Abercromby tenants in Liverpool, the Kirkby strikers, Focus E15, New Era, and the Save Our Homes LS26 residents showed that there are many creative ways to resist housing financialisaton, to spotlight marginalised voices, to reject the shame of housing insecurity imparted by the governing elite, and to express the solidarity and friendships of tenant communities. None of these women-led campaigns have won the big fight against eviction: none have resulted in lasting affordable rents, meaningful maintenance guarantees, or multigenerational tenancies. Yet, all have shone a spotlight or chipped away at a broken system in ways that have forced important concessions and changes. It is not enough, but it matters.

While the Save Our Homes LS26 story got national attention, we regularly received messages from other communities that were undertaking similar fights beneath the public radar, and losing them. What my parents were going through was clearly not unique. Moreover, looking at the history of Cardboard City and other Coal Board estates, it's clear that these patterns of landlordism, managed decline, and eviction span more than a century – and cross all landlord types: private, industry, and municipal. The reality of renting in modern Britain is that poorer tenants have never had housing security – even during the small window in post-war Britain when political consensus seemed to be behind the construction of affordable homes with local authorities as landlords.

The whole system needs an overhaul, from architect to developer, from builder to mortgage lender, from landlord to letting and managing agents – and above all, tenancies. The structure of the housing market, where skyrocketing profits are made through land-banking and sales, means that private builders can't be neutral constructors of affordable rented houses. Competition, and the commercial pressures of innovation and cost-cutting mean that rushed (often poor-quality) but eye-wateringly expensive houses are inevitable.

The solution to this 150-year-plus eviction crisis isn't for the state to enable the building of more houses for affordable rent (or should I say Affordable Rent), build-to-rent, or sale. I join a growing number of commentators who point out that more building risks worsening the problem of costs – exacerbating land value, sales prices, rent rates, and ultimately feeding speculators.[13] The future landlords in this simplistic build-more terrain will continue to be investors, large and small, with a smattering of housing associations charging 80 per cent of an escalating market rate.

The build-more strategy also risks missing the essence of housing security. Social surveys from the interwar years reported that people wanted more than just new buildings to replace their overcrowded slums. What they valued was feeling secure in family and neighbourhood communities. Evictions created a sense of dislocation and isolation and put a greater strain on household budgets – regardless of whether tenants eventually settled into new homes elsewhere.[14] Little has changed since.

Interdependence between neighbour households and multigeneration homes should not be the preserve of the owner-occupier class. Renting is a valid choice that suits many households. Renters deserve the chance to make homes marked by genuine affordability, stability, and social connection. It might not sound like a revolutionary idea, but it requires a radical transformation of how we think about housing – one that prioritises people over profit, security over speculation, and tenant communities over landlord commodities.

Acknowledgements

This book is first and foremost about a tenant community that desperately tried, and failed, to save their homes. The biggest acknowledgement is for them – for their energy, determination, and the inspirational way they fought Pemberstone and badgered Leeds City Council for more than half a decade, despite having no previous campaign experience. Mum and Dad (Hazell and Mark Field), Cindy and John Readman, Mavis and Barry Abbey, Susan Gould, Linda Elsworth, Robert Walker, Liz and Paul Murgatroyd, Sadie Somers, Wendy Richardson, and everyone else on the estate – I have learned so much from you all and I'm so proud of everything we've achieved, even if it wasn't what we hoped for in the end. I finished writing the book in the summer of 2024. Lots will have inevitably changed since, but I hope you've all finally got a place to call home.

I am so grateful to everyone who sat down for interviews and discussions about the estate's history and their experiences of living there: Cindy and John Readman (on 15 February 2023); Mavis and Barry Abbey (15 February 2023); Lynn Abbott, Diane Lilley, Angela Kellett, Janet Richardson, and Gill Taylor (16 February 2023); Howard Benson (9 March 2023); and 'Auntie' Linda Elsworth (a conversation always ongoing). I hope I have done your stories and experiences justice. Thank you, too, Mick Wagstaff, for agreeing to share snippets of his family history in the book, and to everyone on the Coal Boarders Facebook group whose memories and photos keep the estate alive today. Much appreciation also to the councillors who had our backs – particularly Karen Bruce (plus husband Stuart) and Stewart Golton.

There are so many people who have been involved in the Save Our Homes LS26 campaign over the years who deserve acknowledgement and gratitude: John Davis from Hands Off Our Homes; Jay from Judicial Domicide; John Lynch; Chris Kitchen from the NUM; friends at ACORN; Sisters Uncut Leeds; and so many others. Alfie Barker, Hollie Bryan, and the whole Cosmosquare team, your attention and care meant so much – and what a fantastic documentary short you've made. Thanks to the Prefab Museum and Twentieth Century Society for supporting the campaign and sharing resources. And to all the helpful staff at the National Archives, West Yorkshire Joint Services, and the National Coal Mining Museum.

A massive thank you to Leo Hollis at Verso who took me on for my first book and believed me when I said this story about a neglected Coal Board estate and tenant community matters. Your encouragement and proverbial red pen improved the draft immeasurably – though all mistakes are, of course, my own. The wider team at Verso have been excellent to deal with at each step of the way, too. Thank you to you all.

I might never have got this book off the ground if it wasn't for the friends of Dawn Foster, the inspiring and fierce writer and commentator who focused so much of her energy on housing and inequality. Dawn sadly passed away in 2021 and her friends set up the Dawn Foster Memorial Essay Prize in her honour in 2022. I entered that competition with my essay 'Fighting for Cardboard City' and somehow won. The article was published in *Red Pepper* magazine in summer 2022. Thank you to everyone involved in that competition – Lynsey Hanley, Sarah Woolley, K Biswas, Kirsty Connell-Skinner, Kimon Daltas, and the wider *Red Pepper* team. Especially Lynsey and Sarah, who supported me to take the article further. I hope I would have made Dawn Foster proud.

My writing has also been supported by a Society of Authors and K Blundell Trust grant, which is awarded to authors under forty whose works in progress seek to raise social awareness.

I am extremely grateful for this timely financial support, which helped me fill in research gaps, make vital connections, and funded a bit of time and space (and childcare!) to finalise the project.

I want to say a heartfelt thank you to all the friends and family whose ears I have chewed off about this topic – campaign and book – over the years. Birte Vogel, you are my rock! Hannah Kaplan, Hayley Rhodes, Angie Musgrove, Nicolas de Zamaroczy, Deepanshu Mohan, Sally and John Stringer, Sarah Jeal, and Shelley Savage for always taking time to check in on the book's progress, and my sanity with it. To Max Field, who lived through this all, too. Special thanks and massive appreciation to Rob Stringer, Helen Cox, and Howard Benson, who read through a draft of the book, making it infinitely stronger and pointing me down other interesting research paths.

Finally, the hardest thanks to write: for James Stringer, Mum, and Dad. James, you have been a constant source of love, support, and encouragement – giving me time and space to write, reading countless versions, providing invaluable feedback and ideas. I simply could not have written this without you. Our precious daughter Summer arrived midway through writing, and I can't wait for her to read it herself one day (and probably eye-roll at millennial oversharing).

Mum, you are an inspiration to me, and I hope this book conveys to the world what an amazing woman you are. Thank you for letting me tell so much of your story; I know this is not without emotional cost. We never did a formal interview – it's been a conversation over several long years. If I grow into even a fraction of the kind, principled, and determined woman you are, I'll be mighty happy.

Dad will never read my deep thanks to him, but I hope he knew it in his heart before it gave way. We never sat down for a full interview – one of my biggest regrets. But we spoke frequently about the eviction and the campaign, as it consumed all of our lives for many years. His love, support, and our shared sense of social justice kept me going – they still do. Dad was a kind, generous man who would do anything for his neighbours, friends, and family – they were often all one and the same in his eyes. This book's for him.

Notes

Introduction

1 Brenda Vale, *Prefabs: A History of the UK Temporary Housing Programme* (London: Taylor and Francis, 1995), 2.
2 Keith Ross, *Non-traditional Housing in the UK – A Brief Review* (London: Building Research Establishment, July 2002).
3 Notable exceptions: Vale, *Prefabs*; Greg Stevenson, *Palaces for the People: Prefabs in Post-war Britain* (London: B.T. Batsford, 2003); and Elisabeth Blanchet and Sonia Zhuravlyova, *Prefabs: A Social and Architectural History* (London: Historic England, 2018).
4 Alfie Barker, *Hanging On* (2021), alfiebarker.com.
5 Pam Currie, '"A Wondrous Spectacle": Protest, Class and Femininity in the 1915 Rent Strikes', in Neil Gray, ed., *Rent and Its Discontents* (London: Rowman & Littlefield, 2018), 4.
6 Anne Power, *Property Before People: The Management of Twentieth Century Council Housing* (London: Allen & Unwin, 1987), 44.
7 For other non-southern English examples, see Lynsey Hanley, *Estates: An Intimate History* (London: Granta Publications, 2007). John Boughton's *Municipal Dreams: The Rise and Fall of Council Housing* (London: Verso, 2018) contains a number of northern English council estate examples, including Hulme and Wythenshawe in Manchester.
8 Boughton, *Municipal Dreams*.
9 House of Commons Debate [HC Deb], 27 November 1984, vol. 68, cc883–4.

1. It's for your own good

1 Thomas Cubitt quoted in the House of Commons, *Report from Select Committee of the House of Commons on the Health of Towns*, Session 1840, vol. 28, 29 May 1840, 205.
2 John Burnett, *A Social History of Housing: 1815–1985*, 2nd edn (London: Methuen & Co., 1986), 149.
3 Anne Power, *Property Before People: The Management of*

Twentieth-Century Council Housing (London: Allen & Unwin, 1987), 17.

4 Office for National Statistics (ONS), 'Private Rental Affordability, England, Wales and Northern Ireland: 2021', 19 December 2022, ons.gov.uk.

5 Burnett, *A Social History of Housing*, 149.

6 Ibid., 144–5.

7 Wendy Wilson, 'Overcrowded Housing (England)', House of Commons Library, Briefing Paper no. CBP1013, 3 November 2023.

8 Ibid.

9 John Boughton, *Municipal Dreams: The Rise and Fall of Council Housing* (London: Verso, 2018), 16.

10 Power, *Property Before People*, 28–32.

11 Sarah Glynn, 'If Public Housing Didn't Exist, We'd Have to Invent It', in Sarah Glynn, ed., *Where the Other Half Lives: Lower Income Housing in a Neoliberal World* (London: Pluto Press, 2009), 12.

12 Power, *Property Before People*, 32–3.

13 J. A. Yelling, 'L. C. C. Slum Clearance Policies, 1889–1907', *Transactions of the Institute of British Geographers* 7, no. 3 (1982), 292–303.

14 Power, *Property Before People*, 14.

15 Boughton, *Municipal Dreams*, 30.

16 Neil Gray, 'Introduction', in Neil Gray, ed., *Rent and Its Discontents* (London: Rowman & Littlefield, 2018), xix.

17 Ibid.

18 Quintin Bradley, 'Leeds Rent Strike 1914', n.d., criticalplace.org.uk.

19 Howard Benson, 'Thomas Henry Killingbeck', *Woodlesford: The Story of a Station*, newwoodlesford.xyz.

20 Thomas Killingbeck, quoted in ibid.

21 Gray, 'Introduction', xviii.

22 Howard Benson, discussion with author, 9 March 2023.

23 Burnett, *A Social History of Housing*, 227.

24 House of Lords Debate (HL Deb), 8 February 1944, vol. 130, cc730–1.

25 Shelley Savage, '"We Have Saved the Land": The Land Settlement Movement of the 1920s', *Herts Past and Present* 3, no. 39 (2022), 2.

26 Anne Meredith, 'From Ideals to Reality: The Women's Smallholding Colony at Lingfield, 1920–39', *Agricultural History Review* 54, no. 1 (2006), 105–21.

27 Savage, '"We Have Saved the Land"', 5.

28 Carol A. Lockwood, 'From Soldier to Peasant? The Land Settlement Scheme in East Sussex, 1919–1939', *Albion: A Quarterly Journal Concerned with British Studies* 30, no. 3 (1998), 439–62.

29 Power, *Property Before People*, 51.

30 'Bristol Slum Problems', *Western Daily Press*, 12 October 1927, 4.
31 CHAC Report, 1939, cited in Power, *Property Before People*, 25.
32 Pam Currie, '"A Wondrous Spectacle": Protest, Class and Femininity in the 1915 Rent Strikes', in Gray, *Rent and Its Discontents*.
33 Gray, 'Introduction', xvii.
34 Currie, 'A Wondrous Spectacle', 8.
35 Bradley, 'Leeds Rent Strike 1914'.
36 Currie, 'A Wondrous Spectacle', 7.

2. Public money for private contracts

1 HL Deb, 4 May 1943, vol. 127, c334.
2 HC Deb, 30 November 1943, vol. 395, cc258, and 23 March 1945, vol. 409, cc1172–7.
3 Nicklaus Thomas-Symonds, *Nye: The Political Life of Aneurin Bevan* (London: I. B. Tauris, 2016), 158–9.
4 Peter Malpass, *Housing and the Welfare State: The Development of Housing Policy in Britain* (Basingstoke: Palgrave Macmillan, 2005), 82; HC Deb, 4 December 1951, vol. 494, c2229.
5 Wendy Wilson, 'A Short History of Rent Control', House of Commons Library, Briefing Paper no. 6747, 30 March 2017, 7.
6 John Burnett, *A Social History of Housing: 1815–1985*, 2nd edn (London: Methuen & Co., 1986), 283.
7 Malpass, *Housing and the Welfare State*, 82.
8 Audrey Whiting, 'This Is a "Home" to Them: Leeds Families Herd in Cellars', *Yorkshire Evening Post*, 2 February 1948; Audrey Whiting, 'The Rats Play on Bedroom Floor', *Yorkshire Evening Post*, 3 February 1948.
9 The half million figure is based on number of households – 160,000 – multiplied by average household occupancy rates – around three – in England during the 1960s. Department for Communities and Local Government, '50 Years of the English Housing Survey', Ministry for Housing, Communications and Local Government, November 2017, gov.uk.
10 'Man Must Quit Farm Cottage', *Lincolnshire Echo*, 18 May 1946.
11 HC Deb, 2 April 1947, vol. 435, c2185.
12 Howard Newby, 'Tied Cottage Reform', *British Journal of Law and Society* 4, no. 1 (1977), 96.
13 Helen Hay and Dave Fordham, *New Coalfields, New Housing* (Doncaster: Fedj-el-Adoum Publishing, 2017).
14 HC Deb, 6 March 1947, vol. 434, c638.
15 John Boughton, *Municipal Dreams: The Rise and Fall of Council Housing* (London: Verso, 2018), 68.

16 William Beveridge, 'Social Insurance and Allied Services', Cmd 6404, HMSO, November 1942.
17 Daniel Renwick and Robbie Shilliam, *Squalor. The Five Giants: A New Beveridge Report* (Newcastle: Agenda Publishing, 2022), 42.
18 Malpass, *Housing and the Welfare State*, 64.
19 HC Deb, 16 March 1949, vol. 462, cc2123–8.
20 Chris Holmes, *Housing Equality and Choice* (Institute for Public Policy Research, 27 August 2003), 6.
21 Malpass, *Housing and the Welfare State*, 67.
22 Peter Malpass, 'Private Enterprise in Eclipse? A Reassessment of British Housing Policy in the 1940s', *Housing Studies* 18, no. 5 (2003), 649.
23 Renwick and Shilliam, *Squalor*, 46.
24 Malpass, 'Private Enterprise in Eclipse?', 654.
25 The National Archives (TNA), COAL 45/3, 5 January 1953, M. W. Hudson to Sir Geoffrey Vickers.
26 Thomas-Symonds, *Nye*, 159.
27 TNA, COAL 45/3, 5 January 1953.
28 Department of Energy and Climate Change, *Appraisal Report from Department for Energy and Climate Change ("DECC") relating to records of the former National Coal Board ("NCB") latterly British Coal Corporation ("BCC")*, August 2013, 20.
29 'To Build Houses for Miners', *Bradford Observer*, 21 March 1952.
30 TNA, COAL 45/3, 5 May 1952, Statement of Housing Requirements.
31 TNA, COAL 45/3, 16 July 1956, Local Authority Provision of Miners' Housing.
32 Ibid.
33 TNA, COAL 45/3, 25 February 1952, Housing for Miners. Second Interim Report.
34 Ibid.
35 Brenda Vale, *Prefabs: A History of the UK Temporary Housing Programme* (London: Taylor and Francis, 1995), 1.
36 Greg Stevenson, *Palaces for the People: Prefabs in Post-war Britain* (London: B. T. Batsford, 2003), 13.
37 HL Deb, 26 October 1943, vol. 129, cc327–33.
38 Winston Churchill, 'Our Greatest Effort Is Coming', broadcast from London, 26 March 1944, *Vital Speeches of the Day*, vol. 10, 354–8.
39 Stevenson, *Palaces for the People*, 41.
40 Ibid.
41 Nick Hayes, 'Prefabricating Stories: Innovation in Systems Technology after the Second World War', *History of Technology* 25 (2004), 7–28.
42 HL Deb, 4 May 1943, cc349–51.

43 HL Deb, 4 May 1943, cc335–9.
44 Mr O'Mahoney, quoted by Elisabeth Blanchet, '100 Buildings 100 Years. 1946: 17 Meliot Road, Excalibur Estate, London', Twentieth Century Society, c20society.org.uk.
45 Stevenson, *Palaces for the People*, 40.
46 Oonagh Gay, 'Prefabs: A Study in Policy-Making', *Public Administration* 65 (1987), 407–22, 411.
47 Eveleigh Bradford, 'Sir Edwin Airey (1878–1955)', Thoresby Society, May 2018, thoresby.org.uk.
48 Ibid.
49 'Leeds Death of Sir Edwin Airey', *Bradford Observer*, 15 March 1955.
50 Michael Foot, *Aneurin Bevan: A Biography*, vol. 2, *1945–60* (London: Faber & Faber, 2009).
51 HC Deb, 16 October 1940, vol. 365, oral answer 15; HC Deb, 27 November 1941, vol. 376, cc892–3; Fred Wellings, *British Housebuilders: History and Analysis* (New Jersey: Wiley-Blackwell, 2006), 58.
52 Keith Ross, *Non-traditional Housing in the UK – A Brief Review* (London: Building Research Establishment, July 2002), 11.
53 Malpass, 'Private Enterprise in Eclipse?', 646.
54 'N. Kesteven Has 20 Houses Being Built "But Should Do Better"', *Lincolnshire Echo*, 18 May 1949.
55 Renwick and Shilliam, *Squalor*, 50.
56 Daniel O'Neill and Samantha Organ, 'A Literature Review of the Evolution of British Prefabricated Low-Rise Housing', *Structural Survey* 34, no. 2 (2016), 204.
57 TNA, COAL 45/3, 5 May 1952, Statement of Housing Requirements in Areas of High Priority from Production Stand-point.
58 Hayes, 'Prefabricating Stories'.
59 Gay, 'Prefabs: A Study in Policy-Making'.
60 Stevenson, *Palaces for the People*, 208.
61 HC Deb, 7 November 1952, cc556–65.
62 Peter Scott, *The Making of the Modern British Home: The Suburban Semi and Family Life between the Wars* (Oxford: Oxford University Press, 2013), 229.
63 'Against the Public Interest', *Builder* 187, no. 5824 (1 October 1954), 527–8.
64 TNA, WORK 58/17, 22 January 1954, London Building Panel Hearing, Monopolies and Restricted Practices Commission.
65 HC Deb, 13 March 1950, vol. 472, cc799–803.
66 HC Deb, 7 November 1952, vol. 507, cc556–64.
67 TNA, COAL 45/3, 7 March 1952, Central Housing Advisory Committee – Minutes of the 55th Meeting.

3. 'My own cupboard'

1 Greg Stevenson, *Palaces for the People: Prefabs in Post-war Britain* (London: B. T. Batsford, 2003), 208.
2 Nick Hayes, 'Prefabricating Stories: Innovation in Systems Technology after the Second World War', *History of Technology* 25 (2004), 9.
3 Brenda Vale, *Prefabs: A History of the UK Temporary Housing Programme* (London: Taylor and Francis, 1995), 40–1.
4 HL Deb, 4 May 1943, vol. 127, cc317–24.
5 John Boughton, *Municipal Dreams: The Rise and Fall of Council Housing* (London: Verso, 2018), 78.
6 Helen Hester and Nick Srnicek, *After Work: A History of Home and the Fight for Free Time,* (London: Verso, 2023), 23.
7 Judy Giles, 'A Home of One's Own: Women and Domesticity in England 1918–1950', *Women's Studies International Forum* 16, no. 3 (1993), 239–53.
8 Stevenson, *Palaces for the People*, 103, 108.
9 Neil Gray, 'Introduction', in Neil Gray, ed., *Rent and Its Discontents* (London: Rowman & Littlefield, 2018), xxii.
10 Vale, *Prefabs*, 47.
11 West Yorkshire Archives, Leeds Collection [WYA-L], Rothwell Urban and District Council Minute Book, 5/59 1952–1953, July 1952, Non-traditional Houses, 110; December 1952, Erection of Houses, Oulton, 223.
12 Jeremy Paxman, *Black Gold: The History of How Coal Made Britain* (London: William Collins, 2021), 20.
13 Howard Benson, 'Oulton Hall', *Woodlesford: The Story of a Station*, newwoodlesford.xyz.
14 Howard Benson, 'Stone Quarries', *Woodlesford: The Story of a Station*, newwoodlesford.xyz.
15 Howard Benson, 'Water Haigh Colliery', *Woodlesford: The Story of a Station*, newwoodlesford.xyz.
16 Howard Benson, 'Miners', *Woodlesford: The Story of a Station*, newwoodlesford.xyz.
17 Leeds City Council, 'Oulton and Woodlesford Community Design Statement', 2014, leeds.gov.uk.
18 UK Land Registry, Title Deeds, 8 Wordsworth Drive, Oulton, LS26 8EP.
19 Boughton, *Municipal Dreams*, 78–9.
20 Mick Wagstaff, correspondence with author, 14 February 2018.
21 Maria Rentetzi, 'Cardboard Box: The Politics of Materiality', in Susanne Bauer, Martina Schlünder, and Maria Rentetzi, eds, *Boxes: A Field Guide* (Manchester: Mattering Press, 2020), 452–3.

22 John Greve, 'Preface: Homelessness Then and Now', in Nicholas Pleace, Roger Burrows, and Deborah Quilgars, eds, *Homelessness and Social Policy* (London: Routledge, 1997), xii–xiii.

23 DECC, *Appraisal Report from Department for DECC Relating to Records of the Former National Coal Board*, 7–8.

4. Robbery without violence

1 TNA, COAL 45/6, 18 January 1956, R. E. Megarry, The Rent Acts: Applications for Possession.

2 TNA, COAL 45/6. n.d., c.1955, The Board vs. James Francis Hopkins.

3 'Miners' Union Protest on Eviction Orders', *Birmingham Post*, 24 July 1961.

4 TNA, COAL 45/6, August 1952, New Housing Programme for Miners.

5 'Council Alleges Eviction of Two Arley Ex-miners', *Midland Counties Tribune*, 13 October 1950.

6 TNA, COAL 45/6, 18 August 1952, NCB Personnel Committee Minutes.

7 Ibid.

8 Neil Gray, 'Introduction', in Neil Gray, ed., *Rent and Its Discontents* (London: Rowman & Littlefield, 2018), xviii.

9 TNA, COAL 45/6, 11 September 1952, Houses for Miners.

10 Ibid.

11 Anne Power, *Property Before People: The Management of Twentieth-Century Council Housing* (London: Allen & Unwin, 1987), 70–1.

12 TNA, COAL 45/8, 21 April 1953, NCB General Purposes Committee, Memorandum by Sir Geoffrey Vickers.

13 Ibid.

14 TNA, COAL 45/8, 18 October 1954, Suggested NCB Line Nationally in Relation to Government Slum Clearance Policy.

15 West Yorkshire Archives, Wakefield Collection [WYA-W], WYW186/2/3/2/8/4, 5 April 1983, Mr W. B. Williams, to Mr Birchall.

16 WYA-W, WYW186/2/3/2/8/4, 11 April 1983, JCB to Mr W. B. Williams.

17 TNA, COAL 77/6899, 19 January 1955, Minutes of the Meeting of the Colliery Consultative Committee.

18 'Strike of 2,455 Miners over Housing Dispute', *Yorkshire Observer*, 31 August 1954.

19 TNA, COAL 77/6899, 31 March 1954, Minutes of the Meeting of the Colliery Consultative Committee.
20 Phil Child, 'Landlordism, Rent Regulation and the Labour Party in Mid-Twentieth Century Britain, 1950–64', *Twentieth Century British History* 29, no. 1 (2018), 87.
21 'Tenants Organise to Fight Rent Increases', *Chelsea News and General Advertiser*, 8 September 1950.
22 'Solihull Tenants Launch Campaign against "Model" Rents Scheme', *Birmingham Daily Post*, 21 January 1955.
23 The *Holloway Press* reports 1,000 but a pamphlet published by Pluto Press in 1972 documented the numbers as above 2,000. 'A Turbulent Year in St Pancras', *Holloway Press*, 30 December 1960; Dave Burn, *Rent Strikes: St Pancras 1960* (London: Pluto Press, 1972).
24 Burn, *Rent Strikes.*
25 Kim Singleton, 'Thousands Say, We Won't Pay! Merseyside Tenants in Struggle, 1968–1973', PhD thesis, University of Liverpool, 2010, 93.
26 '1969 Abercromby Rent Strike', *Liverpool Anarchist* 9, October 2020.
27 Leslie Clare, 'It Must Be Awful', *Daily Express*, 16 May 1969.
28 Singleton, 'Thousands Say, We Won't Pay!', 121.
29 Ethel Singleton, cited in ibid.
30 John Davis, 'Rents and Race in 1960s London: New Light on Rachmanism', *Twentieth Century British History* 12, no. 1 (2001), 90.
31 Ben Parkin, cited in ibid., 72–3.
32 Child, 'Landlordism, Rent Regulation and the Labour Party', 97.
33 J. E. Trice, 'Report of the Committee on the Rent Acts', *Modern Law Review* 34, no. 4 (1971), 428.
34 Seumas Milne, *The Enemy Within: The Secret War against the Miners* (London: Verso, 1994).
35 Quintin Bradley, 'Leeds Rent Strike 1934', n.d., criticalplace.org.uk.
36 Burn, *Rent Strikes.*

5. Declared defective

1 Sarah Glynn, 'If Public Housing Didn't Exist, We'd Have to Invent It', in Sarah Glynn, ed., *Where the Other Half Lives: Lower Income Housing in a Neoliberal World* (London: Pluto Press, 2009), 26.
2 TNA, COAL 45/69, 14 June 1978, T. G. Robinson to Mr Shepherd. Sale of NCB Owned Properties.

3 Ibid.
4 TNA, COAL 45/69, 29 June 1978, Alan Dickie to F. D. Perryman.
5 John Grayson, 'Tenants, Unions and Councils in South Yorkshire from 1945 to the 1990s', available at 'South Yorkshire Tenants', AdEd Knowledge Company, 16 October 2009, adedknowledge.wordpress.com.
6 Ibid.
7 John Boughton, *Municipal Dreams: The Rise and Fall of Council Housing* (London: Verso, 2018), 170.
8 John Davis, 'Rents and Race in 1960s London: New Light on Rachmanism', *Twentieth Century British History* 12, no. 1 (2001), 72.
9 Boughton, *Municipal Dreams*, 170.
10 Daniel Renwick and Robbie Shilliam, *Squalor. The Five Giants: A New Beveridge Report* (Newcastle: Agenda Publishing, 2022), 103.
11 HC Deb, 13 January 1987, vol. 108, c236; National Coal Mining Museum [NCM] archives, British Coal Corporation, Report and Accounts 1987/88, 13.
12 Boughton, *Municipal Dreams*, 175.
13 Renwick and Shilliam, *Squalor*, 105.
14 The BRE originated in 1921 as an arm of the government focused on housing quality. By the 1980s it was an executive agency of the Environment and Transport Department, before it, too, was fully privatised in 1997.
15 Keith Ross, *Non-traditional Housing in the UK – A Brief Review* (London: Building Research Establishment, July 2002), 12.
16 WYA-W, WYW186/2/8/14/3/2, 7 September 1982, Department for the Environment Press Notice.
17 Ross, *Non-traditional Housing in the UK*, 16.
18 Boughton, *Municipal Dreams*, 136.
19 HC Deb, 13 January 1987, vol. 108, c241.
20 HC Deb, 27 November 1984, vol. 68, cc886.
21 Ibid., c889.
22 WYA-W, WYW186/2/8/14/3/2, 11 March 1983, Structural Defects in Airey Houses.
23 HC Deb, 6 December 1985, vol. 88, c599.
24 HC Deb, 22 October 1986, vol. 102, c1267.

6. Going, going, gone

1 TNA, COAL 45/69, 24 January 1979, Sale of Workmen's Houses.
2 TNA, COAL 45/69, 2 April 1979, Sale of Board Houses.

3 TNA, COAL 45/69, 14 December 1978, Coal News Readers – Sale of NCB houses.
4 TNA, COAL 45/69, 3 January 1979, Mr C. Utley to G. C. Shephard.
5 TNA, COAL 45/69, 25 July 1979, Sale of Workmen's Houses.
6 TNA, COAL 45/69, 14 December 1978, House Sales, Memo from G. C. Shephard to A Dickie.
7 TNA, COAL 45/69, 2 April 1979, Sale of Board Houses.
8 HC Deb, 13 January 1987, vol.108, c241.
9 John Grayson, 'Tenants, Unions and Councils in South Yorkshire from 1945 to the 1990s', available at 'South Yorkshire Tenants', AdEd Knowledge Company, 16 October 2009, adedknowledge.wordpress.com.
10 Shelter, *Pits and Mortar: Cashing in on Coal Homes* (London: Shelter, 1987), 1.
11 HC Deb, 13 January 1987, vol. 108, cc236–44.
12 Ibid.
13 Ibid.
14 Ibid.
15 'Row over Sale of Coal Houses', *Evening Sentinel*, 8 October 1986.
16 R. Dunn, R. Forrest, and A. Murie, 'The Geography of Council House Sales in England – 1979–85', *Urban Studies* 24, no. 1 (1987), 47–59, fn. 2.
17 WYA-W, WYW186/2/8/14/3/2, 11 March 1983, Structural Defects in Airey Houses.
18 HC Deb, 13 January 1987, vol. 108, cc237.
19 Nic Cicutti, 'Johnson Fry Unveils New Look', *Independent*, 29 August 1995, independent.co.uk.
20 Corporate Watch, 'Pemberstone Group: We Profile the Company Trying to Demolish 70 Homes in a Leeds Estate', corporatewatch.org, 24 September 2020.
21 Daniel Renwick and Robbie Shilliam, *Squalor. The Five Giants: A New Beveridge Report* (Newcastle: Agenda Publishing, 2022), 46.
22 Stuart Hodkinson, 'From Popular Capitalism to Third-Way Modernism: The Example of Leeds, England', in Sarah Glynn, ed., *Where the Other Half Lives: Lower Income Housing in a Neoliberal World* (London: Pluto Press, 2009), 101.
23 Ibid., 108.
24 TNA, COAL 45/69, 18 May 1979, W. W. Burke to Arthur Scargill.
25 Phil Reed, 'SOLD: Estate of 210 houses', *Rothwell Advertiser*, 8 January 1987.
26 'Massive Rent Increases for Coal Estate', *Rothwell Advertiser*, 22 January 1987.
27 'House Prices Go Up', *Rothwell Advertiser*, 30 July 1987.

28 Phil Reed, 'Shocker for Homeless Couple', *Rothwell Advertiser*, 29 January 1987.
29 'Average Rent Will Be £14', *Rothwell Advertiser*, 26 February 1987.
30 Wendy Wilson and Bryn Morgan, *Rent Levels, Affordability, and Housing Benefit*, House of Commons Library, Research Paper 98/69, 22 June 1998, 9–10.
31 'Stormy Rents Meeting', *Rothwell Advertiser*, 5 February 1987.
32 Grayson, 'Tenants, Unions and Councils in South Yorkshire', 13–14.
33 Shelter and Wakefield Ex British Coal Tenants Federation cited in ibid., 13.
34 For example, *Public Service Action* 27 (February 1987) features an article on the 'British Coal Homes Rip Off', which mentions the sale to, and by, Manchester Square Associates; *Militant*'s 18 September 1987 issue ran with the headline 'Homes Before Profits'.
35 'Aid for Housing Estate', *Rothwell Advertiser*, 11 June 1987.
36 Phil Reed, 'Council to Investigate Estate', *Rothwell Advertiser*, 26 November 1987.
37 Letter: 'Repair or Demolish', *Rothwell Advertiser*, 10 December 1987.
38 'Landlord Is Ordered to Carry Out Repairs', *Rothwell Advertiser*, 25 February 1988.
39 Kim Clayton, 'Tenants Move Out of Oulton Estate', *Rothwell Advertiser*, 26 January 1987.
40 Jane Foot, *We Are Not for Sale: Part Two* (Sheffield: SCAT [Services to Community Action and Trade Unions Publications], 1989), 19.

7. Subcontracting accountability

1 'Demolition Starts at Oulton Park Estate', *Rothwell Advertiser*, 9 August 1990.
2 Wendy Wilson and Bryn Morgan, *Rent Levels, Affordability and Housing Benefit*, House of Commons Library, Research Paper 98/69, 22 June 1998.
3 Coalfields Task Force, *Making the Difference: A New Start for England's Coalfield Communities*, June 1998, 28.
4 John Boughton, *Municipal Dreams: The Rise and Fall of Council Housing* (London: Verso, 2018), 217.
5 Sold price data taken from Land Registry: landregistry.data.gov.uk.
6 Chartered Institute of Housing, Average Regional House Prices, ukhousingreview.org.uk.
7 Daniel Renwick and Robbie Shilliam, *Squalor. The Five Giants: A New Beveridge Report* (Newcastle: Agenda Publishing, 2022), 109.

8 Peter Apps, *Show Me the Bodies* (London: Oneworld Publications, 2022), 184.
9 Stuart Hodkinson, *Safe as Houses: Private Greed, Political Negligence and Housing Policy after Grenfell* (Manchester: Manchester University Press, 2019).
10 Renwick and Shilliam, *Squalor*, 111.
11 Andrew Leyshon and Shaun French, ' "We All Live in a Robbie Fowler House": The Geographies of the Buy to Let Market in the UK', *British Journal of Politics and International Relations* 11, no. 3 (2009), 438–60.
12 Cambridge Centre for Housing and Planning Research, 'Guide to Local Rents, 2006. Part I: Cross Tenure Rents', cchpr.landecon.cam.ac.uk, December 2006.
13 Valuation Office Agency, 'Private Rental Market Summary Statistics – October 2016 to September 2017', gov.uk, December 2017.
14 Citizens Advice Bureau, *Let Down: CAB Evidence on Letting Agents and Their Charges*, CAB Briefing, May 2009.
15 Lisa Harker, *Chance of a Lifetime: The Impact of Bad Housing on Children's Lives*, Shelter, September 2006.
16 Liam Reynolds, *Safe and Secure? The Private Rented Sector and Security of Tenure*, Shelter, May 2005.
17 Citizens Advice Bureau, *The Tenant's Dilemma: Warning: Your Home Is at Risk If You Dare Complain*, June 2007, 6.
18 Robbie de Santos, *Asserting Authority: Calling Time on Rogue Landlords*, Shelter, September 2011.

8. #SaveOurHomesLS26

1 Vickie Cooper and Kirsteen Paton, 'Everyday Eviction in the Twenty-First Century', in Neil Gray, ed., *Rent and Its Discontents* (London: Rowman & Littlefield, 2018), 81.
2 'Renters Compete with 20 Others in Battle to Find a Home', BBC News, 26 July 2023.
3 Wendy Wilson, *Can Private Landlords Refuse to Let to Benefit Claimants and People with Children?*, House of Commons Library Research Briefing, 30 October 30, 2023.
4 Jenny Preece and Emma Bimpson, *Forms and Mechanisms of Exclusion in Contemporary Housing Systems: An Evidence Review*, UK Collaborative Centre for Housing Evidence, 23 April 2019.
5 Emma Ryan, 'This Is How Long It Takes to Get a Council House in Different Parts of Leeds', *Yorkshire Evening Post*, 28 September 2019, yorkshireeveningpost.co.uk.

6 Sarah Wilson, 'Revealed: At Least 30,000 People Have Waited 10 Years for Social Housing', *Big Issue*, 12 July 2022, bigissue.com.
7 James Riding, 'Leeds Council Considers Removing 18,000 People from Social Housing Waiting List', *Inside Housing*, 24 February 2024, insidehousing.co.uk.
8 Ibid.
9 Leeds City Council, *Homelessness and Rough Sleeping Strategy 2023–2028*, n.d., leeds.gov.uk.
10 See alfiebarker.com.
11 Alfie Barker, 'Why I Made *Hanging On*', Save Our Homes LS26, 13 October 2021, saveourhomesls26.org.
12 Adam Tinson and Amy Clair, 'Better Housing Is Crucial for Our Health and the COVID-19 Recovery', Health Foundation, 28 December 2020, health.org.uk.
13 Deborah Garvie, Jenny Pennington, Hannah Rich, and Martha Schofield, *Still Living in Limbo*, Shelter, 9 March 2024, 52–4.
14 Tinson and Clair, 'Better Housing Is Crucial for Our Health'.
15 Cindy Readman, '"We're So Scared": Cindy Readman on Her Family's Fears after Receiving Eviction Notice', Save Our Homes LS26, 12 August 2021, saveourhomesls26.org.
16 Corporate Watch, 'Pemberstone Group: We Profile the Company Trying to Demolish 70 Homes in a Leeds Estate', corporatewatch.org, 24 September 2020.
17 Jennifer Sizeland, 'Britain's Working Class History Is Disappearing', *Lead*, 4 April 2024, thelead.uk.
18 Zach Boren, 'Leading Housebuilder Pushed for Weaker Climate Targets', *Unearthed*, 5 July 2021, unearthed.greenpeace.org.
19 Sam Gruet, Lauren Woodhead, and Paul Bradshaw, 'Renting: Six out of 10 Renters Live in Energy-Inefficient Homes', BBC, 6 April 2023.
20 Peter Apps, *Show Me the Bodies* (London: Oneworld Publications, 2022).
21 'Sasha White KC', Landmark Chambers, landmarkchambers.co.uk.
22 Richard Clegg, Appeal Decision, 15 January 2021, Appeal Ref: APP/N4720/W/20/3250249, leeds.gov.uk.
23 Stephen Delahunty, 'New Delivery Target for Affordable Homes Programme Expected Shortly as Government Admits "Very Unlikely" to Hit Original Aim', *Inside Housing*, 18 April 2024, insidehousing.co.uk.
24 'Residents and Councillors Mark Major Milestone for Affordable Housing Scheme,' press release, Leeds City Council, 14 November 2023, news.leeds.gov.uk.
25 Jess McCabe, '10 Years of Affordable Rent', *Inside Housing*, 20 December 2021, insidehousing.co.uk.

26 Andrew Kersley, 'Housing Association Rent Arrears Rise 8.4% to Record High of Nearly £800m', *Inside Housing*, 11 March 2024, insidehousing.co.uk.

9. Taking up space

1 John Boughton, *Municipal Dreams: The Rise and Fall of Council Housing* (London: Verso, 2018), 49.
2 Amelia Hill, 'New Era Estate: How US Pension Fund Manager Fuels London Rent Rise', *Guardian*, 19 November 2014; Adam Gabbatt, Oliver Laughland, and Dominic Rushe, 'Westbrook Partners: The Global Landlords Using Property Like an ATM', *Guardian*, 21 November 2014.
3 Brett Christophers, *Our Lives in Their Portfolios: Why Asset Managers Own the World* (London: Verso, 2023), 9.
4 Merle Chricton, 'London's Historic Dolphin Square Enters Next Chapter', *PERE News*, 9 November 2020, perenews.com.
5 Hill, 'New Era Estate'.
6 Sophie Barnes, 'New Era: One Year On', *Inside Housing*, 22 February 2017, insidehousing.co.uk.
7 Socialist Worker, 'New Era Housing Campaign: Meet the London Tenants Fighting the Corporate Spivs', *Socialist Worker* 2431, 25 November 2014, socialistworker.co.uk.
8 Deborah Garvie, Jenny Pennington, Hannah Rich, and Martha Schofield, *Still Living in Limbo*, Shelter, 9 March 2024.
9 Keith Cooper, 'What Happened to the Dolphin Living Dream?', *Inside Housing*, April 27, 2022, insidehousing.co.uk.
10 HC Deb, Public Bills Committee, 'Renters (Reform) Bill (Eighth Sitting)', 23 November 2023, cc268–9.
11 Cooper, 'What Happened to the Dolphin Living Dream?'.
12 Ibid.
13 ESG Reporting 2023, Dolphin Living, dolphinliving.com.
14 See 'About Us', Focus E15 Campaign, focuse15.org.
15 Samira Shackle, '"Those Two Weeks Felt How the World Should Be": The Young Single Mums Who Took on the Housing Crisis – and Won', *Guardian*, 2 May 2024.
16 Lucie Parker, *Hers and His: Opening Up the Household Budget*, Fawcett Society, 2020.
17 Anna Johnston, 'Spring Budget 2022: Housing and Gender', Pre-Budget Briefing, Women's Budget Group, 8 March 2022, wbg.org.uk.
18 Olivia Barber, 'Number of People in Temporary Accommodation Up 14%', *Housing Today*, 20 December 2023, housingtoday.co.uk; Johnston, 'Spring Budget 2022'.

19 Vicky Spratt, *Tenants* (London: Profile, 2022), 52.
20 See Leeds City Council, *Homeless and Rough Sleeping Strategy, 2023–2028*, leeds.gov.uk.
21 Harvey Jones, 'Sex-for-Rent: The Rogue Landlords Who Offer Free Rooms in Return for "Favours"', *Guardian*, 2 April 2018; Rowenna Hoskin, 'Cost of Living: Women Feel Trust Was "Violated" on Housing App', BBC News, 25 March 2023.
22 Dawn Foster, 'Mums against Austerity', *Dissent* 63, no. 4 (2016), 47–52.
23 David Madden and Peter Marcuse, *In Defense of Housing: The Politics of Crisis* (London: Verso, 2016).
24 Pam Currie, '"A Wondrous Spectacle": Protest, Class and Femininity in the 1915 Rent Strikes', in Neil Gray, ed., *Rent and Its Discontents* (London: Rowman & Littlefield, 2018), 10.
25 Neil Gray, 'Afterword', in Neil Gray, ed., *Rent and Its Discontents* (London: Rowman & Littlefield, 2018), 207.
26 Currie, '"A Wondrous Spectacle"', 10.
27 Kim Singleton, 'Thousands Say, We Won't Pay! Merseyside Tenants in Struggle, 1968–1973', PhD thesis, University of Liverpool (2010), 217.
28 Ibid., 129.
29 Kerrie McGiveron, 'Notes on a Community Struggle: Big Flame, the Kirkby Rent Strike and the "Mass Struggle of Housewives"', *Women's History Review* 32, no. 4 (2023), 517–39.
30 Ibid.
31 Kerrie McGiveron, '"Empowered Working-Class Housewives" – Big Flame, Women and the Kirkby Rent Strike 1972–73', *The History Blog*, 6 March 2018, liverpool.ac.uk.
32 Christine Wall, 'Sisterhood and Squatting in the 1970s: Feminism, Housing and Urban Change in Hackney', *History Workshop Journal* 83 (2017), 79–97.
33 Ibid., 84.
34 Ibid.
35 Loretta Lees and Phil Hubbard, '"So, Don't You Want Us Here No More?" Slow Violence, Frustrated Hope, and Racialized Struggle on London's Council Estates', *Housing Theory and Society* 39, no. 3 (2022), 342.
36 See Focus E15 Campaign, focuse15.org.
37 Lisa McKenzie, 'Resisting and Surviving Organised Politics: The Case of the London Housing Movement', in Adam Fishwick and Heather Connolly, eds, *Austerity and Working-Class Resistance: Survival, Disruption and Creation in Hard Times* (London: Rowman & Littlefield, 2017), 24.
38 Lindsey Garrett, 'I Don't Want to Be London Mayor, but Who

Else Will Do What Needs to Be Done?', *Guardian*, 15 May 2015.

39 Danielle K. Brown and Summer Harlow, 'Protests, Media Coverage, and a Hierarchy of Social Struggle', *International Journal of Press/Politics* 24, no. 4 (2019), 509.

40 McKenzie, 'Resisting and Surviving Organised Politics', 18.

41 Owen Jones, *Chavs* (London: Verso, 2020 [2011]).

42 Thomas Hunter, 'UK Local Newspaper Closures Update: 293 Now Gone since 2005', *Press Gazette*, 14 August 2024, pressgazette.co.uk.

43 Grayson, cited in Singleton, 'Thousands Say, We Won't Pay!', 33.

44 Nick Bano, *Against Landlords* (London: Verso), 177.

45 Vidhya Alakeson, *The Challenges of Build to Rent for UK Housing Providers*, Resolution Foundation, June 2013, resolutionfoundation.org.

46 'Track Key Build to Rent Values', Colliers, 2022, colliers.com.

47 Christophers, *Our Lives in Their Portfolios*, 9.

Conclusion

1 Ruth Neill, Conor Cunningham, Maeve O'Doherty, Lee Smith, and Mark A. Tully, 'Pet Ownership and Physical Activity in Older Adults: Cross-Sectional Analyses from the NICOLA Study', *Journal of Ageing and Longevity* 3, no. 2 (2023), 142–52; Joanna Elson, 'Without Urgent Action, There's a Bleak Future for Older Private Renters', *Inside Housing*, 12 June 2024, insidehousing.co.uk.

2 Imogen Blake, 'Growing Gap in Early Heart Disease Death Rates between Poorest and Richest in England', British Heart Foundation, 21 May 2024, bhf.org.uk.

3 'How Inequalities Contribute to Heart and Circulatory Diseases', British Heart Foundation, bhf.org.uk.

4 Amelia Hill, 'Record Number of Over-50s in UK Working Part-Time, ONS Data Shows', *Guardian*, 25 September 2023.

5 Morgan Vine, *Keys to the Future: Projecting Housing Tenure and Poverty Rates in Later Life*, Independent Age, June 2024.

6 David Madden and Peter Marcuse, *In Defense of Housing: The Politics of Crisis* (London: Verso, 2016).

7 Frank Eardley, 'Right to Buy: Past, Present and Future', House of Lords Library, 17 June 2022, lordslibrary.parliament.uk.

8 Peter King, *A Social Philosophy of Housing* (Abingdon: Routledge, 2018 [2003]), 96–7.

9 Anna Minton, *Big Capital: Who Is London For?* (London: Penguin, 2017), 119.

10 Cara Pacitti, 'Through the Roof: Recent Trends in Rental Price Growth', briefing, Resolution Foundation, April 2024, resolutionfoundation.org.

11 'Refuge Launches "Unsocial Spaces" – A Report on the Online Abuse of Women', Refuge, 29 October 2021, refuge.org.uk.

12 'Crowdsourced Twitter Study Reveals Shocking Scale of Online Abuse against Women', Amnesty International, 18 December 2018, amnesty.org.

13 Minton, *Big Capital*; Nick Bano, *Against Landlords* (London: Verso); Josh Ryan-Collins, *Why Can't You Afford a Home?* (Cambridge: Polity, 2018).

14 Peter Shapely, 'Social Housing and Tenant Participation, History and Policy', Policy Paper Series, History and Policy, 25 March 2008, historyandpolicy.org.

Index